D0426900

More Praise for *The Dumbest Generation Grows Up*

"Rootless, screen-addicted, fragile, aggressive, censorious, aliterate, and culturally ignorant—Millennials have been betrayed by Baby Boomers, Mark Bauerlein shows. Want to understand the woke tyranny? Read *The Dumbest Generation Grows Up*."

> —**R. R. Reno,** editor of *First Things* and author of *Return of the Strong Gods: Nationalism, Populism, and the Future of the West*

"Where did the Cult of Wokeness come from? Mark Bauerlein makes a rich, detailed case that older Americans ruined the Millennial generation by raising them to believe that there should be no constraints on human nature—and by handing their developing minds over to Silicon Valley. This book is in no way a middle-aged man's ranting against youth. Rather, it is a serious and persuasive analysis of the damage our society has done to its young—wreckage that the Millennial utopians are now visiting on society—and an urgent plea to refuse and resist the mass culture of idiocracy before we condemn another generation."

> —**Rod Dreher,** author of *The Benedict Option: A Strategy for Christians in a Post-Christian Nation* and *Live Not by Lies: A Manual for Christian Dissidents*

"Mark Bauerlein is one of our most percipient and insightful cultural pathologists. In *The Dumbest Generation Grows Up*, he outdoes himself, showing how the effort to build utopia by jettisoning tradition has bred an entire generation addicted to the mute and dehumanizing platitudes of a sophomoric and self-indulgent nihilism. This is an essential book for our times—clear-sighted, admonitory, mature."

> —**Roger Kimball,** editor and publisher of *The New Criterion*

"A very moving book about the first generation of people raised in the Digital Age, showing the costs children pay as adults when they grow up without being given strong general knowledge and, with it, linguistic proficiency in the public sphere. This is especially tragic for the black students of the new generation, who score in reading (and in income) below 80 percent of their white counterparts. The widespread language of equality needs to be backed up with results."

—**E. D. Hirsch Jr.,** author of *Cultural Literacy: What Every American Needs to Know* and founding chairman of the Core Knowledge Foundation

"In this penetrating and searingly honest book, Mark Bauerlein continues the project he began thirteen years ago, tracking the intellectual and moral devolution of the generation we call the Millennials. In this book he has followed their path as they have moved into an uneasy, unwelcome, and unhappy adulthood. What he sees are failures: our massive (and massively expensive) failure to educate our young or to form in them the traits that are needed for a life of character and generativity. The wondrous hopes of a coming Digital Age have crashed and burned, leaving behind an entire cohort of young Americans wandering around, dazed and directionless, haunted by apocalyptic fears, with faces glued to the empty enchantments of their telephones, ill-equipped for the tasks of living productively in today's world. If we are to figure out what to do about this disaster, a catastrophe we have imposed upon ourselves, we first must take the full measure of our failure. No one has done that with more tenacity and insight than Mark Bauerlein, and his book will be required reading for all Americans for many years to come."

—**Wilfred M. McClay,** professor of history at Hillsdale College

"Poor Cassandra, cursed by Apollo to utter true prophecies that no would believe: *You'll regret it if you haul that wooden horse left by the Greeks inside the gates of Troy*, etc. Mark Bauerlein must have offended Apollo too; how better to explain why his 2008 book, *The Dumbest Generation: How the Digital Age Stupefies Young Americans and Jeopardizes Our Future*, fell on deaf ears? He warned us that catering to the self-infatuation of the digital generation would have consequences. Among other acts of negligence, ignoring our responsibilities to instruct students how to read worthy literature; how to hear sublime music; how to enjoy sweet, silent thought; or how to weigh the perplexities of self-government would leave those young people unprepared for real life. They would face the world bereft of knowledge, faith, and sound judgment. Bauerlein now bravely faces the results. The 'Dumbest Generation,' now in its early thirties, wanders bewildered through the decade in which it should shoulder a serious public role but remains dazzled by utopian fantasies, a pseudo-moral imperative that *'everyone should be happy,'* and the callow pleasures of the callout culture. Bauerlein, writing gracefully, reflects his own immersion in our rich civilizational heritage. I cannot think of a better cure for cultural dumbness than reading *The Dumbest Generation Grows Up* with a mind towards really understanding the authors, ideas, and works of artistic genius that thread through its pages."

—**Peter Wood,** president of the National Association of Scholars

"A richly argued jeremiad against a generation that is ignorant of the past and is therefore condemned to repeat it—and that has thus also embraced the ideas of communist totalitarians, with little sense that they are doing so or of what the consequences will be. Mark Bauerlein has provided an invaluable service with this remarkably informative book."

—**David Horowitz,** founder of the David Horowitz Freedom Center and author of *Radical Son: A Generational Odyssey* and *I Can't Breathe: How a Racial Hoax Is Killing America*

"I would like to be able to praise Mark Bauerlein's *The Dumbest Generation Grows Up* as a cautionary tale warning us about what will happen to young minds if their education introduces them to no great books and offers for imitation no transcendent cultural heroes and is bereft of any vision except the empty one of perpetual and unearned happiness. I can't do that, because Bauerlein's lesson—delivered in tones elegiac, world-weary, and surprisingly gentle—is that it's already happened: 'The fractious, know-nothing thirty-year-old is what we got when we let the twelve-year-old drop his books and take up the screen.' Entirely persuasive and entirely sad."

—**Stanley Fish,** Floersheimer Distinguished Visiting Professor of Law at Yeshiva University

THE DUMBEST GENERATION GROWS UP

The
Dumbest Generation
Grows Up

From Stupefied Youth to
Dangerous Adults

Mark Bauerlein

REGNERY GATEWAY
Washington, D.C.

Copyright © 2022 by Mark Bauerlein

All rights reserved. No part of this publication may be reproduced
or transmitted in any form or by any means electronic or mechanical,
including photocopy, recording, or any information storage and retrieval
system now known or to be invented, without permission in writing
from the publisher, except by a reviewer who wishes to quote brief
passages in connection with a review written for inclusion in a magazine,
newspaper, website, or broadcast.

Regnery Gateway™ is a trademark of Salem Communications
Holding Corporation
Regnery® is a registered trademark and its colophon is a trademark of
Salem Communications Holding Corporation

Cataloging-in-Publication data on file with the Library of Congress

ISBN: 978-1-68451-220-1
eISBN: 978-1-68451-221-8

Published in the United States by
Regnery Gateway
An Imprint of Regnery Publishing
A Division of Salem Media Group
Washington, D.C.
www.Regnery.com

Manufactured in the United States of America

10 9 8 7 6 5 4 3 2 1

Books are available in quantity for promotional or premium use.
For information on discounts and terms, please visit our website:
www.Regnery.com.

Contents

CHAPTER ONE

Making Unhappy—and Dangerous—Adults

W hat have we done to them?

"Them"—the Millennials, the first Americans to come of age in the Digital Age, the cutting edge of the tech revolution, competing like never before for college and grad school, ready to think globally and renounce prejudice and fashion their profiles to achieve, achieve, follow their passions and be all that they can be—but ending up behind the Starbucks counter or doing contract work, living with their parents or in a house with four friends, nonetheless lonely and mistrustful, with no thoughts of marriage and children, no weekly church attendance or civic memberships, more than half of them convinced that their country is racist and sexist. This is no longer the cohort that in 2010 was "Confident, Self-Expressive, Liberal, Upbeat, and Open to Change."[1] It is a generation with a different theme: "53 Reasons Life Sucks for Millennials."[2]

And we—the educators, journalists, intellectuals, business and foundation leaders, consultants, psychologists, and other supervisors of the young—who flattered them as *Millennials Rising: The Next Great Generation*,[3] cried, "Here Come the Millennials,"[4] left them to their digital devices and video games and five hundred TV channels and three hundred photos in their pockets, fed them diverting apps and stupid movies and crass music, and stuck them with crushing student debt and frightful health-care costs, a coarse and vulgar public square, churches in retreat, and an economy of "creative destruction" and "disruptive innovation" (which the top 10 percent exploited, but the rest experienced as, precisely, destructive and disruptive), all the while giving them little education in history, art, literature, philosophy, political theory, comparative religion—a cultural framework that might have helped them manage the confusions.

No generation had had so many venues for self-realization and could explore them without the guidance of the seniors—Facebook, online role-playing, YouTube (whose original motto, remember, was "Broadcast Yourself"). After all, if Millennials were individuals who could "*think and process information fundamentally differently* from their predecessors,"[5] their minds conditioned to operate in alternative ways by digital immersion in their developing years, then the opinions of Boomers and Generation Xers of what the kids proceeded to do wasn't altogether relevant. If an eleven-year-old "community volunteer and blogger" could blow away a prominent education consultant with her international network and organizational savvy ("She's sharing and learning and collaborating in ways that were unheard of just a few years ago"[6]), then the rest of us were forever fated to play catch-up. "The Internet and the digital world was [*sic*] something that belonged to adults, and now it's something that really is the province of teenagers," a Berkeley researcher told the producers of "Growing Up Online," a 2008 episode of PBS's *Frontline*.[7] So who are forty-five-year-olds to judge? As a distinguished academic put it in a keynote discussion at the 2008 South by Southwest festival (SXSW), "Kids are early adopters of all new technologies. And they do it outside the watchful eyes of their parents. So there's a sense of fear among parents."[8] Lighten up, we were told. Instead of fearing these kids who were passing them by, said the most progressive admirers of this new generation gap, the elders had a better option: "What Old People Can Learn from Millennials."[9]

A dozen years ago, those of us watching with a skeptical eye couldn't decide which troubled us more: the fifteen-year-olds averaging eight hours of media per day or the adults marveling at them. How could the older and wiser ignore the dangers of adolescents' reading fewer books and logging more screen hours? How could they not realize that social media would flood the kids with youth culture and peer pressure day and night, blocking the exposure to adult matters and fresh ideas and a little high art that used to happen all the time when authors and their new books appeared in a standard segment on Johnny Carson or when Milton Friedman appeared repeatedly on *Donohue* in the late '70s, teenagers played *Masterpiece* and *Trivial Pursuit*, and even little kids heard Leonard Bernstein's beloved children's concerts or got their classical music on *Bugs Bunny*. In a 2010 speech, George Steiner warned, "Nothing frightens me more than the withdrawal of serious music from the lives of millions of young children"—Chopin and Wagner replaced by "the barbarism of organized noise." That was the inevitable outcome once technology enabled youths to become independent consumers. But for every George Steiner, there were dozens of intellectuals and teachers willing to cheer the multi-tasking, hyper-social young. Maybe it was that those figures who surely knew better were unwilling to protest for fear of appearing to be grouches, fogeys. Steiner himself admitted, "I sound like a boring old reactionary." Nobody wanted to be that—though Steiner added, "I don't apologize."[10]

There should have been many, many more critics. The evidence was voluminous. Even as the cheerleaders were hailing the advent of digital youth, signs of intellectual harm were multiplying. Instead of heeding the signs, people in positions of authority rationalized them away. Bill Gates and Margaret Spellings and Barack Obama told Millennials they had to go to college to acquire twenty-first-century skills to get by in the information economy, and the schools went on to jack up tuition, dangle loans, and leave them five years after graduation in the state of early-twentieth-century sharecroppers, the competence they had developed in college and the digital techniques they had learned on their own often proving to be no help in the job market. The solution? Be more flexible, mobile, adaptive! High school students bombed NAEP exams ("the Nation's Report Card") in U.S. history and civics,[11] but, many shrugged: Why worry, now that Google is around? The kids can always look it up! An August 2013 column in *Scientific American* featured an author recalling his father paying him five dollars to memorize the U.S. presidents in order and reflecting, "Maybe we'll soon conclude that memorizing facts is no longer part of the modern student's task. Maybe we should let the smartphone call up those facts as necessary."[12] As boys began stacking up heavy sessions of video games, Senator Charles Schumer worried that they might become desensitized to violence and death, prompting a columnist at *Wired* magazine to scoff, "But dire pronouncements about new forms of entertainment are old hat. It goes like this: Young people embrace an activity. Adults condemn it. The kids grow up, no better or worse than their elders, and the moral panic subsides."[13]

Such "no big deal" comments didn't jibe with the common characterization of the digital advent as on the order of Gutenberg, but few minds in that heady time of screen innovations bothered to quibble. Something historic, momentous, epochal was underway, a movement, a wave, fresh and hopeful—so don't be a naysayer. In December 2011, Joichi Ito, then director of the MIT Media Lab, stated in the *New York Times*, "The Internet isn't really a technology. It's a belief system."[14] And Silicon Valley entrepreneur and critic Andrew

Keen was right to call its advocates "evangelists."[15] John Perry Barlow, the renowned defender of open internet who coined the term "electronic frontier," imagined virtual reality as the Incarnation in reverse: "Now, I realized, would the Flesh be made Word."[16]

Given how pedestrian Facebook, Twitter, and Wikipedia seem today, not to mention the oddball auras of their founders and CEOs, it is difficult to remember the masters-of-the-universe, march-of-time cachet they enjoyed in the Web 2.0 phase of the Revolution (the first decade of the twenty-first century). Change happens so fast that we forget the spectacular novelty of it all, the days when digiphiles had all the momentum, the cool. As a friend who'd gone into technical writing in the '90s told me recently, "It was *sooo* much fun back then." Nobody wanted to hear the downsides, especially when so much money was being made. SAT scores in reading and writing kept slipping, but with all the texting, chatting, blogging, and tweeting, it was easy to find the high schoolers expressive in so many other ways, writing more words than any generation in history. The class of 2012 did less homework than previous cohorts did—a lot less—but at the Q & A at an event at the Virginia Military Institute, after I noted their sliding diligence, a young political scientist explained why: they were spending less time on assignments because all the tools and programs they'd mastered let them work so much faster—they weren't lazy; they were efficient!—at which point the twelve hundred cadets in attendance, tired of my berating them for their selfies, stopped booing and burst out in applause. A much-discussed 2004 survey by the National Endowment for the Arts (NEA), *Reading at Risk: A Survey of Literary Reading in America*, found an astonishing drop in young adults' consumption of fiction, poetry, and drama, with only 43 percent of them reading any literature at all in leisure hours, 17 percentage points fewer than in 1982,[17] but in my presentation of the findings at dozens of scholarly meetings and on college campuses (I had worked on the NEA project), the professionals dismissed them as alarmist and reactionary, arising from a "moral panic" no different from the stuffy alarm about Elvis and comic books fifty years earlier.

Some public intellectuals defended the digitizing kids because they, too, loved Facebook and Wikipedia. "The early signs of a culture of civic activism among young people, joined by networked technologies, are cropping up around the world," wrote two Harvard scholars in 2008, endorsing the networks for, among other things, helping organize resistance against authoritarian regimes—and thus putting opponents of the internet into the role of supporting repressive forces.[18] Others wouldn't criticize the trends because they didn't much care about the tradition-heavy materials that dropped out as kids logged on and surfed and chatted—the better books, films, artworks, symphonies and jazz solos, discussion shows, and history no longer present. In an April 2001 story in the *New York Times* with the revealing title "More Ado (Yawn) about Great Books," reporter Emily Eakin quoted a top professor: "You can conceive of a curriculum producing the same cognitive skills that doesn't use literature at all but opts for connecting with the media tastes of the day—film, video, TV, etc. It's no longer clear why we need to teach literature at all." Such critical thinking skills are the key aim, Eakin wrote, and "those, some English professors are willing to admit, can be honed just as well through considerations of 'Sex and the City' as 'Middlemarch.'"[19] From the notion that *Sex and the City* serves to promote higher-order reflections, it's only a small step to the satirical videos on collegehumor.com, founded by undergraduates in 1999 and a few years later pulling in $10 million annually. Still others defending digital youth had a personal reason for countenancing the turn to the screen in spite of its intellectual costs: they didn't want to chide the kids. It made them uncomfortable. They didn't want to embrace the authority that licensed criticism of others for their leisure choices, and they didn't want anyone else to assume it, either, and especially not to direct it at the (putatively) powerless adolescents. It sounded too much like get-off-my-lawn bullying.

Whatever the motives, the outcome was a climate of acceptance. Even some of the most conscientious studies of digital youth chose to play it neutral, not to judge. *Hanging Out, Messing Around, and Geeking Out: Kids Living and Learning with New Media* was a large entry in a series on digital media funded by the MacArthur Foundation and published by MIT Press in 2010. Mizuko Ito of the University of California, Irvine, led a team of twenty-one researchers on a three-year ethnographic project, building case studies, collecting data and contextual information, and providing analytic insights in order to describe the role of digital media, devices, and communications in the ordinary hours of youth in the United States. It was a superb profile of adolescent behavior and the new media environment. The researchers enumerated "intimacy practices" that kept peers close to one another. They explored "fansubbing practices," the rising status of kids as "technology experts" in their families, what went into profiles on MySpace, the interpretation of "feedback" on open sites such as YouTube, the widening category of "work," and so forth.[20]

I skimmed the book when it came out and corresponded briefly with Professor Ito. I just looked back at it and found that the chapters hold up, though some of the technologies are dated, of course. At the beginning of the book, however, the authors briefly declared a certain suspension of judgment that pulled me up short. Stating that they proposed to approach media as "embodiments of social and cultural relationships," Ito and her coauthors concluded, "It follows that we do not see the content of the media or media platform (TV, books, games, etc.) as the most important variables for determining social or cognitive outcomes."[21] That is, the specific stuff the youths consumed was *not* a primary influence on their development—not in the eyes of the observers. This was a crucial withholding of critical judgment, flattening the character of the actual subject matter passing through the screens. Whether text messages talked about Shakespeare homework or party gossip, whether an individual browsed the web for Civil War battles or for pets at play, shared photos of Modernist architecture or of party scenes...the researchers were determined to remain indifferent. The methodology demanded it: to document, not assess; to describe, not prescribe. The goal was to render habitats and habits, to show how a new tool produces new activities and alters the environs and beings within it. The content and quality of the materials consumed and created, their aesthetic, moral, and intellectual merits, were to come second or third or last, if at all. The inquirers wouldn't evaluate the substance of a video game, only how it was situated in the home, how parents regulated it, how kids identified with the figures.... What the kids did with it, not what it was: that was the key. Not what, but how: that was the question.

This is the standard ethnographic posture, of course—disinterested, unbiased, and open-minded—but how much of themselves did the investigators have to suppress in order to stay true to the method? One profile of a young anime expert in the book noted that, though he was at the time a graduate student in electrical engineering at a top school, he spent "about eight hours a day keeping up with his hobby." His own words: "I think pretty much all the time that's not school, eating, or sleeping."[22] One might have called this an obsession or an addiction—every leisure moment devoted to a cartoon genre, a habit that disengaged the young man from people and things in his immediate surroundings. If that was too extreme a diagnosis, the authors could at least have pondered the opportunity costs: no exercise, no dating, no volunteering or churchgoing, no books or museums or concerts or other hobbies. I would have asked about, precisely, the content of anime. What was so appealing about it? Was there a particular character or storyline that grabbed him? What were his first feelings at the first viewing? That line of investigation would get to the heart of his case: Is this really how he wishes to spend his teens and twenties? How long does he plan to keep it up? Apart from the pleasure, what does anime do for him that other, more educational diversions might do just as well?

That wasn't the tack taken by the investigator here, however. Instead, after the young man confessed his every-free-moment groove, the sole comment was, "Building a reputation as one of the most knowledgeable voices in the online anime fandom requires this kind of commitment as well as an advanced media ecology that is finely tailored to his interests."[23]

True enough, but when I read that final remark now in 2021, I don't think about anime, the young man's extraordinary "commitment," and his advanced media skills. Yes, his fixation is off the charts, and there is an etiology to trace. But I let it go because I don't have the information. Instead, I consider the mindset of the observer, the researcher doing the project, an intelligent and caring academic who has somehow turned off her taste, who refuses to ask whether the young man's lifestyle is healthy or whether anime is really worth so many precious hours of his formative years. What did the observer think about this habit? She must have had an opinion. Did she approve of what anime was doing to him? Would she be happy to see her own child diving into anime and shunning everything else in leisure time? Did she project forward five or ten years and envision this man heading into middle age still hooked, or perhaps no longer hooked and regretting the months and years that might have been?

She couldn't say; this was a case study, and the proper ethnographic stance preempted such a reckoning. The observer must be all eyes and ears; no value judgments. It was, as I said, a legitimate academic posture, and I admire the dedication of the researchers, but such disinterested examinations went smoothly along with the general unwillingness of elders in the spheres of culture and education in the 2000s to criticize the well-equipped, hyperactive Digital Natives. Our young anime man made that easy because he was exceptional. Obviously high-IQ, energetic, heading toward an advanced degree in a vibrant field, he dived into anime in every free moment without appearing to suffer any injury at all. Why should a kid who could run circles around all of us in the digital space have posed a problem? We had to admire his expertise; he was daunting, a front-runner, a fit representative of the newly entrepreneurial young, endowed with a technology he wielded better than we ever would. The kids were alright.

On October 26, 2018, a story appeared in the *New York Times* about a surprising trend in Silicon Valley. It bore the title "The Digital Gap Between Rich and Poor Kids Is Not What We Expected," and it cited the common concern during the late 1990s and 2000s that well-off kids would have abundant access to digital tools and the internet, while poor kids, lacking a computer, would fall further behind in academic achievement and workplace readiness. The digital revolution wouldn't be a great equalizer. The fear was that it would exacerbate inequalities, with privileged students "gaining tech skills and creating a digital divide," the story said.

In 2018, however, eleven years after the first iPhone was sold and fourteen years after Facebook was founded, something different and unexpected was happening: "But now, as Silicon Valley's parents increasingly panic over the impact screens have on their children and move toward screen-free lifestyles, worries over a new digital divide are rising." As public schools serving poor and minority kids were pushing one-to-one laptop programs, the reporter observed, executives in Palo Alto and Los Altos were sending their children to vigilantly low-tech private campuses such as the Waldorf Schools. A psychologist who had written a recent book about the hazards of screens told the reporter that when he urged poor families in the East Bay to pull their kids away from the internet, they blinked in surprise, while parents in Silicon Valley crowded his seminars, having already read and appreciated his work.

The troubled parents quoted in the story were the opposite of Luddites. Neither were they social conservatives, fundamentalist Christians, or Great Books–types. They came right out of the belly of the digital beast, including the ex-Microsoft executive who noted the customary hype ("There's a message out there that your child is going to be crippled and in a different dimension if they're [*sic*] not on the screen") and added an understated fact that communicates his disdain nicely: "That message doesn't play as well in this part of the world."[24] The story doesn't mention him, but Steve Jobs himself famously kept his own household and kids fairly tech-free, and a parallel *Times* story published at the same time and by the same reporter, Nellie Bowles, found more tech celebrities doing likewise. Why? Because, explained Chris Anderson, ex-editor of *Wired* and head of a robotics company, "We thought we could control it. And this is beyond our power to control. This is going straight to the pleasure centers of the developing brain. This is beyond our capacity as regular parents to understand." He actually compared it to crack cocaine. No ideological or principled objections to social media on these defectors' part, just a desire not to have their kids swallowed up in screen time. They want their children to go to Stanford and Caltech, and they know that hours online don't help. They've seen how much money tech companies make selling tools to school districts ("Apple and Google compete furiously to get products into schools and target students at an early age"), because once a youth adopts a brand, he tends to stay with it. They are familiar, too, with the many psychologists helping companies with "persuasive design," the science of getting people onto a site and keeping them there.[25] They didn't have to watch the *60 Minutes* segment the year before on "brain-hacking" in order to realize the manipulations at work or to hear Bill Maher comment on it thus: "The tycoons of social media have to stop pretending that they are friendly nerd-Gods building a better world and admit that they're just tobacco farmers in T-shirts selling an addictive product to children."[26] Nobody could claim that these parents were uninformed alarmists. They knew too much.

The people interviewed in the story weren't outliers, either—not within their elite group. They exemplified a national trend, a contrary digital divide: kids in lower-income households in the United States tally 42 percent more minutes of screen diversions per day than kids in upper-income households (487 minutes to 342 minutes, according to a Common Sense Media study cited in the "Dark Consensus" story).[27] While academics insisted for years, in urgent and radical terms, that youths needed to acquire the latest tools in order to get ahead and join that elite ("To keep pace with a globalized technological culture, we must rethink how we educate the next generation[,] or America will be 'left behind'"[28]), the most successful and aware individuals in this super-competitive techno-culture acted the opposite way. When they observed their own children at the screen, these high-tech wizards regretted what they had created. That these skeptics inhabited the very industry that produced the tools and nonetheless warned against the damage they do more loudly than the professional guardians of education and tradition; that people who worked at Google showed more circumspection than humanities teachers, school consultants, and culture journalists; that public school leaders pressed ahead on wiring devices into classrooms in a way that led the inventors of those very devices to pull their kids out—this wasn't merely an ironic twist. It was a condemnation of the professionals.

From the very start, they should have been telling everyone to slow down—above all the kids. As far back as the 1980s, academics were arguing that a sweeping transformation had begun. For instance, a distinguished Renaissance scholar stated in one of the leading scholarly journals of his field, "Digitized communication is forcing a radical realignment of the alphabetic and graphic components of ordinary textual communications."[29] Such drastic pronouncements multiplied in the 1990s and were a cliché by 2000 but no less widely believed. If this was a historic cataclysm, though, the stewards of tradition and mentors of the young should never have stepped back and let the least mature and informed among us plunge into it without caution or reproof. Nobody could have predicted the full impact of such a radical discontinuity with the past. The value of books hadn't changed, but the value, and possible pitfalls, of the cellphone remained to be seen. Educators and intellectuals should have been the first to rise up and shelter the budding American mind from the billion-dollar onslaught of screens. When Nielsen reported in October of 2010 that the average 13- to 17-year-old with a mobile device sent more than 100 texts per day (3,339 per month),[30] they should have issued grave proclamations of dismay and commanded parents to seize those tools immediately. When the Kaiser Foundation reported earlier that year that 8- to 18-year-olds averaged 7 hours and 38 minutes of media consumption per day, often of more than one medium at a time (for example, watching TV and browsing the web simultaneously),[31] the National Council of Teachers of English (NCTE) should have sent weekly alarms to parents ordering them to preserve an hour a day with books.

We needed brisk advocacy of Homer and Mozart, not rosy tales of creative things kids were doing online—which I heard too many times to count, as when, in a meeting of educators to craft standards for high school English, a woman next to me questioned whether we should uphold rules of spelling and punctuation, given all the inventive locutions kids were trading on social media. (She was outvoted, though standards developers now typically allow violations of Standard English in student writing and speaking when they are "appropriate.") At the VMI event mentioned before, after I had announced to the crowd that I'd told my wife the day before to put on my tombstone "He never took a selfie," a group of local schoolteachers in the crowd rebuked me by proclaiming that they had integrated social media into their lessons and assignments, kids loved it, and reading scores were climbing (see chapter three for widespread evidence to the contrary). In other dismaying cases, instead of praising the new digital culture, our mentors downgraded the tradition. After *Reading at Risk* came out in 2004[32] and *The Dumbest Generation* in 2008,[33] it happened again and again, as I presented the evidence to live audiences. At one event, when I listed figures from the Arts Endowment's surveys showing young people listening to classical music and jazz at meager rates, an academic respondent objected to the Endowment's neglect of rock 'n' roll. At another, when I mentioned low attendance at ballet and musical theater, a respondent wondered why we hadn't included Spanish/Latino dance on our questionnaire. In one discussion, after I noted that humanities teachers were increasingly dropping novels of more than two hundred pages from their syllabi, finding that fewer undergrads would read them all the way through, a University of Chicago English professor pointed at his computer screen and huffed, "What do you mean they're not reading? Whaddya think this is?"

Not once at any of the one hundred–plus speeches I gave at libraries, conventions, and campuses, however, did an engineer or software developer challenge me for denouncing texting, *Grand Theft Auto*, and Facebook. It was the "softer" professionals, the English professors and reading specialists, rhet-comp lecturers and middle school teachers, who took offense. The guardians of the liberal arts had raised critical thinking to the highest goal of humanistic instruction, but strangely the tech folks had five times more critical a perspective on Facebook and the web. Graduate students in literature departments, eager to lay claim to the *avant garde*, thought hypertexts were really neat, gushing that these electronic texts with live links readers could pursue broke up the cramped "linearity" of print. Community college students who were assigned to edit Wikipedia pages on scholarly subjects combined the old and the new in a compelling way, we were advised. The marvelous technology of "clickers" let freshmen and sophomores give instant feedback that appeared on a screen behind the teacher in college classes, thus transforming bored nineteen-year olds into active learners. Sure, abuses happened and mistakes were made, but those would disappear in the normal course of adoption as teachers and administrators learned to use the technology well. Tweedy traditionalists regretting the decline of Western Civilization in the curriculum weren't going to change any of it.

This was the import of the digital revolution for history and civics, literature and art, philosophy and religion. The rising generation didn't need that knowledge. They heard their elders proclaim that the digital breakthrough had altered the way we think and read and communicate—and didn't they know it better than anyone else? The past was obsolete; how intoxicating was that idea to eighteen-year-olds! Not only did it save them the effort of studying all that old stuff; better, it lifted the burden of the monuments, the greats, the heroes and geniuses, all the things that can make an adolescent feel small. They were told they deserved the towering title "Millennials," even though they had never accomplished much. A new age had come. We saw no violence in this revolution, no political or economic convulsions, but certainly two earmarks of breakthrough were clear: a radical departure from the past and a select population forging the future. "Bliss was it in that dawn to be alive, / But to be young very heaven!" William Wordsworth famously said of the French Revolution in its early stage, which he witnessed firsthand.

Values switched places, as they always do in a revolutionary situation. With history disrupted and language transformed, a full paradigm shift was underway, so that being informed and learned was now an actual disadvantage. The fifty-year-old English professor had passages of Wordsworth in his head line by line, and he could recite the arguments of all the best scholars on Romantic poetry, but his expertise didn't apply so much anymore. He assumed that his many years of study and teaching had formed him into a worthy mentor. In truth, they had only conditioned him to old ways of knowing. And because the digital event reached all the way down to the very cognitive mechanisms of users, he could never fully enter the twenty-first century. The more he knew about the past, the more immersed in old sonnets and Old Masters and in non-digital ways, the less he could connect with his pupils. The passage from a no-computer ecology to computers-everywhere was comparable to the evolution from an oral society into a literate society, it was said. The brain itself functioned in a new way; there really was a distinct "Net Generation Brain" (a chapter title in Don Tapscott's *Grown Up Digital*)[34]—a contention that recent neurological research supports. "The act of learning to read added an entirely new circuit to our hominid brain's repertoire," said cognitive scientist Maryanne Wolf, and when we shifted from print reading to screen reading, that circuit was modified (as we shall discuss later, Wolf believes the modification causes damage).[35] The professor "processes" in one way; the sophomores "process" in another. He was tied to the printed page; they scanned screens. He single-tasked; they multi-tasked. He read a sole text in linear sequence; they jumped around, clicked on links, kept twelve tabs open on the desktop. He had been formed in another environment; the gulf was too wide; he couldn't relate.

As for the Millennials, "The world was all before them," as Milton says of Adam and Eve as they leave the Garden. This was liberation; the withdrawal of the mentors granted them freedom to roam, to experiment. Nothing confirmed the old ed-school saw that exhorted teachers to switch from sage-on-the-stage to guide-on-the-side better than the PC, which could be personalized to each user, and social media, which let kids learn from one another, not just from the teacher. When the Center for Teaching Innovation at tier-one Cornell University advised professors to "[c]reate a digital learning environment by using online technology such as bulletin boards, blogs, Canvas, or social networking sites where students can interact, ask questions, and share information relevant to the course at any hour," it frankly diminished the authority of the scholar at the podium and in office hours waiting for undergraduates to drop by. And rightly so: "This generation thinks in many dimensions at once." Hence, a good instructor won't impose himself too firmly. Instead, he will "[p]rovide opportunities for students to be creative in how they approach assignments."[36]

Such teaching centers opened everywhere in the '90s and '00s, and they all said the same thing: use the tools; empower the kids; understand the difference between them and you. Don't be too controlling; let them discover on their own. Be interactive, we now have the tools, Facebook is your friend! Don't worry about the fact that the 2011 National Survey of Student Engagement (sample size: three hundred thousand–plus) showed that fully 42 percent of first-year students *never* spoke with their teachers outside of class about readings and ideas (another 37 percent only "sometimes"). Why is that a problem when at the same time an impressive 45 percent of them did discuss such things with fellow students (41 percent "sometimes," only 14 percent "never")?[37] Apparently, the kids had realized on their own what the pedagogy experts had had to explain to the grey-haired profs. They were already tugging at the teacher's leash, "taking ownership" of their education (another ed-school dogma). What they didn't get from those two and a half hours per week of class time with the teacher they got from one another—a pleasing sign that the much-recommended "collaborative learning" was taking place.

That same year, however, researchers Richard Arum and Josipa Roksa uncovered a piece of evidence that suggested peer learning wasn't necessarily so helpful. The book was called *Academically Adrift: Limited Learning on College Campuses*, and it evoked more commentary in education circles than any book published around that time. Citing the standard premise that peer-to-peer contact involves more equality and trust than peer-to-teacher contact—and thus more receptivity to learning—Arum and Roksa nevertheless found that "students who entered college with higher academic aptitude spent proportionally less time studying with their peers than students who came in with less prior demonstrated ability." It wasn't a huge discrepancy, but it did cast doubt on the notion that when peer-to-peer learning didn't happen it was due to conservative influences from above. Instead, it appeared that stronger students chose not to join groups. They worked better alone.[38]

That glitch, however, didn't slow the narrative of fruitful collaboration. We didn't hear many educators change their orders and command, "Stop studying with your friends and get over to your professor's office right now." Professor Arum is currently dean of the School of Education at UC-Irvine, but right across the way is the UCI Learning and Academic Resource Center, which defines its mission thus: "To advance academic success through proven active learning strategies, peer-to-peer collaboration... LARC connects 'what to learn' with 'how to learn' in a student-centered, collaborative learning experience."[39]

Back in April 1969, three decades before the digital revolution, a surprising thing happened at the campus of State University of New York, Old Westbury, when radical theorist Herbert Marcuse visited to give a lecture to the students. Michael Novak describes the episode in his memoir *Writing from Left to Right: My Journey from Liberal to Conservative*, which includes a full chapter on Novak's time teaching at Westbury, where he had joined the school as a willing participant in a new way of educating. The college had just opened with a small set of faculty and a hundred students or so. It was a deliberate experiment in precisely the kind of youth empowerment that would take a digital form thirty years later. In this new institution "all students would be 'full partners,' and new ways of weaving together learning and action would be explored," Novak remembers.[40] Here, finally, teachers would respect the finer consciousness of students, who hadn't been corrupted by the Establishment. Undergrads arrived fired up by Vietnam and youth revolt, convinced that the grown-ups had botched the world and wouldn't let go unless the young forced them, and they demanded that Westbury show how authentic reform works. Many of the teachers agreed.

Novak was in sympathy with the protests of the time, which he paints as part of a "tumultuous quest" for "honesty, courage, and community,"[41] but he retained enough common sense to recognize that a college needed some structure and hierarchy. The students' call for equality became "*hatred* for authority," he recalls, a full-on "contempt for normality and 'bourgeois' norms."[42] It was ludicrous: students coming to class barefoot and dirty, ordering teachers to approve their independent projects no matter what direction they took, denying the expertise of the very professors appointed to grade and accredit them, worshipping Viet Cong guerrillas and harassing teachers who seemed noncompliant (one day Novak found on his door a note signed by "The Committee" threatening him and his family). The whole experience pushed Novak toward views that would land him squarely among the neoconservatives in the 1980s.

Soon Novak and a few others split off to form their own college-within-a-college, in which the classics would be studied in a traditional manner. There, as provost, he could invite suitable outsiders to come and address the students, one of them being Marcuse. It was a logical choice. Nobody had better credentials than the famed German émigré, who had woven Marx and Freud together to create a compelling indictment of capitalist society in *Eros and Civilization* (1955) and *One-Dimensional Man* (1964). His thesis of "repressive tolerance," which authorized minority revolutionaries to deny free speech rights to conservative foes, thrilled Angela Davis and Abbie Hoffman. Students at Westbury would love to hear him.[43]

Novak doesn't mention it, but a year after Marcuse's visit, an account of it appeared in *Playboy* magazine under the heading "Portrait of the Marxist as an Old Trouper."[44] It was written by Michael G. Horowitz, a young journalist who had been a student of Marcuse's at Brandeis a few years before. People "came in droves" to see Marcuse at Westbury, Horowitz stated, students and nonstudents, eager to savor the man whose "revolutionary broadsides [had] always been too delightfully apocalyptic to be anything but explosively alive." The article recounted Marcuse's flight from Nazi Germany in the '30s, his patriotic work for the U.S. Office of War Information during World War II, positions at institutes at Columbia and Harvard in the 1950s, and professorship at Brandeis in the '60s, which he held until his anti–Vietnam War stance and fervent Marxism poisoned the relationship and he had to go (Marcuse compared America in 1965 to "the terror of Nazi Germany"), eventually relocating to UC–San Diego. By then, *Time* and the *New York Times* had named him the star theoretician of the New

Left. Student radicals who were otherwise contemptuous of anyone over thirty idolized him. The attendees at Westbury, Horowitz observed, were "as crass in their adoration as the crowd cheering Johnny Winter that night at the Fillmore East." Novak himself appears in the *Playboy* account as the "Catholic theologian . . . whose arguments for the New Left were giving the Vatican fits." Horowitz spotted him sitting "penitently on the floor, so as to be at Marcuse's feet."

Horowitz foresaw that the students' adulation would be tested, though. He had previous experience of Marcuse, from when he was a sophomore at Brandeis. Just before Marcuse quit the campus, students had held a reception in his honor at which a revealing exchange occurred. Marcuse's secretary had asked him, in an apparent reference to his formal teaching style, "Why don't you ever talk to your students?"

"But I do talk to them!" he replied.

Horowitz, standing right there, jumped in: "Ok, let's talk!" Marcuse let him proceed. "What do you think of student power?" the young man queried.

It was a common challenge at the time, to ask educators in authority how they conceived of their students—as children to be tutored or as budding adults to be set free? Given those polar alternatives, Marcuse was unambiguous: "On Vietnam, on dormitory rules, I am with you. But in the classroom, I believe in only one power—faculty power. When we were students in Berlin, we never dictated to our professors[;] we listened to them."

That response stuck with Horowitz, who judged Marcuse's approach "disturbingly authoritarian," and he didn't believe Marcuse had changed his educational views since then. What proceeded to unfold at Westbury didn't surprise him.

"What do you think of black studies?" came a shout from the back once Marcuse took his place at the front and the discussion began.

"I don't believe in black studies or white studies," Marcuse answered. "There's a certain amount of material that every intelligent person should learn."[45]

As Horowitz noted, this approach could only sound hopelessly reactionary to the revolutionaries in the room—a core, a tradition, a static canon of hoary works imposed upon a rising generation in order to tame it. The logical challenge would be: What "material"?

When I came across the *Playboy* article and read the account, such a challenge had an all too familiar ring. It was essentially the same question that was heard throughout academia in the 1980s and '90s, when multiculturalists discredited the traditional syllabus with the accusatory questions "Whose tradition? Why Shakespeare? Who decides?" I heard it all the time in those years and couldn't always figure out why it had so much authority, but it did. The questioners—from 1969 through the next few decades—assumed that those put-downs fully justified displacing Western Civilization from the curriculum: English lit from Beowulf to Virginia Woolf, the Great American Novel, art and architecture from the Parthenon to Picasso, the music of Mozart and Stravinsky, and all the rest. This time, though, it didn't fly with the speaker. Marcuse didn't bother with a specific defense. He didn't offer any names or titles. For him, it was obvious what students should be learning: "I am talking about the basics of history, economics, psychology, philosophy, and so on."

"Are these really relevant to the black student in a revolutionary situation?"

Marcuse acknowledged the apparent irrelevance of the traditional curriculum to kids from the ghetto but insisted that that was all the more reason for the core instruction. The same year he had written that genuine rebellion in an advanced society required "a break with the familiar, the routine ways of seeing, hearing, feeling, understanding things," something that he understood few uneducated persons could achieve.[46] Marcuse didn't go into that point at Westbury, but we can draw the implication. Without the guidance of tradition, the black student wouldn't comprehend his own situation, he wouldn't understand how radical the change must be to transform it, and hence his revolution would never go beyond fruitless gestures of resistance.

"But why bother preparing them?" growled a student Horowitz recognized as a member of SDS (Students for a Democratic Society). "For what? The white man's economics courses? If he's seen rats, junkies, and the General Motors Building, he knows all he has to know!" The crowd brayed its approval.

Marcuse had had enough. His tone remained diplomatic, but not his words. "I detect here…a growing anti-intellectual attitude among the students. There is no contradiction between intelligence and revolution. Why are you afraid of being intelligent?" He gave an example of thoughtful activism at UCSD, when students added scholarly material to their demands of the administration and won a concession from the dean. He noted, too, the roles of Voltaire, Diderot, and Rousseau in the French Revolution, and of Marx, Lenin, and Trotsky in the Russian Revolution, thinkers all. That argument quieted the crowd. A stand-off set in. The students didn't want to go into Voltaire and Marx; they were sure they'd already mastered the tools of revolution. And Marcuse wouldn't back down; he was unwilling to indulge youth just because they were young. You can imagine them sulking in silence, the man they revered sounding just like their square fathers telling them to finish their homework.[47]

It was a telling encounter between American upstarts and an Old-World thinker, a clash over readiness, not ideas or politics. Neither side would budge. They couldn't, because the debate had become too personal. The young revolutionaries wanted to hear about the tactics of the capitalists, yes; but more, they wanted Marcuse to endorse *them* as they were at that very moment ("Give us student power!"), and he wouldn't do it. They were already revolutionaries, they believed; but no, he said. If they really wanted to become revolutionaries, they would have to go to their rooms and read more books. Don't be in such a hurry; you're not ready yet, this sixty-year-old man told them. This wasn't a quarrel over politics. It was a quarrel over youth.

In his memory of the event, Novak saw it that way, too. He devoted only one paragraph to Marcuse's performance. But while at the time that he wrote his memoir, many years after the event, he stood far from the political position of the young reporter, his version of Marcuse's judgment didn't contradict Horowitz's at all: "After mingling with the students, he was affronted and disgusted. At his lecture, he set aside his prepared notes and instead described the severe Prussian discipline of his own education: the classics he had to master; the languages he had to learn by exercises and constant tests. His theme was that no one had any standing on which to rebel against the past—or dare to call himself a revolutionary—who had not mastered the tradition of the West."[48]

In both renditions of the story, the master was a disappointment to his fans, precisely because he couldn't accept them as partners. Not even the tactician of repressive tolerance could bridge the generation gap. Horowitz concludes that Marcuse was a radical thinker but lived a bourgeois life just like the rest of the Establishment, "paying mortgages, getting the car fixed...." He talked and talked but would never provoke a revolution. Though "a despairing youth intelligentsia needs constant resuscitation," they weren't going to get it from Marcuse, Horowitz decided. Novak's final remark records the impact of the guru's refusal to approve the students' rejection of traditional learning: "This was not at all what the students expected. From then on a chill came over quotations from Marcuse."

That was fifty years ago, at the height of a great upheaval, and it's amusing to look back on the turnabout that took place at this gathering of angry young men and women at the historic Long Island estate housing Westbury College. It isn't at all ironic, however, that the guru theorist of the time should be the voice of tradition, for this was Marcuse's fundamental point: nothing can be more reactionary than to cut the young off from the past and overestimate their novel identity. Or, put it this way: the ruling class rejoices over a stupid revolutionary who fails to spot the machinations that hold him back. Late capitalism works in subtle ways, by a misleading commodity fetishism, for instance, and you have to read a lot in order to see through it—that was the gist. Marcuse was formed in a rigid Prussian system, yes, but personal experience wasn't what led him to locate power strictly in the professor. He didn't assign *The Social Contract* and *Candide* because his professors had made him read them when he was a student. He did so out of tried-and-true Marxist principle.

It was a paradox, but no less true for that: if you want to be a canny revolutionary, you must start out an obedient student. Especially in a consumer society of relative prosperity, a compliant attitude in the formative years is necessary to the correct understanding of tyranny later on—of how labor gets "alienated," how bread and circuses cloud people's class consciousness, and so forth. If you simply trust that your generation, by virtue of its unique place in history, has special insight into injustice and power, you live only in the present, and consumer capitalism loves it when you think like that. You lack the tools of revolution; you're anti-intellectual, no matter how much you fancy yourself a rogue. Nothing serves the counterrevolutionary faction better than the puffed-up rebel who ignores Marx and Trotsky, neglects Machiavelli and Rousseau, and misses out on Hegel and *Robinson Crusoe* (a book Marx read closely). Without the background, without the ideas, our self-satisfied subversive is unwary and undiscerning, a shortsighted resister who doesn't realize that a "revolutionary" wearing blue jeans and a beard is fully as co-optable by consumer society as a conformist sporting an Oxford shirt and a crew cut. That's what bothered Marcuse about the youths who revered him. They were the opposite of what they thought they were, and few of their teachers were telling them so.

He understood something that the mentors of '69 didn't—the designers of the Westbury experiment and so many others, Jerry Rubin and the Youth International Party (the "Yippies"), the heroes of Woodstock and *Easy Rider* and *Zabriskie Point*, and the cheering intellectuals such as Charles Reich, whose celebrated paean to the flower children, "The Greening of America," began, "There is a revolution underway—not like revolutions of the past. This is the revolution of a new generation."[49] Marcuse was as politically radical as any of them, but he drew the line at the classroom, reserving it for the priming of students through lessons in the classics (You think revolution is simple?). As Marcuse watched the youngsters toss the tradition into the trash, he must have thought to himself, *What a damning self-conception they've absorbed.* The archetypal leftist could only despise the hip young Westbury faculty member announcing to all that he would approve any project a student brought forward, even one in which the student proposed to lay matches end to end across the Brooklyn Bridge (Novak describes that very declaration in his book).

It is easy to see why that cutting-edge mentor at Westbury would encourage such a thing. The senior project wouldn't force the student to learn much history, economics, or ethics, but it would help instill a certain personal conviction, an attitude these younger teachers admired and fostered: you, young man or young woman, just out of adolescence, but very concerned by what you see and hear, you are in charge; you have the authority. We, the teachers, are but helpers and facilitators, not masters—use us as you will. This would be the lasting impression created by the revolutionary new student-centered education: a ridiculously inflated notion of the students' capacities that would eventually cost them dearly. How would it play once they left the campus?

The undergraduates who ate it up denounced the System and the Establishment, suspected the Suits, refused to accept hierarchy, and claimed a unique perception of the whole rot. That's what their more enlightened mentors licensed them to do. But out in the real world, what would experienced workers conclude after a few weeks in the store or the office or on a work site with this kind of person? These graduates would leave school sure of themselves and suspicious of bosses, older coworkers, and neighbors, aiming to change the world but not really knowing very much about it. The kids at Westbury were outspoken about the irrelevance of the tradition, of the whole Establishment, dumping the old learning and the old ways with unprecedented self-conviction. Five years later, however, the confidence they had acquired in class would turn to bitterness when they found that the mentors' high opinion of them wasn't so widely shared in the larger society. They would discover that the pride they had taken in their youthful rebellion wasn't particularly helpful in the workplace, which values specific competencies more than anyone's self-esteem.

In other words, by praising the young as a special cohort at a pivotal point in history, by flattering them as "partners" in their own upbringing, in granting them political purity by virtue of their mere youth, the sympathetic observers, teachers, and thinkers did the opposite of their intent. They handed the young a tempting self-image that would never hold up. They may have believed that they cared more for the juniors than Marcuse and the old German disciplinarians ever did, but their tender forbearance only fostered illusions. Time would pass, our young idealists would grow older, youth would fade, the revolution wouldn't materialize, illusions would collapse, and the radicals of '69 would have no intellectual resources by which to cope. The world wouldn't make sense, and the novels, treatises, artworks, religions, and chronicles that might have explained their failures to them and offered models for recovery would be unavailable—because the mentors hadn't lodged them in their heads. This was the sorry irony: the more the mentors complimented teens and early-twenty-somethings as a vanguard sufficient unto itself with no need for the guideposts of tradition, the more they ill-equipped them for adulthood.

This brings us to the thesis of this book. The Marcuse affair happened five months before the very first message was sent from one computer to another, the letters *l-o-g*, typed on October 1, 1969, at UCLA and read simultaneously at Stanford (where the computer crashed before the word *login* was complete). Nobody at Westbury, Sproul Plaza, Kent State, or any other site of student protest imagined what was coming. They wouldn't have believed that one day the icon of youth rebellion would no longer be the stormy college student burning a draft card but a bouncy tween on an iPhone. The generational dynamic would be the same, though. The '60s' idealization of youth and denigration of the past got a reprise in the November 11, 2007, *60 Minutes* segment "Here Come the Millennials," which started with a warning to employers: "A new breed of American worker is about to attack everything you hold sacred: from giving orders, to your starched white shirt and tie." The querulous longhairs of '69 self-righteously suspicious of the Man were reincarnated in the networked high schoolers whose teachers hailed them with this encomium at Edutopia, the influential project of the George Lucas Educational Foundation: "I'm giving my students an award. A major award! I'm honoring them for stepping outside the comfort zone of the school system that they have been subject to for most of their

lives, authoring their own learning, and in the process, enjoying it."[50]
Marcuse's rebuke to the mentors who had encouraged that same adolescent confidence in 1969 could well be applied to these youth
watchers of the 2000s: in telling the kids that they were a pioneering
cohort, marking them as heralds of the next millennium, casting the
past as error or irrelevance, these false prophets were doing a terrible
thing. But this time, as they argued just as heartily for the special
acumen of the young and the mustiness of tradition, they could point
to material evidence: the phenomenal tools kids wielded so much
better than their parents and teachers. Those handheld devices and
Facebook profiles were delivering the independence youth had long
deserved, we were supposed to agree; the mentors never considered
this could be a disaster.

It was a disaster, and it was never going to be anything but a
disaster. We shouldn't even have to enumerate what the kids didn't
get, what they missed out on as the compliments poured in, but
when things get this screwy, the basics must be reiterated. To cut the
young off from a living past was to deprive them of a profound and
stabilizing understanding of life, of themselves. To immerse them
with one another, the private space of the teen's bedroom now a
bustling social space open for business all night long, was to ramp
up peer pressure like crazy. To neglect the masterpieces of art and
ideas, epic events and larger-than-life personages, was to level their
enjoyments to the mundane. To allow their religious impulses to
flicker, not to expose them to the orderly ministrations of Sunday
mornings, was to leave them among the "Nones," a label with sad
undertones. The bold and giddy digiphiles exhorted them, "You're
free—be creative—change the world—you're the future—the iPhone
4 is out next month!" But there was a grim subtext: "There is no
tradition for you—you have no usable past—no greatness to
revere—you're on your own."

Gaming, chatting, surfing, browsing, trolling, texting, tweeting, photoshopping...superficial ventures all, as the words suggest, and the kids rode the waves with abandon, unable to dive beneath the surface. The little screens and their all-too-present buddies and "friends," rivals and sex partners, bullies and mean girls, avatars and game characters barred the apprehension of the Good and the True. This was no place for the sublime, and there were only fleeting sightings of the Beautiful. Prayer, contemplation, aesthetic distance, a silent walk in the woods, Beethoven's Fifth, an hour in an easy chair with Jane Austen and no interruptions...they wouldn't happen. Digiphiles promised that the internet would bring the universe of knowledge to everyone with a device, but only the rare fourteen-year-old used it that way. The social side counted most. Pew's 2010 report on "Teens and Mobile Phones" astonished no one when it stated, "Text messaging explodes as teens embrace it as a vital form of daily communication with friends."[51] That those tools tied the kids to one another 24/7 didn't raise much concern. Eleven years before Marcuse's visit to Westbury, his countrywoman Hannah Arendt had warned that child-centered child-rearing would free kids from the tyranny of adults only to subject them to "the tyranny of their own group,"[52] of their peers, which terrified them far more than the decrees of their fathers. But the mentors of the twenty-first century couldn't admit such a thing; nobody wanted to speak of Millennials as dictatorial. They were the most tolerant generation in human history, you see: united against racism, sexism, homophobia, xenophobia...

Millennials couldn't tell you what rights the First Amendment guaranteed, but they had the correct attitude toward same-sex marriage, so we needn't be concerned. They wouldn't rank *Madama Butterfly* above Lady Gaga's "Bad Romance," but that was just a commendable respect for diverse arts. They couldn't detail the hardships

of General Washington at Valley Forge or the significance of his withdrawal to Mount Vernon after the war, but they knew he owned
slaves, and that was the important thing. In sum, the argument went,
if their beliefs weren't founded on very much knowledge, nor their
tastes formed out of the best art and music and verse, nevertheless
what they heard from and shared with one another online, the video
games they played and screen shots they took, the selves they crafted
and projected on Facebook and in Second Life: these were sufficient
to make them into happy grown-ups and good citizens.

But they weren't. We are now fourteen years past the publication
of *The Dumbest Generation*, which documented the anxious hours
of hyper-connected kids and predicted for them a difficult maturity.
I was blunt: "The Dumbest Generation will cease being dumb only
when it regards adolescence as an inferior realm of petty strivings
and adulthood as a realm of civic, historical, and cultural awareness
that puts them in touch with perennial ideas and struggles."[53] It was
obvious to me that a twenty-first-century teenager who didn't read
books or magazines or newspapers, who had no religion and
ignored history, civics, and great art, would grow into an unsatisfied
and confused adult. The pains of aging and parenting, workplace
drudgery, monthly bills and cleaning house, the scattering of
friends and family, an encounter or two with death (a parent or
grandparent)... and the middle-aged Millennial would lack the
solace of the Sermon on the Mount and the calm of Mahler's "Ada-
gietto." Self-portraits by Rembrandt and Van Gogh would have
given them the opportunity to lock eyes with men of profound
sadness; the screens to which they had transferred their attention
would instill no similar thoughtfulness and discernment. A bad
formation was taking place—anti-intellectual, ahistorical, and
vulgar—which cut their attention spans and fed their extended
adolescence, and it had to stop.

As I noted above, reaction to the thesis of *The Dumbest Generation* was swift and feisty. An op-ed in the *Washington Post* by Neil Howe after our debate at the American Enterprise Institute was characteristic: "Generational attitudes, Bauerlein's included, are typically long on attitude and short on facts."[54] How could I call the Millennials dumb? They had just elected the polished, professorial Barack Obama president. What about the fact that more of them went to college than any other cohort? And all the volunteering and service they were doing? In hundreds of interviews, from *CBS News with Katie Couric* to BBC's *World Today* to NPR, the hosts countered, *Wait, doesn't every aging generation do the "Kids these days!" thing?*

Well, as I said, we are now fourteen years past that publication date. The financial collapse of late 2008 happened, college costs continued to rise and student debt soared, the job market stagnated, ISIS emerged and gruesome killings were broadcast, the Arab Spring rose and fell, Barack Obama won a second term (but race relations seemed to worsen), Black Lives Matter broke out on college campuses, Donald Trump (incredibly) entered the White House, #MeToo sprung up and Harvey Weinstein went down, the transgender crusade began, the Kavanaugh hearings unfolded, the economy improved (but then COVID reached our shores), George Floyd died, looting and riots happened...and here we are with another election having left bitter feelings, lockdowns still in place here and there, and revolutionary sentiments in the air. The Twixters of the '00s reached their majority in the up-and-down '10s, and it had to be tough for them as they made their way toward manhood and womanhood. The sixteen-year-old of *The Dumbest Generation* is now twenty-nine years old. The nine-year-old who got her first cell phone in 2008 is now twenty-one. How is he faring? What has she become? How have they experienced and understood the intensities of our era?

Not very well. Whether it comes from media, social science, population surveys, college reports, or anecdotes, the evidence says that the young American psyche is sore and restive. "The truth is," a *Psychology Today* columnist wrote in 2019, "although no one can really agree about the millennial generation, one thing is fairly certain: They're stressed out."[55] An October 2020 story in Business Insider linking to lots of statistics bore the headline "Lonely, Burned Out, and Depressed: The State of Millennials' Mental Health in 2020"[56]—an echo of several hundred other accounts of misery. An April 2020 recap in the *Atlantic* of the Millennials' job and financial condition titled "Millennials Don't Stand a Chance" termed the ones turning thirty a whole new "lost generation."[57] They don't like other people very much, either, with 60 percent of eighteen-to-twenty-nine-year-olds believing that "most people can't be trusted" and 71 percent believing that most people "would try to take advantage of you if they got the chance" (older age groups scored much lower on mistrust).[58] One of the best observers of the Millennials, Jean Twenge, compiled a mountain of data to produce a book published in 2017 with the unsparing title *iGen: Why Today's Super-Connected Kids Are Growing Up Less Rebellious, More Tolerant, Less Happy—and Completely Unprepared for Adulthood (and What This Means for the Rest of Us).*[59]

They believed that they would achieve a fulfilling work-life balance and transform the office (no cubicles for them!), but an August 2016 Gallup poll reported that only 29 percent of them were "engaged in their jobs."[60] They graduated from college only to find they had joined what is now called the "overproduction of elites"—too many people trained for the professions, more than our society needs—and they were stuck with high loan payments and unattractive career options.[61] They insisted that every person be free to love whomever he wants, yet as they've grown older, they've increasingly failed to find a mate for life. A 2014 Urban Institute study entitled "Fewer

Marriages, More Divergence: Marriage Projections for Millennials to Age 40" reported, "We find that the percentage of millennials marrying by age 40 will fall lower than for any previous generation of Americans."[62]

The data are depressing, even if the Millennials overstate their plight. You can understand why members of the Greatest Generation would see them as a bunch of crybabies. If the former spotted a June 2020 column in the *Washington Post* entitled "The Unluckiest Generation in U.S. History," which highlighted the financial pains of young people during COVID,[63] they must have snorted at the absurdity. No Depression, no Dust Bowl, no War in the Pacific, no polio, no Jim Crow, no Iron Curtain, no military draft...gimme a break! When they saw the infamous undergrad at Yale shrieking on the quad at a faculty member for failing to secure a "safe space" and a "home" for her, they must have wondered at the hysteria that could cast Ivy League grounds as dangerous territory.[64] When a 2017 study in the *Journal of American College Health* showed that one in four students suffered "clinically significant symptoms related to the election [of Mr. Trump],"[65] Greatest Generation readers had to have blurted out, "What? You think you get to win every time?"

The Millennials may be exaggerating their suffering, but that only proves how poorly they have been trained for life. "Sometimes we're not prepared for adversity," says Cannonball Adderley, and his advice—plead to the Lord for "Mercy, Mercy, Mercy"—the kids never heard and wouldn't want to follow. It calls for the very humility they were told was unnecessary for a Digital Native. A little knowledge of the presidency going back a hundred years would have revealed how often the wheel turns and the inconceivable happens (as when Teddy Roosevelt took charge in 1901), thus softening the trauma they were experiencing over President Donald Trump. But they'd never really known any other president than Barack Obama, and they assumed that only someone like him, or at least someone pledging to carry on his legacy, deserved to enter the White House. If they'd read one hundred good novels in their teens, they would have developed a fuller cognizance of virtues and vices, the practice of interpreting Ahab and Heathcliff and the Invisible Man being a good tryout for relations with real and often challenging people. It might have prevented the knee-jerk responses to dissenting opinions—such as those we saw when Jordan Peterson and Ben Shapiro took questions from the audience, the "That's racist!" and "That's sexist!" verdicts that shut down the marketplace of ideas.

The Millennials grew up in a world of their own, though, and it didn't provide them with the tools to handle the ordinary pains of life once they had to leave that world. Most of them had no religion to give shape and direction to their mortal careers, no doctrine to explain suffering when it came. The "Nones" phenomenon is widely documented, but even those who had active faith and often went to church adopted a watery, shallow conception of people and things, and of God, too—what sociologists Christian Smith and Melinda Lundquist Denton have termed "moralistic therapeutic deism"— which preaches the goodness and tolerance of God and the rightful happiness of all souls on earth, but which wouldn't help them get over a bitter breakup, a miserable job, or an unwise social media post or photo that brought the ire of a digital mob down upon the poster. Why does a good God let bad things happen? No answer.

If they didn't have recourse to firm scriptural guidance, then perhaps the wisdom of Socrates, the pathos of Ophelia, or the pep talk of *Walden* might have done, but they didn't have those, either. The schools didn't instruct them in the great and momentous, and pop culture certainly didn't pass those things along. It used to, when Sherman and Mr. Peabody travelled back in time on the *Bullwinkle* show, or when the popular 1950s radio and TV series *You Are There*, hosted by Walter Cronkite, covered in news-like fashion the assassination of Caesar and death of Cleopatra, the Battle of Hastings, Joan of Arc, the Salem witch trials.... True, there were lots of little programs like that available online in 2010, and you could watch *You Are There* episodes on YouTube (the ones I just looked up were posted in 2014), but this time they had to compete with a million games and Instagram photos and music videos, and they lost. The kids were too tuned in to one another to listen to the voices of the dead. A dose of patriotism, too, might have given a foundation to their adulthood, but they weren't inclined to feel much loyalty to country, state, or town when the internet had turned the earth into a global village and they could socialize as easily with a stranger a thousand miles away as with a kid down the street. Even a hobby with a little cultural content would help—say, an interest in the Civil War or 1950s American cars, World War II fighter planes (models you could glue together) or 1940s fashions, Victorian novels or the Hardy Boys and Nancy Drew books—but to our sophisticated Millennial with phone in hand, those diversions were silly.

Such things would have shored them up in the way religious faith supported people in earlier times. They could have been coping resources, giving the Millennials a moral meaning relevant to their condition, building the kind of strength you see in the Greatest Generation. Growing up is painful, and tales of awkward youth—*The Catcher in the Rye*, *Great Expectations*, *The 400 Blows*—would bring a little relief. My twin brother and I watched *Star Trek* reruns one summer, and I realized later the lessons in leadership we absorbed from Captain Kirk and his lieutenants, along with the references in different episodes to Shakespeare, *Paradise Lost*, ancient Rome, Lincoln, the U.S. Constitution.... I remember going to bed at night after a hard day in twelfth grade with a Philip Marlowe book in hand—Los Angeles in the '30s, gamblers and dames and a hero trying to keep his scruples. It made the squalor of high school a little less imposing by offering an escape and a promise: life could be serious and romantic, not always this paltry, fearful existence in a Del Mar apartment in 1977.

The nineteenth-century poet-critic Matthew Arnold, writing in an age of dizzying change, had this to say about the benefit of things from long ago: "I know not how it is, but their commerce with the ancients appears to me to produce, in those who constantly practice it, a steadying and composing effect upon their judgement, not of literary works only, but of men and events in general."[66] I cited that observation in *The Dumbest Generation*, and nothing in the progress of the lives of the Digital Natives who ignored it has lessened its truth. As the modern world hits you with one disruption after another, marvelous or not, and as the Digital Age speeds it up as never before,[67] the ancients steady and compose you, keep you balanced. That's the formula: acquaintance with the old helps you accommodate the new. A well-read man won't be so shocked by politicians clamoring for war; Thucydides called it in 431 BC. Or, if a girl's love for a rambling fellow is getting out of control, her mother understands it because she has for comparison the many women who fell for Lord Byron and Picasso, the tale of Cathy and Heathcliff, Richard III's seduction of Lady Anne.... Hard and distressing phenomena don't go away, but they can be apprehended more smoothly, and that feels better. The heroes and villains of the Roman Empire and the French Revolution are a reliable yardstick against which to measure the leaders of today, and the comparison strengthens you to resist manipulation. The best examples of art and literature, the astute wit of Molière and the mournful lines of *The Waste Land* and the beauties of Schubert's *Lieder*...they supply intellectual standards that give you perspective on the consumer society. Such things show the young what it means to grow up.

Arnold is remembered most for his definition of criticism: "a disinterested endeavor to learn and propagate the best that is known and thought in the world."[68] People see him as a conservative because he admitted few contemporary works into that high classification. But Arnold's definition has more, another phrase that by itself sounds quite progressive: "...and thus to establish a current of fresh and true ideas." That makes the past less static. The best that has been known and thought doesn't stifle the present or discourage the living. Instead, it filters out the stale and the false and draws forth the psychically healthy, the authentically new. Most important for the young, it sets them into a current, the river of time that flows from long ago and far away right up to their feet and from them shall proceed to the generations to come. This is a fund of creation bigger and better than the social network. We should have told them so again and again. It can give you a second home. A youth conversing with Dante or Manet, caught up in Civil War battles, collecting stamps and coins, even wearing vintage clothes, joins a lineage that makes him less alone and unacknowledged. He can be like W. E. B. Du Bois, living in a society that knocks him down but making uplifting contact with comrades long gone:

> I sit with Shakespeare and he winces not. I cross the color line and move arm and arm with Balzac and Dumas, where smiling men and welcoming women glide in gilded halls. From out of the caves of evening that swing between the strong-limbed Earth and the tracery of stars, I summon Aristotle and Aurelius and what soul I will, and they come all graciously with no scorn nor condescension.[69]

This balm was always available to Millennials as they tripped over hurdles in the real world—well short of God, but a whole lot better than the twenty-first-century ethos that gave them no inheritance, only a screen and keyboard and whatever in the way of friends and accomplishments they could make of them. Someone had to inform them, though—mentors with the knowledge, confident enough to pass it on. For, besides familiarizing them with particular works from the tradition, the mentors would have had to persuade the young of the value of the past, something that doesn't come naturally to a twelve-year-old. They had to learn that Gettysburg and the Address were not just schoolwork, that there were other reasons to study the fate of Robespierre than the final grade. History is more than knowledge, the mentors should have said; it's moral truth. Literature is more than plot and character; it's personal. A nation isn't just a place; it's part of who you are: you're an American. But the mentors didn't tell them any of those things. In forty years as a student and teacher of English, I watched the humanities at the high school and college levels deliberately drained of this very conviction. Instead of urging eighteen-year-olds to absorb English literature, from Chaucer to James Joyce, as the best inventions in the language we speak, the professors opted for "critical thinking" as the prime goal of learning. Comparative literature scholars and art historians turned ever more to contemporary theory—to Lacan, Foucault, and the rest—and away from subject matter, Flaubert and the Pantheon. They didn't tell students they had to learn the canon; no, students must "interrogate" the canon. They dropped the classics or changed their purpose from things to be assimilated because of their inherent value to things to be picked up so that a student might exercise his critical faculty.

This was asking kids to build while holding back the tools. It emphasized critical thinking over subject matter knowledge, but critical thinking about a subject only happens on top of thorough knowledge of that subject. In a March 2005 essay in the *Atlantic*, Ross Douthat demonstrated the hollowness of this kind of education by describing one assignment in a course he took in his final year as an undergraduate at Harvard: The American West, 1780–1830. The teacher had handed the students two journal articles on the theory and practice of "material history" and sent them to the Peabody Museum to select a pair of objects from the frontier era—one made by Indians, one by Europeans—asking for an in-depth comparative analysis of them. Douthat chose a Sioux war club and a six-shooter but then wondered, "How could I eke out ten pages when I knew nothing about the provenance of the weapons or the significance of the markings?" Well, it turned out to be easy, and he "didn't need to do any reading, absorb any history, or learn anything at all."[70] Douthat merely strung together clever-sounding observations, such as "Chief Antelope's war club is less a weapon than a talisman of supernatural power.... The 'H.A. Brigham' inscription, a [nineteenth-]century version of the modern logo, reinforces the revolver's connection to a capitalist order...." He had heard such abstract insights from many teachers at Harvard, and they could be applied in spite of his total ignorance of everything else about the objects being described. It was easy to wield the standard catchphrases whose bare mention marked the student as an advanced intelligence. Nifty! Douthat concludes, "By the time I had finished, I almost believed it." The paper got an A.[71]

Look at the personal impact, though. Douthat's effort didn't produce a meaningful understanding of the old. It blocked that understanding. Douthat didn't come any closer to imagining the weapons in 1820 in the hands of reckless and deadly men. The whole exercise was trivial, and it left him slightly embarrassed. He didn't learn anything. He faked it, and he admitted it. His teacher had turned the past into a pretext.

It happened a million times to the Millennials, and few of them recognized the sham as Douthat did. After all, that kind of instruction required less reading and less work, and you could still get an

A. Who wanted to raise objections that would only raise the weekly page count? Questions about whether this superficial style of humanities education really formed rising Americans into sturdy citizens and discerning consumers weren't asked. This was Harvard, the best! True, the graduates would become adults with little civic sense, without legends, stories, powerful images, and beautiful songs and Great Books in their bones. So what?

With mentors like that, it's no surprise that we see so much anger, anxiety, fragility, self-righteousness, and dismay among Millennials now in their late twenties and thirties. They were never handed something that everybody needs: the religious and historical and cultural equipment to manage a busy world. They grew up with a gaping hole in their souls, and "the soul has needs that must be satisfied."[72] That line comes from Alexis de Tocqueville in *Democracy in America*, in the chapter entitled "Why Certain Americans Display Such an Exalted Spiritualism." It follows a section on "The Love of Material Enjoyments" and seems to contradict it, but that's the point. In America, Tocqueville said, the "passion for material well-being" was universal, but there was spiritual passion as well. Indeed, the truth that man does not live by bread alone was demonstrated nowhere so well as it was in the towns and hamlets Tocqueville visited. As he toured the States in 1831 and '32, he was surprised to see such otherworldly ardor—"an exalted and almost fierce spiritualism that one scarcely encounters in Europe"— in a nation otherwise devoted to material gain without an established church.[73]

Another factor helped explain it: compared to the Old World, the United States had no authoritative traditions or recognized history. In his preface to *The Marble Faun* (1860), Nathaniel Hawthorne complained that it was hard to write a romance about a country "where there is no shadow, no antiquity, no mystery, no picturesque and gloomy wrong nor anything but a commonplace prosperity, in broad and simple daylight."[74] The landscape had no depth, no "ruined castles," Goethe noted. Young men and women didn't live in the memory of what their grandfathers in the town had done, because the town hadn't existed back then, or if it were an old city such as Boston or Philadelphia, it had changed too much over two generations. People moved around too much to build up a sense of former times. Recent immigrants from Germany didn't remember the Pilgrims. They just wanted space to do their own thing.

But the flatness of daily life, the fixation on middle-class well-being in a present that lacks moral meaning, didn't serve the soul (not then and not now). The more a society pushes "the search for material goods alone," Tocqueville implies, the more thirsty for spiritual nourishment the people will be. Again, man cannot live by bread alone. He has a "taste for the infinite and the love of what is immortal," Tocqueville wrote. Those are "sublime instincts." If a school or a town or a job doesn't feed them, if all that people get is "enjoyment of the senses," they will turn elsewhere for the satisfaction of those deeper desires. That explains the "itinerant preachers who peddle the divine word from place to place" toward whom the most isolated, struggling, and uneducated farmers and their families flocked. People will always crave a higher purpose. Such instincts are eternal, and a man "can hinder and deform them, but not destroy them."

Tocqueville's formula applies here; Millennials are no different. The Digital Age gave them endless diversion and one another, but that wasn't enough. It didn't give them transcendence. Or a grasp of the tragic, either, such as you might learn from the story of the rich young man who couldn't give his goods away and follow Jesus. Nor did they experience an exalted romance, as when Gatsby "knew that when he kissed this girl, and forever wed his unutterable visions to her perishable breath, his mind would never romp again like the mind of God."[75] They knew nothing of the "passion for the past" that Tennyson said he had felt for as long as he could remember, or of the "historical sense," as T. S. Eliot called it—that feeling for what is no more, which makes Hamlet and Pearl Harbor as real as anything coming through the screen. They had no awareness of long shadows of devastation, such as might be acquired from reading the letters of men who fought at Shiloh or Antietam; no knowledge of gothic secrets like the parentage of Charles Bon in *Absalom, Absalom*; no understanding of the world-changing adventures of Cortez and the conquistadors or Nelson at Trafalgar; no appreciation for high oratory from Pericles to Booker T. Washington at Piedmont Park; no appetite for sublime crescendos like the *scène d'amour* in Berlioz's *Roméo*; no sense for piercing conversions or sweeping teleologies or founding myths—just a hectic round of gossip, games, messages, photos...

"The desire for God is written in the human heart," it says on page one of the Catholic Catechism, and Tocqueville was right to believe that that desire can never be expelled, only deformed. Millennials were just as hungry for meaning and design in the world as every other generation, but no cohort had had paraded before them as many distractions from and degradations of that desire as the Digital Natives. The mentors let them plunge into Youth World, and the search for meaning staggered and simmered. They had the will to believe but no organized religion to offer them anything worth believing in. They claimed a historic importance for themselves but had little historical knowledge to back it up. They were known for their idealism, but they didn't read much ethics or social theory. They fancied themselves discriminating consumers, but they had no appreciation of high art that might refine their tastes. Where would their spiritual impulses go?

Consider the question this way: What belief best suits a youth who doesn't want to go to church? What conception of human nature will appeal most to someone who trusts in his own exceptional nature? What vision of the future works best for someone with no sense of the past? What standard of judgment goes with a sensibility that won't distinguish superior from inferior creations? What ultimate meaning will he find on his own?

The answer is: Utopia.

Utopia is an innocent dream of how things ought to be, and a youth raised on Millennial projections can't understand why that blessed condition shouldn't materialize here and now. A 2014 study by Pew Research entitled "Millennials in Adulthood" concluded that Millennials shun religious and political organizations—they are "Unmoored from Institutions."[76] But a Utopian faith doesn't need a formal structure or a priesthood. Life is better without them. Its dogmas are simple—total freedom and equality and happiness—and twenty-first-century believers think that they can communicate them and organize on their own online. Religions warn of the dangers of fabricating heaven on earth, and that's one reason why Millennials go "None." The historical record of Utopia is poor, one collapse into failure or bloody tyranny after another, but if you regard the past as a mistake, a time of unenlightenment, you shrug. Millennials mistrust successful people—Pew found in 2018 that only one-third of them have "a great deal/fair amount" of confidence in political and business leaders, one half of them in religious leaders[77]—which might seem to contradict the idealistic outlook, in that common success might prove that the basic elements of a personal Utopia already exist and that everyone else merely needs to learn how to use them. But Millennials notice, too, how often the success of one comes at the expense of others—for instance, in college admissions, which let one in and keep another out, and that's not right. People shouldn't be so competitive. Some of those successful people made it by forms of injustice, and that makes them suspect. This is how Utopians think. They sharply divide human beings along those lines, into those who are committed and suited to the equalizing paradise to come and those who are not.

Given the formation they received—the withdrawal of the mentors and the avalanche of media and social media—we may assume that the yen for Utopia would inevitably have spread among them after they left the safe spaces of home and college. Like Tocqueville's Americans, they needed a transcendent horizon for their ambitions, and Christianity wouldn't have much appeal—it was too ancient, and that Original Sin thing certainly didn't fit their views. Not the old liberal individualism, either, not when real estate was so expensive in youth hot spots and the ones who went to college had heavy loan payments and the ones who didn't had seen their wages slip. The rigors of an open society, a vibrant public square packed with conflicting voices, would only upset them. In Utopia, people calm down; they don't contend. It's perfect, the logical outlook for the fragile and the self-involved, for the excitable personality profiled by Jonathan Haidt and Greg Lukianoff in their 2018 book *The Coddling of the American Mind*, which predicted that pampered youth would fail once they had to mingle with people uninterested in coddling them. In Utopia, nobody fails.

The result is a fair portion of Americans who've grown into frighteningly illiberal adults. This is not a marginal phenomenon. Surveys and reportage show roughly one-third to one-half of young Americans favor communist ideas when they are presented in the abstract. They mistrust capitalism, support limitations on free speech, regard the United States as a guilty empire, and disrespect privacy rights. They don't like the inevitable inequities of an open society and insist that they be fixed. They can't debate first principles; it agitates them. They get people fired for telling a stupid joke. They believe they've been cheated of a satisfying lifestyle. Many of them have become angry activists. Some of them landed among the rioters of summer 2020.

It is the contention of this book that the process began when they were in middle school. They enjoyed an unprecedented habitat, surrounded by the omnipresent screens, with the bells and whistles obscuring the facts of what they were missing. Their multi-year digital exposure hit them during the very years in which the world takes form in a child's head. Digital tools and lax mentors primed them to flee from history, religion, great literature, and art, from music and ethics and American civics, into the fantasy of a society that would replicate the teenage bedroom, where freedom and friends predominated, games and photos and chats never stopped. When school ended and they hit the workplace, the bills piled up, and bosses weren't so caring, sex partners came and went...they had no religion, no cultural patrimony, and no role models to ease the transition. So they attached themselves to something else: a religion of sorts, a pugnacious, illiberal demand, a twenty-first-century American-youth version of, precisely, Utopia. It has many names— "Black Lives Matter," "Social Justice," "Racial Justice," "Democratic Socialism," "LGBT Rights," "Antifa"—but "Utopia" captures best the breadth and generality of the attitude. They have come to it not by a process of study and reason, but by the opposite, for emotional and psychological reasons, and out of a lack of understanding. In their uncompromising picture of a perfect future, they found what they needed: goals and values, the Good and the True and the Sublime, which the web and the grown-ups promised but didn't deliver. The tools that supposedly empowered them, the hands-off mentoring assumed to liberate them, the friends who reassured them at all times...all of those things sent them into a mythical land of goodness and shelter, relief from the rigors of a pressing social sphere, partisan political scene, and competitive job market. Like every Eden, though, it had a dark aspect: a fury toward anyone or anything that threatened to ruin this sacred preserve. Utopian justice is the harshest.

CHAPTER TWO

They Have a Dream

B ack in April 2016, when I was teaching at Emory University, Milo Yiannopoulos came to campus to speak, and a lot of students were troubled. It was a tense spring semester. Black Lives Matter protests had begun the year before at the University of Missouri and spread to dozens of the most elite campuses in the nation. There was ongoing talk of a "rape culture" on college campuses, too—some of it adopted by the Obama Administration, which in mid-2014 had put fifty-five schools under review for their handling of sexual assault cases, including Harvard, Michigan, Princeton, and Emory (I don't think anything ever came of it, though I recall having to complete some kind of online orientation questionnaire). Donald Trump's unexpected jump to the front of the Republican pack frightened and appalled young people who had idolized President Obama; they couldn't imagine the boisterous, politically incorrect Mr. Trump's taking his place. (That November in the election, Mr. Trump would draw only 37 percent of the youth vote.[1])

Emory had a few BLM activists who organized protests that year, which, though they didn't much affect a campus that is dominated by the business school and biological sciences (the Centers for

Disease Control sit right across the street), predictably earned news coverage and the attention of the administration. In March, when some students found chalkings on the sidewalks endorsing Mr. Trump and his "wall," they stomped to the university president's office and demanded a fix. The president did what all college presidents do when wrathful undergraduates, especially those of color, head their way. He listened, nodded and sympathized, and chided the unknown provocateurs, whom the kids said had "intimidated" them. One student alleged an "environment of hatred that is created by seeing 'Trump 2016.'" The president acknowledged the protestors' "genuine concern and pain," but it wasn't clear what actions might be taken against the perpetrators.[2]

That was it, no big deal. And the university certainly didn't mount an investigation. The president's commiseration was the practical tack, the standard way of making the situation go away, and the whole thing should have disappeared. Only fifteen or so students were involved, and their reactions were obviously overdone. Show them you share their disquiet, issue vague announcements that divisive actions are unwelcome, and the students will relax and head back to the dorms—problem solved. But Bill O'Reilly got hold of the story, and CBS News and Gawker too, all of whom knocked the protesters for their snowflake reflexes. I myself did a spot on an afternoon Fox show, highlighting just how vitalizing it must have been for those pained nineteen-year-olds to speed toward the administration building and have the Biggest Man on Campus defer to their feelings.

That episode is what prompted the Milo event a month later. The high sensitivities of a few dozen vocal kids on campus were a perfect occasion for the in-your-face satire he had crafted against PC censorship and developed into a national sensation. At the time Milo was the most infamous figure in the campus speech business, a maverick needling the feminists, trans activists, and race theorists, who had all the moral weight in higher education and routinely bulldozed the moderate liberals (who made up the majority of the faculty and administration and who habitually bowed to the minority on their left). Milo could be crude and caustic, but he was also handsome, funny, cultured, and intelligent, ready to face leftists on *Bill Maher* and to provoke undergraduates in college auditoriums with his sly smile and bitchy put-downs. For a pro-Trump conservative, he had an unusual identity: gay man, part Jewish, and known for dating black men. It was hard to cast him as a homophobe, anti-Semite, or racist. He was canny, too, in the way he mixed antic theatrics with serious points, alternating between outlandish queen in costume and astute intellectual conversant with the best literature and art. At UC–Santa Barbara that very month, he had entered the hall seated like a pharaoh in a golden chair on a platform carried by six strong men (a spectacle preserved for posterity on YouTube).[3] Every other week, it seemed, a Milo affair erupted, and his speeches and interviews traveled all across the internet. I just checked a CNBC appearance from later that summer that YouTube records as having drawn 1.9 million page views.[4] When he secured a book contract with Simon and Schuster a few months later, preorders sent it to number one on Amazon by the next day.

Naturally, a celebrity who specialized in flouting political correctness during a freakish election season (in which he referred to Mr. Trump as "Daddy") would spark controversy at Emory, as he did everywhere else. The usual thing happened. Milo sent a tweet suggesting he come speak, the College Republicans and Emory's Young Americans for Liberty issued the invitation, Milo arrived and addressed two hundred students, and a pack of protesters lined up outside the hall where he was speaking holding posters that said, "EMORY: NO PLACE FOR HATE," "Milo: Racist Misogynist," and "Emory Is Nothing without Women + POC." No violence or even heated disputes broke out, and it was all in all a good occasion for the airing of contrasting views. In fact, the students who were offended chose not to confront Milo directly, and they advised others to ignore him. One protester told the student newspaper that Milo's act had only one purpose: "to delegitimize the grievances of oppressed peoples,"[5] implying that you can't argue with someone who dismisses your feelings and experiences, your very self. Best, then, to give him as little attention as possible.

I followed the events from a distance. The attacks on Charles Murray at Middlebury and Heather Mac Donald at Claremont McKenna hadn't happened yet, nor the torching of Berkeley in advance of Milo's visit there nine months later. But Black Lives Matter "lists of demands" were coming out every week or two, one ultimatum after another sent to college presidents by dissatisfied students insisting that more personnel of color be hired, more services for students of color be created, and more recognition of ongoing local racism be confessed. (A list of statements from groups at Yale, USC, UCLA, Purdue, Harvard, and other schools can be found at thedemands.org.) We started to hear calls for the removal of names from buildings and programs, usually because of those individuals' implications in slavery or colonization. In late 2018, for instance, Stanford would clear Father Junípero Serra's name from the grounds. Warnings of "cultural appropriation" were heard, such as when students at Bowdoin College were rebuked for donning sombreros at a tequila party. The terms "micro-aggression" and "trigger warning" popped up, and everybody started using them. At Columbia University, students described the traumatizing impact of the core curriculum, which favored white males and Eurocentric tradition. And the notorious *Rolling Stone* tale of rape at the University of Virginia, which appeared November 2014 and instantly became a sensation, bolstered claims about a "rape culture" in the dorms and fraternities and athletic facilities and was accepted by education reporters and deans everywhere, whether they really believed it or not, even after the story was exposed as a fabrication.

The complaints of bigotry and discrimination have become so customary by now that to lay them out is a tiresome activity, not least because of the unappealing character of the complainers. If we step back from the issues, we have to ask how so much attention and sympathy were awarded to twenty-year-olds who didn't come off as particularly smart or talented, perceptive or good. The more we heard about them, the harder it was to like them. A story in the May 30, 2016, *New Yorker*, "The Big Uneasy: What's Roiling the Liberal-Arts Campus?" focused on Oberlin College and included interviews with several activist youths, each one proving deeply self-absorbed and decidedly anti-intellectual. One student—a "trans man" with a Beaver Cleaver haircut and a blue streak on top who had advocated in the *Oberlin Review* for a trigger warning on every syllabus on which Sophocles' play *Antigone* appeared—told the reporter that he encountered micro-aggressions everywhere he went. He didn't provide details. Another student explained that she no longer wasted her time in debate. "I do think that there's something to be said about exposing yourself to ideas other than your own," she conceded, "but I've had enough of that after my fifth year."[6] She identified as "Afro-Latinx," but rejected the "Du Bois, I'm-gonna-sit-back-and-read-my-things state," as she put it. Enough talk, no more books—she wanted action. Another undergraduate, who is white, urged her fellow white students to stay quiet in class so that students of color could feel more comfortable speaking up. The last student interviewed by reporter Nathan Heller showed up in sweatpants and a T-shirt. She had organized "queer" events and workshops in the past and had just finished with a symposium against racism. She was worn out, but the "radical work" of "queer people, people of color, and black people" inspired her. She owed nothing to Oberlin, however. In fact, she resented Oberlin and the other elite schools she had attended (with scholarships). Those places hadn't helped her; they had hurt her. She told Heller that "the past few years have been about 'unlearning' most of what she had been taught."[7] Higher education was just a "tool of capitalism."[8]

I read the story at the time and couldn't understand the students' mood of misery and faithlessness. They were wrapping up college but took no pride in their accomplishment. In the self-dramatics, the kids seemed to lose sight of any specific reform goals. It made me feel like the puzzled and impatient parents in 1969 who couldn't figure out why their children were so fractious and disrespectful or what to do about it. Indeed, I couldn't even connect the protesters back in the '60s with the activists of 2015. The first had the War and the draft; the second had...micro-aggressions. The first talked about Nixon and Dow Chemical; the second about themselves. The first held sit-ins and rap sessions and bounced opinions back and forth nonstop. The second were tired of the discussion. The protesters at Emory who showed up for the Milo event were altogether typical, taking the same personal angle, expressing their conviction that something was being done to them, directly, and asserting that the old ways of responding in the halls of debate and the marketplace of ideas wouldn't fly.

I didn't get it. When I was a student at UCLA in the 1980s, the ones who took up a cause had a whole different mindset. I remember one affair from around 1984, when Asian Americans in California lost their ability to qualify as low-income first-generation minority applicants who would get special consideration in admissions. The University of California system had dropped them from the affirmative action program because Asian enrollments had climbed so fast that they didn't appear to need help any more. In reaction, Asian groups staged some demonstrations and marches around campus that made a simple point: Why should low-income Asians be punished for doing well? Their demand: reverse the decision. There was no personal angst, just insistence on a policy change. Other student groups at the time pushed for divestment from South Africa (still under Apartheid) and Israel (to support the Palestinians), issuing flyers and organizing discussions. They didn't detail their own agonies; they insisted that the University of California alter its investment portfolio. If a reporter had asked them about how the situation in South Africa affected them in their daily lives, they wouldn't have known how to answer. In fact, they would have rejected the premise of the question. To decry an injustice far away is a moral duty whether it affects you or not. Even the Asians whose own group was affected by the change in policy took an impersonal approach to the issue, appealing to the justice of their cause rather than their personal suffering.

Not this time. The protest in 2016 was all personal: stop making me feel bad; stop "delegitimizing" me. This was the gist in the 2010s. In Fall 2017, the president of Wesleyan University, Michael Roth, invited me to speak as part of a "difficult conversations" initiative. Wesleyan is a determinedly left-wing campus, and Roth saw the occasional conservative visitor as good for the intellectual climate. We were eight months into the Trump Administration, and I'd written pieces for Vox, CNN, the *New York Times*, and other liberal outlets that suggested I might praise President Trump in a way that would rise above naked partisanship. I decided on a presentation of Donald Trump as a traditional American rogue figure, a model of Emersonian nonconformity, an outlandish character in a lineage of comic renegades. No other individual in my lifetime mobilized the entirety of respectable opinion in America against himself, I would tell them, and that very fact deserved analysis. Everybody in the elite denounced him—a strange uniformity for a social group that repeats its admiration for thinking outside the box. Hollywood, Silicon Valley, the Swamp, the art world, the media, academia... they hated him with a passion that revealed more about themselves than it did about the object of their enmity. He had to have something going for him to evoke such a monolithic pageant of slurs.

I laid this out before an audience of two hundred, and the faculty in the room more or less got the tongue-in-cheek element (though they asked some tough questions about Trump's sexism). Not the students, though. This wasn't funny at all. They went after Trump's racism and barked objections to the "wall." A couple of them stormed out and slammed the doors after I answered their challenges. I had mentioned Emerson, Thoreau, and Walt Whitman in my short talk—classic voices that hailed the iconoclast and the irreverent—and the very first question I got chided me for selecting those three white males. I wanted to reply, "Who ever taught you to think in this way?", but I didn't want to insult my hosts. Instead, I went with a little sarcasm: "Oh, yes, it's really bad, especially when Emerson says that society is in 'conspiracy' against the 'manhood' of its members" ("Self-Reliance"). I stressed the word "manhood" and waited for the questioner to respond. He remained quiet, so I gave the crowd the historical fact that the "manhood" element in Emerson didn't stop thousands of strong women in the 1840s from reading him and recognizing, *Yeah, that's me!* The questioner still didn't reply—had he read one word of those three men before?—so another student shouted, "But were they black women?!" It was becoming ridiculous. When I praised President Roth for his support of open debate (which he had declared in a *Wall Street Journal* column announcing his visiting speaker program), a student sitting right behind Roth announced that he didn't think much of the op-ed, adding, "But then, I wished that the Vietcong won back in the sixties." As a professor in the room reminded him that the Viet Cong had won the war, I looked out at the students, baffled once again about why these kids attending a great school like Wesleyan and clearly on the way to success were so bitter and humorless. Afterwards, a tall young man, part black and part Hispanic, came up to me and in plaintive tones said that young people of color were dying, yes, dying, from what was happening. He wasn't angry; he was despondent and helpless. I gazed at him and tried to figure out what motives lay behind the overt distress at that otherwise relaxed after-the-event moment. He was sincere; he really meant it; he genuinely wanted to acquaint me with a world of hurt that I had missed, but he didn't get specific. He wasn't arguing; he was emoting. Pain was out there, he insisted, smothering and pitiless, and innocent young men and women were falling. I needed to accept that. This was no time to be ironic or to cite irrelevant writers from long ago.

The exchange lasted only a couple of minutes, and it wasn't contentious. It was mystifying. My interlocutor walked off feeling no better than before. His expression of angst didn't relieve him at all. I appeared to him as just another obtuse character comfortable in my "privilege" (which another student mentioned in the Q & A), and to his credit he had tried to open my eyes and ears, not attack. That he couldn't be any more precise than "People are dying!" was my problem, not his. I didn't tell him that while he was attending an elite private school whose professors and administrators showed an exquisitely solicitous regard for his feelings, I had never attended a private school of any kind in my life, had worked my way through college, and had had teachers who usually couldn't attach my name to my face. Instead, as he reiterated the affliction under way, I actually said something like, "Where?" or "Who?"—only confirming for him the exasperating incognizance of those in power. President Roth had conceived the dissenting-speaker program as a benefit for him and his peers, but when people are suffering so, intellectual diversity doesn't count for very much. He was at Wesleyan, one of the topmost schools in the country, but academic ideals paled before the grand anguish he saw near and far.

This called for an explanation. A student at Emory who had taken a few courses with me often dropped by to discuss her work and ponder going to graduate school. I paid her now and then to assist with an undergraduate program I had started a few years before. She didn't have the typical background of the selective private school undergraduate nor the attitude of the on-her-way, busy-busy Millennial. She had transferred from a two-year college, had to work to pay her rent, and had shared the dysfunction in her family with me. She wasn't an outright conservative, but a few comments she had made about welfare and grievance hinted at some sound mistrust of identity politics. On the day Milo arrived, she happened to be in my office, and I asked her if she knew who he was.

"Oh, yes," she answered with a smile, as if Milo were a common topic of student conversation. She added something about local happenings always going back and forth on social media. I wondered whether I could ask her to sum up what looked to me like a foolish overreaction on the part of the protesters and give me a straight appraisal of him.

"Tell me, what about Milo bothers these guys? Why are they so upset?"

I expected one more impression of a fellow everyone was talking about, but she ignored the first question. The real issue was her peers.

"Well," she answered, pausing and choosing her words carefully, "they believe that everyone...deserves...to be happy."

I waited for her to go on, but she stopped and said nothing further. She had thought about this before, I could tell, and apparently didn't want to explain until the bare truth had had time to sink in. It was three o'clock on a spring afternoon in my dim office, I had papers to grade, she had a draft on Thoreau she wanted me to examine, and the hallways were quiet, but *everyone deserves to be happy*. There was something vatic and otherworldly about that statement. It was as if she had put a higher truth into the air and everything else had halted. Not often does a fresh moral absolute break the ordinary course of a teacher's day. It had the shape of an axiom, like an article of faith in pop psychology ("I'm OK, You're OK"), plus the force of a commandment—a positive one, not a thou-shalt-not. You could utter it as casual fact: "Well, you know, everyone really deserves to be happy, that's only fair"—or as a stiff injunction: "Listen carefully; everybody *deserves* to be happy, and I mean *everybody*. You got that?" She was right to let it hang there.

I stopped, too, needing a moment to let this oracular line settle into my head. The meaning of each word in her sentence was clear, but not the meaning of the whole. *Everyone deserves to be happy*—really? There was too much here for me to answer one way or the other, "Yes, they do," or "No, they don't." The sentiment was simple, but as she vocalized it an entire worldview condensed and flowed through it. You could sense Life, Fate, and Meaning in play, as when Whitman effuses near the end of "Song of Myself," "Do you not see O my brothers and sisters? / It is not chaos or death—it is form, union, plan—it is eternal life—it is Happiness."[9] *Everyone deserves to be happy*—there you go; a new rule of human existence, a binding but odd expectation—and unrealistic, too, because never, not ever, will everyone actually be happy. That occurs only in a place called heaven. Where could they have gotten this notion, I wondered, and how could they sustain it against so much evidence against it right in front of them on a daily basis? Two girls love the same guy, and at least one of them will end up unhappy…intramurals are taking place right now in the gym, and only one team will win it all…the

popular business school at Emory admits a certain number of sophomores and turns away the rest of the applicants.... Sources of unhappiness are everywhere. There was simply no way to square this
everyone-deserves-to-be-happy principle with the things I taught or
with the tense ambitions of these high-achieving undergrads or with
the general unhappiness in the air that year. (Lots of them would
apply to medical school, for instance, and only a few would get their
first choice.)

Besides that, the whole notion of permanent happiness was foreign to me. I had never assumed that I deserved to be happy, never
once in my life. I wanted to be happy, but the frequent days of unhappiness never struck me as a violation of the universal order. My
Catholicism tells me that happiness comes from God, and God's
blessings are *un*deserved. I fully accept that. And even before I joined
the Church, my militant atheism ruled out the possibility of any
rightful or fateful outcomes at all, good or bad; I saw the whole idea
of just deserts as nothing more than a pleasing illusion. *Everyone
deserves to be happy?* Even evil people who do horrible things? No
way. From where does this birthright to happiness come? Who says
so? It sounded like a child's notion of life, a bit of wish-fulfilment
puffed up into an ontological truth. If that's what they believe, I
thought, it can't have come from what they've observed in the world.
It must spring from a source deep in their psyches.

All this ran through my mind in the minutes following this astonishing claim. We moved on to other business, but the claim stuck
with me. It wasn't a rational demand, but it explained a lot. The longer
it sat on the desk between us, the more significant it seemed. I had
watched clips of students at California State University–LA bedeviled
by the arrival of Ben Shapiro, whose slogan now clarified more
sharply the source of their fury: "Facts don't care about your feelings."[10] Dammit; they should! If it comes down to choosing facts or

feelings, I imagined the protesters saying, "We'll take the feelings." Why shouldn't reality guarantee my happiness—and why shouldn't my happiness determine reality? Yes, that's what they believed, or at least that's what they wanted to believe. It certainly went along with the widespread "moralistic therapeutic deism" mentioned earlier that prevails among Millennials, a benign faith in a benign God who wants everyone to be happy, so let's not get too judgmental with one another. Be yourself, it counsels, and let others be themselves, and don't get picky.

I shouldn't have needed this one Millennial to explain the faith. The students were, in fact, open about this let-me-be-happy-and-don't-make-me-unhappy pose. The formal demands they issued around that time, the angry ones included, were largely about themselves and their feelings. A smoldering protest message delivered in November 2015 to the president of Amherst College was typical. It objected first to the "negative social climate created towards [their] peers of color and other marginalized groups." Three of the initial four demands called for apologies from the college president and the board of trustees. Another demand was that the flyers posted around campus by persons unknown saying "All Lives Matter" and "Free Speech" should be denounced as "racially insensitive." The campus mascot, Lord Jeff, had to go because of his "inherent racist nature." These demands would be "part of a short-term healing" that would prepare the campus for more material changes later on. The diction was telling. This was about "healing," not money or procedures. The painful experiences of oppressed students had to come first—Amherst needed more empathy.[11]

Everyone deserves to be happy explained it. Without that principle, such emotive episodes of turmoil didn't make sense. Too many aspects of the students' lives were enviable for allegations of harm to hold up. These were youths enjoying comfy dorms, fancy facilities, and fast Wi-Fi. You couldn't find a more sympathetic ear than college presidents, who took every opportunity to show their social consciousness, as when a bunch of protesters crashed the holiday party at the home of the president of the University of Pennsylvania and staged a "die-in" for Michael Brown (shot in Ferguson, Missouri), lying on the floor as if they were corpses and ordering the president to join them—which she did—or when the president of Penn State stepped outside his office to be photographed with black demonstrators in a "hands up, don't shoot" pose (and Fox News and the *Patriot-News*, respectively, published photos of each spectacle).[12] These Millennials heard the blessings of diversity broadcast nonstop throughout academia and in advertising, the military, corporate America, the Democrat and Republican Parties, and pop culture, too, which attached an essential value to minorities of every kind. The very presence of a person of color could be transformative! What more did they want? They had a black president and attorney general, the *Obergefell* decision granting marriage rights to gays and lesbians, pledges from Silicon Valley to handle its alleged sexual harassment problem, and guarantees of affirmative action in admissions and hiring to guarantee equity in American society at large. Only some higher goal than a good education, attentive student-life services, and a decent job could justify undergraduates in being so sour and dissatisfied.

And there it was: the happiness mandate. *Everyone deserves to be happy.* The idealism of it, the selflessness and equality, the suspension of the meritocratic competition that dogged them constantly... who could object? I was convinced. It offered a different interpretation, a less political one, of why the restive Millennials were marching against Milo, Trump, Islamophobia, and the rest. Logic would tell us that the twenty-year-olds' emotional distress required an emotional cure, not just policy reforms. Concrete bureaucratic solutions such as a new diversity course in the general education requirements and hiring a new diversity officer would help, but only so much. A little groveling by the dean, earnest confessions of the institution's guilty past and its systemic racism in the present, solemn pledges of more diversity, more sensitivity...that was better. "Make us happy; make everyone happy!"—that was the core. Not Marxism, not liberal bias or multiculturalism, which I had considered as central to student dissatisfaction when writing about the campus climate in my years as a blogger for the *Chronicle of Higher Education*. This was different, more visceral. When protesters decried oppression, racism, and patriarchy, they meant them emotionally, not politically or histori-cally or institutionally. The catchwords "diversity, tolerance, inclu-sion" that schools broadcast so earnestly were but translations into pale administrative idiom of the undergrads' tremulous yearning to feel better.

My student's encapsulation was tighter and truer. It had the appearance of self-evident rightness, a plain appeal to those of a humane complexion. It wavered between plea and accusation, hope and regret, everyone-shall-be-happy and why-isn't-everyone-happy?—a sure sign that there was a defense mechanism at work. I could see it as psychic compensation for the losses they and their friends had experienced when they took the ACT and scored lower than they hoped, applied to colleges and weren't among the tiny frac-tion of applicants admitted by the top ones, shot for premed and got shot down in Calculus II, found a true love that didn't last, scanned Facebook pages of former classmates and couldn't believe how much better other people's lives were than the ones they were living, couldn't find a good job in Boulder or afford rent in Manhattan...no matter, none of that should curb happiness for all. I'd watched closely how digital hype in the 'oos had convinced Millennials of their fabu-lous destiny, and the inevitable disappointments of college and work undercut it, but this was a devotion no adverse events would shake. Not all of us can be doctors and lawyers and MBAs, handsome or beautiful, rich and famous, and we don't always get the girl of our dreams or go viral online, but all of us can and should be happy. No exceptions, not even individuals unhappy in their own bodies, for what tests the happiness proposition more than persons whose own genitalia thwart their fulfilment? If we can make trans people happy, we can make everyone happy.

In 2019, my son attended a strings camp in Vermont, one of the many Suzuki Institutes he has joined over the years that offer violinists, violists, and cellists individual and group lessons during the day and fun at night. At this camp, sessions were held in an elementary school, with kids shuffling from room to room hauling their instruments and music stands while parents lounged in the halls and strolled in and out of the building. As I sat in a common area after lunch when meetings had started, I overheard a teacher in the room next to my son's class coaching children aged five to seven in a choir practice. I had spotted her entering the room a few minutes before. She looked about thirty years old, overweight and sloppily dressed, but she sounded warm and joyful as she led the kids in song. It was a sort of babysitting feature of the camp for parents who had brought their twelve-year-old musicians and their younger children, too, who weren't ready yet for instrumentals. On the last day of camp, the youngsters would line up with the choirmaster in the auditorium to perform a few pieces for the ooh-ing and ah-ing adults before the final recitals began. The particular jingle she was practicing with the children that afternoon had a curious message, though: "It doesn't matter who [sic] you love." I'm not sure if that was the song's refrain or if the teacher simply chose to repeat it at each pause in the singing, but she said it several times. Not "This land is your land" or "You are my sunshine," but "It doesn't matter who you love."

My initial reaction was the same as when I first heard *Everyone deserves to be happy*: "Wait a minute; that's not so." I peered through the small window in the classroom door and saw her clapping and singing and swaying back and forth with the kids, repeating the refrain with a kindly maternal glee, everything about her posture, countenance, motions, and voice reinforcing the warmth of the message. The contrast between the gaiety of the mood and the patent falsity of the statement was jarring. What kind of assertion was this? Certainly not an empirical one. The disconfirming cases were too obvious. What about the woman who loves the man who beats her? He hits her, she calls the police, he's arrested, and a week later she drops the charges...because she loves him. What about Oscar Wilde's ardor for Bosie, which placed him in "a position at once grotesque and tragic" and produced "appalling results," as Wilde admitted in *De Profundis*.[13] What about the ancients who regarded erotic love as hazardous, sometimes verging on a disease, as when Virgil describes Dido's rising passion for Aeneas:

> The queen, for her part, all that evening ached
> With longing that her heart's blood fed, a wound
> Or inward fire eating her away....[14]

They and countless others spoke right back at our choir teacher, "*It does matter whom you love; it matters a lot.*" If she had read those many love stories with bad endings or undergone a destructive longing or two herself, she might not have treated love so blithely. She was working with children, and it was reasonable for her not to want to broach the dark side of desire, but that doesn't excuse selling cheery fictions that will only mislead those who buy them.

All of this was beside the point, of course. "It doesn't matter who you love" was really just a slightly more tepid way of saying, "It's okay to be gay." You hear it all the time in the public square, but I never expected it to pop up in choir practice for kids who had barely learned to read. While someone played one of Bach's cello suites next door and a chamber group of thirteen-year-olds in the auditorium struggled with a Schubert piece, a dozen six-year-olds were learning not to judge, never to judge—not in matters of the heart. It was a foul dose of propaganda, a subtle insertion of sexual politics into the heads of children who couldn't understand it, made worse by the supreme satisfaction the teacher took in her instruction. Little ones were getting their first lesson in antiheteronormativity—wonderful! That she had to tell a sentimental myth about love in order to "naturalize" homosexuality, that she was foolishly levelling every kind of love to an indifferent and innocent impulse—well, let's not get fussy. We know what she meant, and she meant well.

She was good, yes—the kids laughed and sang, they loved her, a better, happier specimen of Millennial utopianism, I had to admit, than the protesters enraged by Milo three years earlier. She too believed that everyone deserves to be happy, but hers was a cozier rendition. The protesters denounced hate; she proclaimed love. They wanted someone out of the community; she wanted everyone in. They had to address other students heading into the building who rolled their eyes at the signage and enjoyed Milo's banter; she had a 100 percent captive and willing crowd. The protesters couldn't enact the hate-free, all-are-welcome diversity that they envisioned, not with Milo and his fans nearby, but at that very moment in the Vermont classroom, *It doesn't matter who you love* was fully real and true and undisputed. None of those kids was going to say, "But what about Emma Bovary?"

The hour ended, my son proceeded to his next class, and I walked back to our room. When I described the scene to friends later, they shook their heads and muttered, "Can't they leave these kids alone?" I agreed; yes, it was perverse to peddle erotic notions of any kind to wide-eyed first-graders. She didn't mean, "Love your neighbor," a devotion unmingled with sex—nothing so brotherly as that. Even the kids probably picked up, in some hazy way, the sexual subtext of *It doesn't matter who you love.* They may have dimly understood enough to realize that she wanted to dispel any idea that marks certain kinds of "love" as wrong. If it was necessary for her to say, "It doesn't matter who you love," if the rule had to be repeated until the kids internalized it, then someone else must have said at some other time, "*It does matter who you love—be careful.*" That pointed to sex. The statement had a juvenile tenor, but the implications were entirely adult.

This was another occasion to think through the mindset, the bigger outlook, implied by an ostensibly simple remark characteristic of the Millennial worldview. Once again, a far-reaching wisdom seemed to boil down to a maxim that didn't work. It was puzzling. When an assertion flies against a mountain of contradictory facts, when a controversial or delicate issue is settled in so smooth a fashion, when the answer flows in such ingenuous tones, we assume that either a conscious ideology or an unconscious anxiety is at work. Maybe this was just a rhetorical tactic, inducting impressionable minds into liberal politics through slogans that sound like the moral at the end of a fable. After all, she was speaking to children—get them when they're young!

But that's not the full story. She didn't come off as manipulative or canny. Our Millennial believed too fervently in her juvenile patter for it to be merely strategic. You could see that clearly in her performance; she took too much pleasure in the act itself. This is the way things should be, she seemed to be saying, precisely in these empty-headed terms. We don't need any more sophistication. *It doesn't matter who you love*—that's it, that's all. Forget the complications and distortions that go with hot passions, the deceits and seductions, abandonments and desperations. Don't think about those cases when love (or lust) goes terribly wrong. The people who have paid for their illicit desires, from Paolo and Francesca to Bill and Monica, shouldn't have been punished that way, for no desire is illicit. They wanted one another; don't bother me with the consequences; there are no exceptions.

The simplicity of her teaching, the untroubled affirmation, the taming of something that ancient myth and nineteenth-century novels paired with mortality, the easy disregard of the tragedy inherent in human desire... it was impressive. "Love and death, a fatal love—in those phrases is summed up, if not the whole of poetry, at least whatever is popular," wrote Denis de Rougemont in his remarkable *Love in the Western World* (1940), a meditation on the ruins of romantic appetite. "Happy love has no history," he continued, taking the story of Tristan and Iseult as the prime example: "...actually passionate love is a misfortune."[15] But that was long ago, today's twenty-nine-year-old says—a repressive time. Love is good; it is always good; only torpid conventions make it bad. Fifty years after the sexual revolution began, on a sunny day in rural New England, this Millennial had brought it to its final stage, the flat assertion of all-out liberation. What canon could be more ultimate than this: *It doesn't matter who you love*? Straight or gay, old or young, couples or "throuples"... it doesn't matter. There was no ideology in her expression and no psychological involutions in her head. The dogma was too artless for that. I got the impression she would sound just the same way if she were speaking to adults. The dumbing-down was not a concession to the age of her audience. It was precisely how she understood the nature of love. "Love is love," no matter where it goes. Love *is*; let's respect it; it's pure and sweet, what the world needs now. *Everybody deserves to be happy*. The choice of an object doesn't matter; never should it cause unhappiness. Love of all kinds is ever deserving, the joys of it open to everyone everywhere anytime.

This is a utopianism that doesn't require you to know very much or think very hard. The slogan says it all. The Millennials who subscribe to this faith haven't deduced or read their way to it. You don't need a college degree to believe that everyone should get a fair share of well-being. Love is natural and good—we all feel it. If it runs in diverse directions, don't start ranking choices—celebrate diversity! "Hate has no home here," and neither does critical thinking. The knowledge my humanities colleagues and I have spent our professional lives imparting to students (without ever assuming we had to justify our work) is no longer wanted, not in the area of sexuality. The fates of Medea, Heloise and Abelard, Quentin Compson . . . irrelevant. The shame of Hester Prynne or of Byron after his divorce . . . forget about it. The bare assertion of *It doesn't matter who you love* makes that clear. It is aggressively anti-intellectual. It has to be, because the faith it expresses is so empirically fragile. It takes only a little reflection to kill it. It can't survive the knowledge of Narcissus and Anna Karenina, nor a personal experience with a clever seducer, nor familiarity with what psychologists call "emophilia," the knack of falling in love too often and too fast, especially with the wrong guy or gal over and over. The slogan pushes those disagreeable data away. That's how you have to read it—as wary defense. History and art, literature and psychology—they muck things up, disturb the catechism of inclusion with inconvenient truths. This utopianism, in other words, is founded upon a conviction that the goods of sexual experience are patent and overt and ever-enjoyable, if we would just lighten up, and the only way for that conviction to hold is for the Millennial to dodge the evidence of *Brave New World*, the Marquis de Sade, and all the treacherous figures of daimonic energy outlined in *Sexual Personae*, Camille Paglia's compendious survey of liminal desires, primitive to modern. Only when you drain your mind of the great love stories of the past, real and fictional, along with what they imply about human nature, can you affirm love as uncomplicated perfection. More than that, you have to turn this naïveté precisely into the right way to be, the only correct way to think about passion. Our choirmaster hailed this simplicity as one of the nicest things about her creed. How wonderful to find that a source of pain may be stopped with a homely motto! If you think this is just a puerile locution, a bit of kindergarten wisdom bound to collapse in the light of experience, that's because you've grown old and weary, or skeptical and cavillous, or maybe you're just too uptight to let go, or you resent the possibility that a younger, better generation might succeed.

"As young adults with the privilege of remarkable educations and opportunities ahead of us, we should be as idealistic about our ability to change the world for good as we ever will be."

That sentence comes from a statement originating in the University of Virginia Student Council and signed by fifty-eight student body presidents from schools across the country, from NYU to Florida, Rice to Wisconsin-Oshkosh, the University of Connecticut to UCLA. Many more signed on in subsequent weeks, their names grouped under the heading "Signatures of Solidarity." It came out November 12, 2017, in response to the demonstrations and riots during the "Unite the Right" rally in Charlottesville, Virginia (where UVA is located), which pitted white nationalists against Antifa-types, left one woman dead, and brought outcries of white supremacy across the media, academia, and the public sphere. Signers of the statement at Berkeley, UC–Santa Barbara, James Madison University, the University of Oklahoma, and elsewhere created videos of the message word-for-word, and campus newspapers reprinted it. The *Washington Post* ran the entire statement on November 13.[16]

The statement runs for four paragraphs, citing first the neo-Nazis' coming to Charlottesville, then the threat that such events posed to the students' faith in American institutions. There was a line about responsibility from JFK's *Profiles in Courage* in the third paragraph, then a concluding demand that leaders in our country step up and "use their power to transcend politics as usual, take risks, and fight for justice and equity." The students acknowledged that the schools had "crafted [their] characters and molded [their] minds," but they worried over "coming of age in a period of such substantial tumult." They called themselves "future leaders of this nation's workforce," but demanded that current leaders act now: "[W]e require your full dedication to this collective work of fighting white supremacy, anti-Semitism, and all others [*sic*] forms of hate." It has to happen soon, they said, because they had "witnessed hate and hostility settle in institutions nationwide." The students were discouraged, saying, "This past year has hardened many of our loftiest conceptions," but they refused to step back. Here in this declaration to college leaders and to anyone reading the message, they presented their "unyielding and uncompromising commitments to fight for equity and justice in all that [they] do."[17]

At the time the statement first came across my desk, it didn't seem particularly noteworthy. It looked too much like a dozen other collective announcements issued by the conscientious young in the first year of Donald Trump's term. As with the "lists of demands," the activist promises on the Black Lives Matter "What We Believe" page before it was scrubbed in 2020 ("dismantle cisgender privilege and uplift Black trans folk"), and the signs popping up in yards with elemental slogans such as "No Person Is Illegal" and "Everybody Welcome," the signers strove to voice their solemn concerns, and I could imagine lots of teachers and journalists and older activists impressed by their mindfulness and zeal. But to anyone not already disposed to the cause, the pathos in the statement was buried in too much empty chatter to have much impact.

As I reread it now, however, five years later, with the call to fight racism having evolved into a sweeping project of social engineering that includes racial quotas, new forms of segregation, Critical Race Theory rituals that require degrading confessions of white guilt, and a Democrat Party and corporate America eager to back illiberal, "woke" aims, the verbal flaws of the #StudentsAgainstHate document have acquired a deeper significance. However much the signers of the statement avowed their sincerity, it's hard to overlook the statement's clumsy style and banal semantics. If I were grading it, I'd circle the errors and slips in red pencil, then give it a C–, but that wouldn't get to the real problem with this lumbering callout. For there is a pathology here, an effectual one. The statement contains many errors, and they stem from educational failings, but those errors, paradoxically, only toughen the position of the signers. Look at it in terms of its rhetorical qualities, not its substance. The clichés ("opportunities ahead of us," "change the world for good") certainly betray an absence of thought, but this mindlessness only makes their accusations all the harder to answer: you can't debate with obtuse people utterly convinced of their own rectitude. They don't want to debate, and they're not going to. The pairing of "should be as" with "as we ever will be" doesn't make sense. It signifies a confusion about who and where they are, which actually proves the neglect of the elders, our failure to offer them a stable world and a sure place within it. They say that recent events have "hardened" their "loftiest conceptions," but surely what they mean is that those events have undermined or eroded those conceptions, or else that they have hardened their sensibilities. They fused those two points into a nonsensical locution, which has the perverse virtue of trapping the elders into a response of "Huh?" They are preoccupied with themselves ("we" and "our" occur twenty-four times in the statement), but in fact they don't express who they are and how they feel very clearly, and that very well could be because we let them grow up in an unjust and uncertain habitat. The generalities ("privilege," "remarkable education," and "change the world"), which are meant to evince the capacious intelligence of the signers, only reveal the fuzziness of their ideas. Maybe if the mentors had handed them a righteous future with solid moral poles they could speak more precisely about their wants.

In other words, the hack language and lax thinking of the signers of this statement are our fault, not theirs. After all, these are some of the best and brightest eminences at the best schools, heads of student bodies. They're smart, not stupid. They want to persuade. They work hard; they care; they compliment their teachers. They strive to improve the conditions of others, and they still believe in America in spite of the legacy of racism and conquest (two weeks after issuing the statement, the UVA Student Council opened its meeting with an acknowledgment that the school was built by slave labor on land belonging to the Monacan Nation). They have proven their talent by attending elite schools and winning election to office—not out of personal ambition, either, but from selfless motives. Social reform isn't a career path for them; it won't run Monday through Friday, nine to five. It's their way of life: "[T]o fight for equity and justice in all that we do." We can't blame them for their bad rhetoric and outsized commitments. They're good kids—better people than we are, in fact. They sit on the moral high ground, and if the mentors have not given them the intellectual tools to operate in that thin air, that's not their fault.

That is, the bad rhetoric strengthened their case. They got to have it both ways, to accuse the elders and demand reform *and* not to be responsible for their own errors. This is the way of children, but we can't knock them for their adolescence. The kids really were right, you see, righter than they realized. The ones who signed #StudentsAgainstHate and the millions of Millennials who agreed with them had launched explicit moral charges against the mentors, calling out the racism and exploitations that Boomers and Xers hadn't managed to expel entirely, and the elders accepted the terms as swiftly as an eighteenth-century courtier would the minor grumblings of the king. At the same time, unconsciously, with their flawed expressions, underwhelming grammar, and ridiculously inflated expectations, the students levelled intellectual charges that were worse, though the mentors wouldn't have cared to acknowledge them. Each defective sentence and trite usage betrayed what their teachers and parents had failed to teach them, the poor training of which the kids were unaware. The students presumed to understand more than they did, assumed that they spoke and wrote better than they actually did, and their inability to judge themselves went straight back to the shirked duties of the mentors. Did the signers of the letter never pause to consider that they should run their statement by an English or journalism teacher for a quick line edit? Didn't anyone have the knowledge to point out that citing philanderer JFK in a message of equity might be a little dicey? No, they believed that the statement was fine as is—which proved that their teachers hadn't taught them to catch verbal solecisms, avoid clichés, and dig deeper than the pop culture versions of historical figures. When they pledged to do *everything* in their power *at all times* [my emphasis] to "fight for equity and justice," the exaggeration showed that they had absorbed a conception of daily life that a decent humanities curriculum would have confounded long before. Dramas about middle-class striving (think of *Death of a Salesman*), satires of annoying idealists such as *Sullivan's Travels* (in which a rich Hollywood liberal learns some common humility), social comedies of love and marriage such as *The Country Wife* and *The Barber of Seville*, ex-radicals' memoirs such as *The God That Failed* and *Radical Son*—anything to bring their expectations of postcollege existence back to earth. Getting to know such works would at the very least have improved the quality of their protest.

But that hadn't happened. They came to current affairs solemn and perturbed—and uninstructed, too. The first two were a result of the third. The idealism of these college stars was only slightly more developed than the everybody-deserves-to-be-happy pipe dream of the Milo protesters and the all-love-is-pure paradise of the choir teacher. That you should be constantly fighting for justice and equity, in all that you do, in private and in public, at work and at home, every waking minute, was a utopian aspiration just as fantastical as the others. That has never happened before, and it never will. Only the most sheltered and impractical sensibility wouldn't realize that people want rest now and then; they need a break. Such zeal doesn't go far when you have kids waiting for dinner and a stack of bills on the table. "Fight ever and always" erects a social hope into a rule of conduct for life that nobody could ever follow, even if everyone agreed about what "justice" and "equity" mean. It's a standard that makes everyone guilty, too, for every action that doesn't, in some way or another, explicitly advance equity and justice is unjust and inequitable. That includes wearing the wrong costume to a Halloween party, voting for Donald Trump, buying goods from a company that advertises on Tucker Carlson's show, refusing to use *they* as a singular pronoun, pulling your kids out of a public school, enjoying *Gone with the Wind*.... A social conscience heightened to this level can never rest. The humdrum tasks of buying food, decorating your room, watching TV with your kids, choosing where to vacation...nothing is innocent. Everyone has done a bad deed here and there. Except for the young, that is, who aren't responsible for the many injustices that preceded them.

The only way to uphold this absolute is to ignore the facts and wisdom of history and art and literature and philosophy and religion.

Or rather, to turn that around: when a youth with a social conscience grows up unexposed to the best records of civilization, when his mentors haven't presented the turning points of history and the creations of the masters, when he hasn't read "Ozymandias" and heard "To be or not to be" and watched the last five minutes of *City Lights*, this is where he ends up—with unrealistic expectations, over-self-confidence, and insistent demands. When the novels, memoirs, and music that would draw him out of adolescence never show up, his adolescent arrogance remains in place long after its sell-by date. There is no tragic sense of life in him. The fates of poor Werther and Lily Bart and Van Gogh haven't touched him, nor the colors of Monet and the editing of Orson Welles, nor the sublime cadences of *La Traviata* and "All Blues." To him the human stain is a trait we can overcome and erase if we only try; nothing in his Millennial formation has shown him otherwise. The pitfalls of hubris and ideological purity and utopia are everywhere in the tradition, but a young person will encounter them only if the tradition enters into his classrooms, his movies and TV shows, and his talks with his parents—and they didn't. People delude themselves all the time, say Marx, Nietzsche, Freud, Sartre, Orwell... read them and you learn to slow your "loftiest conceptions." People hurt each other unintentionally again and again—Orpheus and Eurydice, Aeneas and Dido, Lear and Cordelia—and social injustice usually has nothing to do with it. They drift into mischief by slow degrees, like some of the miscreants in *Sherlock Holmes*, or Kate Croy and Merton Densher in *The Wings of the Dove*, who demonstrate the slippery course that runs from not entirely bad motive to really bad action. But none of this entered the youth's consciousness, and he's not aware of its absence now that he's graduated. The tutelages of those thinkers and characters take time, anyway. Google's teaching is faster and simpler: "Don't be evil."

It's also stiffer; it's tenacious, unyielding. Don't be evil, don't do evil, stop doing evil, stop it—right now! As with our other twenty-first-century slogans, Google's is boldly simplistic, proudly *not* clever. This is the thought of a mind that has closed down—righteously so. It doesn't need wit; it has moral perfection. Philosophers and theologians and writers have pondered the nature of evil forever, but why bother? Evil is evil. Don't muddy things up. If the thinkers of the past were so wise and good, then why is the world in which the Millennials find themselves so awful? You tell them to study the Founders, but they've heard some pretty bad things about those characters. Why should they take advice from rich white men who owned slaves? Why should they appreciate the technical brilliance of D. W. Griffith, given the race-baiting of *Birth of a Nation*? You tell them to read Ezra Pound, the genius of high modernism, but a few nasty quotations from his World War II broadcasts cancel any insights they might find in *Hugh Selwyn Mauberley* ("The age demanded an image / Of its accelerated grimace, / Something for the modern stage, / Not, at any rate, an Attic grace…").[18] It isn't complicated. In 2016, English majors at Yale circulated a petition asking the department to "decolonize" the coursework,[19] and the logic of their call couldn't be more incontrovertibly plain. The introductory courses are all white male authors, and that "creates a culture that is especially hostile to students of color." Haven't they been victimized enough?

The mentors have no rejoinder. They may believe that students must learn the basics of Chaucer, Shakespeare, Milton, and Blake before they proceed to contemporary authors and social issues, but they can't explain why, or they won't. They know that great art and artists cross current moral codes all the time, but they don't have the pluck to tell the upright young that they should study them anyway. The Renaissance humanists, though devout Christians, preserved and passed on the pagan authors nonetheless, dividing their artistry from their gods, but that's a distinction the mentors will not draw and the Millennials cannot draw, not if it means someone is going to get hurt. Should a traditional idea of cumulative learning hold when it causes historically disadvantaged youths pain? No: Yale English adjusted its courses one year later.

Knowledge is power, but not this time. The defects of non-learning that show up in the letters and petitions and protests, the bad syntax and oafish catchphrases and juvenile history—they don't disempower the youths at all, not in this situation. On the contrary, they're daunting. Confronted by angry students with ridiculously utopian demands and complaints, the mentors simply abandon the intellectual standards that have brought them to their mentoring position. It's a bizarre self-disabling. Academics and scholars and teachers who live by the scientific method and critical thinking and empirical, historical, or textual inquiry have to reject their own expertise and all its tools precisely because the kids are so vulnerable to them. They don't want to embarrass their juniors. The mentors can't call on the knowledge and skills they have acquired in their many years of training and practice, or they would have to disqualify the protesters from protesting and tell them to go back to their dorm rooms and read some books, as Marcuse told the Westbury radicals. That's something that no American academic today could say. Look at the face of a hapless college president in discussion with a flock of irate undergrads. He's nervous and glassy-eyed, frightened of making the wrong move, terrified to offer anything but sympathy and apology. The second he turns to substance—makes a quibble over an impractical demand or wants to discuss problems with a change in the general education requirements—he's in danger, and it is precisely the crude demands and utopian desires of the kids, for whose lack of education and culture he and his faculty are responsible, that have put him in jeopardy. College leaders can't respond to safe-space pleas with anything other than "I'm sorry you feel unsafe; we'll try harder." When Professor Nicholas Christakis at Yale University, pushing back only gently, tried to reason with the crowd of students furious at the Halloween email sent by his wife, they exploded at him. The issue was safety, and it was not up for discussion, only acknowledgment and submission, so shut up and listen. No specific plans or initiatives would guarantee the kind of utopian safety the kids demanded. A college president can't make the campus safe by decree, and policies that would attempt to make it fully "safe" would penalize speech and movement and pedagogy, too, to the point of compromising liberal education. It is, however, the very impracticality, the irrationality, of the demand that stymies the mentors, who know that a reply of "I can't do that" will only incense the kids, spread protests across the quad, and perhaps lead to a resignation. Every administrator who saw the outrageous Yale video took a lesson: don't discuss; never argue; only conciliate, appease, apologize. The very thing that cries out for correction—that is, the thickheaded utopianism of the aggrieved students—prevents it. When protesters object to a Western Civilization proposal because, they say, it fosters white supremacy, they don't want to debate the merits of Dante and Bernini. They can't; they don't know anything about those masters. More than that, they don't want to know; they don't care about the debate. They just want an irritant to go away.

That's the thing about utopian wishes: they can't be moderated or refuted by the facts, or by contrary visions. Once it is formed, the dream is immune to criticism. It's so neat and clean and appealing—and easy, too. The Roman Republic didn't last. "What is truth?" Pilate asked. Dante put Ulysses deep in hell. Whittaker Chambers died believing that ruthless Communists would inherit the earth. But the questions those cases pose mean nothing to the young dreamer. They only threaten to undermine the universal comfort supplied by his utopian dream. If you don't know much history, historical evidence doesn't sway you. You've already learned to disrespect it. If you haven't studied great literature and oratory, you're content with clichés. Your justice doesn't need eloquence, and you certainly don't want any comedy around: it might remind you of the foibles and imperfections that could prevent the realization of your demand for perfect justice. And laughter isn't easily governed, either. It can turn against the just themselves, against you. Utopians insist that they be taken seriously—very seriously.

In February 2020, as the primaries were beginning, a poll by YouGov and the *Economist* showed that 60 percent of Democrats younger than thirty years old backed Bernie Sanders or Elizabeth Warren. A month before, a Quinnipiac poll of Democrats thirty-five and younger had Senator Sanders ahead of Joe Biden 53 percent to 3 percent—an astounding statistic, in light of how things turned out. A *New York* magazine article that year, "This One Chart Explains Why the Kids Back Bernie," cited those numbers, reviewed what they meant, and attributed them an "aberrant fondness for socialism."[20]

The curious revival of youth socialism had in fact been a commonplace in political commentary for several years. Millennials were identified as socially quite liberal as soon as they started to come of age in the '00s, but with the 2008 financial crisis and its effect on twenty-year-olds on the job market, an increasing number of them drifted farther left and called for more government action to relieve economic pain.[21] Political observers, marking them as a crucial voting bloc, followed the direction of their loyalties closely. In 2008, eighteen-to-twenty-nine-year-olds made up 17 percent of the electorate, casting more than twenty-two million votes, two-thirds of them for candidate Obama,[22] prompting stories such as this from the Huffington Post: "Why the Youth Vote Is the Big

Story—for 2008 and for Decades to Come."[23] In 2012, however, Obama's proportion of the youth vote slipped to 60 percent,[24] perhaps because, as one young idealist put it in a commentary entitled "I'm a Millennial, and I'm Disappointed in Obama," his actions in office were mostly "symbolic measures" that "weren't representative of the more radical ideologies Obama had . . . once exhibited."[25] The author meant radically left, of course. As the 2010s proceeded, especially when Bernie Sanders arose to challenge Hillary Clinton for the Democratic nomination with massive support from the young, we didn't see much discussion of Millennials as radicals, though. *Socialism* became the keyword for their politics.

From the first time I heard that description—having charted the knowledge levels and intellectual habits of this generation for years—I knew it was a misnomer. To label Millennial activists "socialists" is a mistake. It grants them way too much intellectual heft. It overlooks the deepest sources of their activism, the emotional, even anti-intellectual, side of utopianism. True, according to a 2019 Cato Institute survey, 50 percent of adults under thirty expressed "favorable views" of socialism (capitalism got 49 percent), while older Americans were in the mid-thirties.[26] Likewise, in 2018, Gallup reported that 49 percent of Americans from eighteen to thirty-nine years old approved of socialism, while 51 percent approved of capitalism.[27] And a YouGov poll from October 2020 reported that 35 percent of Millennials "support the gradual elimination of the capitalist system in favor of a more socialist system."[28] Clearly, those with socialist sympathies were not a minor group within the generation, and the trend was continuing.

But *socialism* was the wrong term to describe it. To call someone a "socialist" is to presume he has some knowledge of the social contract, of surplus value and the alienation of labor, the New Deal and the Great Society, Christian social doctrine, utopian projects such as

Brook Farm and '60s communes, the various revolutions of the twentieth century...not a lot of knowledge, mind you, just a little familiarity with some of those things. But Millennials don't know anything
about socialism in theory or practice. They haven't read Marx on
private property or Trotsky on revolution or the welfare writings of
the '60s, such as Michael Harrington's influential *The Other America:
Poverty in the United States*. They haven't tracked the fiscal performance of socialist governments in the twentieth century, nor have
they read critiques of them by Friedrich Hayek and Milton Friedman.
They don't understand how Social Security or Medicare-for-all work.
Speak the words "collectivization," "central planning," or "Tito," and
they stare blankly. Their "socialism" is much simpler than that. It's
not a philosophy, and it's not an economic model. It means "fairness,"
or "someone to watch over me." It's a chance to get out from under
their student loan payments and find a good job, free health care, and
affordable housing in a Millennial hot spot (Austin, Seattle,...).

It's a mistake, then, to call one-third to one-half of Millennials
"socialists" or to assume they have acquired real knowledge of socialism and weighed socialist ideas. No, they are utopians, and they are
utopians precisely because they haven't acquired any political knowledge or weighed any political ideas. Their worldview fits into neat
catchphrases; it doesn't get any more sophisticated than that. P. J.
O'Rourke pared it down to this in a column entitled "This Is Why
Millennials Adore Socialism": "As soon as children discover that the
world isn't nice, they want to make it nice. And wouldn't a world
where everybody shares everything be nice? Aw...kids are so
tender-hearted."[29] A May 2019 column at Fox Business by Connor
Boyack, head of a free market think tank in Utah, lays out "Why
Socialism is So Popular Among Young People" by citing similarly
childish motives: "When your life is ahead of you, it's tempting to
want to live at others' expense and seek an easy path in life." Boyack

adds the ignorance factor, which he chalks up to left-wing teachers who are "unlikely to extol the virtues of capitalism and point out the historically disastrous results seen in countries that embrace social-ism."[30] Tucker Carlson and Neil Patel took on the question at The Daily Caller six months later, pinpointing student loan debt that burdens grads for decades and leads them to believe that "our current system isn't working," an inference the authors accept as entirely natural, though shortsighted.[31] A few years before, a column at The Federalist by editor Joy Pullmann and Emily Ekins of the Cato Institute had addressed "Why So Many Millennials Are Socialists." One section of that article rightly notes that "Millennials Don't Know What Socialism Is." It cites another survey, this one by CBS and the *New York Times*, which found that only 16 percent of Millennials understood the definition of socialism as "government ownership of the means of production." The article goes on to describe what socialism does mean to the young: mainly a generous social safety net with government in the role of "benevolent caretaker." Millennials don't understand the drawbacks of socialism because, the authors explain, they came along after the Cold War ended, when the evils of life behind the Iron Curtain had come to belong to another, unremembered time.[32]

These commentaries are right on target: Millennials don't know much about what they're talking about. But don't get the impression that the unserious views of the young have unserious consequences. Yes, our current thirty-year-old has a shallow, presentist conception of socialism—too shallow, in fact, to deserve the label. As we've seen, "utopian" is a better description of their faith in an imaginary society of no misery, free from the inequalities that ruin everything. It's a fantasy upheld by know-nothing-ness—or rather, it's a fantasy caused by know-nothing-ness. As O'Rourke puts it, Millennials call for aggressive government plans to end inequality "not because young people learned left-wing lessons from the Soviets and the Red Guards. It's because they didn't." They backed Bernie Sanders, but they couldn't create a redistribution project if they tried. They pledge to fight racism, but they don't know anything about antidiscrimination laws that are already in place. They call for universal happiness, but the many tales of people getting exactly what they want only to find that it produces disaster, from Midas onward, cause them no doubts (cosmic irony is a foreign concept). They may proclaim themselves socialists, but they don't know how to do anything socialist. They haven't a molecule of the brutal savvy and organizational brilliance of Lenin and Stalin and Mao. We may laugh at their naïveté, or we may worry that they're going to elect more AOC types, but we don't worry too much, trusting that their stupidity won't assume any more dangerous form than that.

But this is a particularly restless kind of stupidity, a keen and impatient utopianism. Ignorance of this sort isn't going to stop with foolish expectations and entitlements. Millennials are active and entrepreneurial, we are told; they want to change the world. They don't know much about the world as it was before they came along, but the impulse is no less mighty because of that. Ignorance plus self-righteousness is a dangerous mix. As avid and unbending utopian desires go unfulfilled, you know what will happen next: idealism will slide into frustration, the promised happy fellowship to come veering into a merciless search for the enemies who must be obstructing it; the positive will turn negative.

When, in an August 2016 speech at West Philadelphia High School, presidential candidate Hillary Clinton called Millennials the "most tolerant and generous generation that we've ever seen in America,"[33] she was echoing what cultural commentators and other observers of the young had been announcing for more than a decade. On matters of sexuality, race, marriage, drugs, and religion, according to social scientists, Millennials were significantly more accepting than Boomers and Xers.[34] "Millennials Are Tolerant, Educated, Enterprising, and Hyphenated," announced the Huffington Post in a December 2014 story that summarized contemporary research[35]—news that was repeated a thousand times from 2000 forward. You could sense the glee of left-wing reporters as they detailed the increasingly left-wing outlook of a cohort nearly the size of the Boomers, one that promised to put conservative opinion in a permanent minority in America. "The left is back—and millennials are leading the way," gushed a *Washington Post* story in July 2017.[36]

But they were a new kind of left wing that was eager to dump liberal values. Here's what liberal-leaning Pew Research recorded in November 2015: "40% of Millennials OK with limiting speech offensive to minorities." The First Amendment is a cornerstone of liberalism, yet here were Millennials willing to curb free speech in the name of niceness. The rate of Millennials who believed that "government should be able to prevent people from saying offensive things about minority groups" jumped way above the numbers for Xers (27 percent) and Boomers (24 percent), while the Silent Generation was at only 12 percent. Two years later the left-leaning Brookings Institution issued the results of a First Amendment survey of college students conducted August 2017 showing that they embraced further restrictions:

- 44 percent of students believed that the First Amendment does not protect hate speech. Another 16 percent marked "don't know."
- 51 percent of students believed that a group of protesters is fully justified in shouting down a speaker if that speaker utters "offensive and hurtful statements."
- 19 percent believed that a group may rightly use violence (!) to prevent that speaker from speaking.

- 62 percent of respondents believed that a campus organization that invites a controversial speaker is "legally required" to invite another speaker who will present an opposing view.
- Finally, 53 percent of respondents favored a school environment that prohibits "speech or expression of viewpoints that are offensive or biased against certain groups of people." The other option, an "open learning environment" that allows such speech, drew 47 percent approval.[37]

These were not unusual results. Gallup, the Knight Foundation, and the Foundation for Individual Rights in Education (FIRE) documented the same illiberalism in their own surveys, distressing conservatives and liberals alike. President Obama himself objected, telling an NPR interviewer in December 2015, "My concern is not whether there is campus activism. I think that's a good thing. But let kids ask questions and let universities respond. What I don't want is a situation in which particular points of view that are presented respectfully and reasonably are shut down, and we have seen that sometimes happen."[38] Here was a position on which moderates on both sides could agree, especially after they saw Bill Maher, Michael Bloomberg, and other liberal friends hooted and cancelled just as Condoleezza Rice and Jordan Peterson had been in other episodes. Leaders on both the Left and Right who were disturbed by the illiberalism had enough experience to realize that the meanings of *hate*, *offensive*, and *biased* are too fuzzy to serve as standards for speech codes, that today's heroes—Rosa Parks, for example—were often classed as offensive troublemakers in their own time. Or maybe they just wanted to hold true to principles of pluralism and academic freedom. In a 2020 survey of speech on campus, pollsters found that

71 percent of students opposed allowing a speaker on campus to argue that "[s]ome racial groups are less intelligent than others."[39] Would that bar an education researcher from talking about the large black-white score gap on SAT and NAEP exams? It probably could. Fully 49 percent would boot a speaker who argues that "[a]ll white people are racist," which would keep a lot of Black Lives Matter figures away from the podium. One could also construe much of the content on the syllabi of their courses as offensive, from sixteenth-century explorers to Nazi Germany to *Huckleberry Finn*, which, along with *To Kill a Mockingbird* and *Of Mice and Men*, was banned last year in the Burbank school district.[40]

For close observers of higher education, this was a surprising development. The head of FIRE, Greg Lukianoff, often notes that when the organization began in the 1990s, the people it defended were mostly students and teachers whose speech rights and academic freedom were violated by zealous administrators. Now, he finds, the aggressive ones are the activist students themselves, who are presumably at the bottom of the academic hierarchy but who've acquired extraordinary moral authority and have professors and deans thoroughly intimidated and ready to apologize, apologize. These social justice warriors have no bureaucratic excuses for their hostility to a robust First Amendment climate; their illiberalism is heartfelt. It's visceral. The respondents to these surveys who approved the strictures and shout-downs were wrong on the law and wrong on education, but they don't care. Offense is offense; it has to go. If we want a world of benign inclusivity, we must exercise a vigilant exclusivity until we no longer have to. To create a comforting home of no discrimination and happiness for all, we must pass through a purifying period of antidiscrimination—so watch yourself. Eggs have to be broken. A law professor at Emory drops the *n*-word in a discussion of a 1967 incident of Jim Crow, and students file a complaint, hold a rally, and get the professor removed from the classroom—good![41] Millennials raised in conservative religious traditions find their churches' positions on homosexuality wrong ("Younger Americans are the least homophobic generation in our nation's history"[42]), and so they leave and become "Nones," trusting their twenty-four-year-old opinions more than the venerable scriptures—and rightly so. To spread happiness you must expel the source of unhappiness. Milo wasn't going to end affirmative action or sway education authorities about anything, but he did poke fun at feminists and trans persons, and that hurt. Hate has no home here. Charles Murray argued in the 1990s for an element of heritability in IQ, a message said to discourage African Americans entering the jam-packed achievement path, so chase him off. Jordan Peterson had no record of abusing gays or lesbians or trans individuals in his thousands of hours of clinical practice, but he refused to follow an Ontario directive mandating preferred pronouns, and so young trans activists pressed the University of Toronto to fire him. Why waste time refuting when you can remove? Target stocked a book by Abigail Shrier entitled *Irreversible Damage: The Transgender Craze Seducing Our Daughters* until a lone nose-ringed Millennial in Colorado accused the store of transphobia on Twitter, and one day later Target pulled the book from its inventory: mission accomplished (though only temporarily, as the subsequent outcry led Target to reverse the decision).[43]

The altruistic wish, the noble dream of diversity, the unquestionable goodness of the plotters of cancellation...they don't contradict the targeting; they demand it. We cannot question the motives of the aggressors, of those people so intent on justice. We must admire their consistency, their willingness to act according to their stated principles. The feverish identification that well-off white and Asian students at $60K-per-year schools have formed with low-income African Americans and the historical burdens they carry proves their benevolence. Their flight from an open society is not a betrayal of their utopian faith. It is instrumental to it. The turn has been taken. I saw it spelled out in one particularly threatening component of the "List of Demands" issued by the group Black Students at Emory in December 2015 and published in the student paper. Following demand number three, which asked for "psychological services that cater to [the authors'] unique psychological needs," demand number four addressed course evaluation forms that professors hand out to students at the end of the semester and that are collected and reviewed confidentially by department leadership and stored in professors' personnel files. The protesters asked that two questions be added to the evaluation, which already addressed workload, pacing, clarity of presentations, fairness of assignments, and the like:

- "Has this professor made any microaggressions towards you on account of your race, ethnicity, gender, sexual orientation, language, and/or other identity?"
- "Do you think that this professor fit into the vision of Emory University [*sic*] being a community of care for individuals of all racial, gender, ability, and class identities?"[44]

Of course, the university would never approve those questions. Microaggressions and "does this professor fit?" are blurry standards, leaving everyone uncertain as to what counts as a crime. They would poison the atmosphere in the room, with students prompted to be suspicious of their teachers and teachers prompted to be wary of their students. Once a few reports of microaggressions transpired because of the new evaluations, word would get around, and free and open discussion in class would decline. Too much of the ordinary instruction in humanities classes could fall into a subset of "microaggressions"—for instance, the appearance on a syllabus of violent or sexual materials with no accompanying trigger warning. The question would effectively pressure teachers to banish delicate and controversial material from their classrooms. If I taught Frederick Douglass's *Narrative*, with its grisly whippings and many appearances of the *n*-word, I would expect my injudiciousness to show up in student responses.

As for the second question, it places the nineteen-year-old in the remarkable position of appraising the teacher's overall fitness to serve at the school. It doesn't focus on the course, but on the character of the instructor and his contribution to or obstruction of the "community of care." The sophomore is assumed to have the competence to judge what the campus climate is supposed to be and whether his professor fits that ideal. Both questions, we might add, could encourage nineteen-year-olds angry about a bad grade to get back at the professor with anonymous accusations of bias. (By the way, students at Emory were not the only ones to make microaggression and "care" demands; such pleas were quite common on other campuses at the time.)

That these youths should have made such destructive proposals and arrogated to themselves powers of academic judgment far beyond their capacities was yet more evidence of the toxic combination of moral certitude and missing knowledge. The proposal would only harm their own education, but the power that would come with it was too tempting for them to resist. They didn't have the learning to anticipate that adding such questions to teacher evaluations would only empower the yearning to turn the tables on who gets to grade whom and undermine their expensive educations. The utopia they envisioned—expressed in the paradisal description of this selective, high-powered research university as a "community of care"—had to involve a levelling of hierarchy if the power imbalance between students and teacher was going to end. The logic of progress required it. Safe spaces cannot be maintained if the ones who need protection have no voice in the maintenance of safety. A one-way relationship isn't fair; professors judge me, so I should get to judge them. Everyone is an equal member of the community.

Except that an equal balance of power is not quite what these proposed questions projected. We have here, instead, an imbalance of power. Consider the two distinct evaluations taking place. The professor delivers course content, assigns tests and papers, and records grades. That's his authority. He appraises one thing: the quality of the student's work. He does his job; his labor is academic, affecting a small part of the overall record of the student, one class among thirty-two in each undergraduate's career. The student, however, assumes a bigger responsibility, these new questions handing him the role of professional evaluator. This is a greater authority. The answers he gives judge the teacher's very suitability for employment. A charge of microaggression coming from enrollees in a class could start an investigation that invokes Federal law, Title VII or Title IX. A professor so charged would have to defend himself from allegations that he might not even comprehend given the vagueness of the standard "fits into the vision of…a community of care." The students who initiated the whole thing, of course, would justify it on the grounds of the damage they had suffered from this insensitive professor for fourteen weeks, a damage that reaches far beyond the present, back to legacies of discrimination that have affected the entire student body (in the words of the fifth demand in the Emory document, "to the historic and current systematic oppression of Black persons in America"). The professor presumes he teaches Shakespeare or the French Revolution, but to social justice–minded students, the essential question is: Does the professor help or not help the cause? Is he ending the longstanding injustice, or is he keeping it going?

A mentor cannot function this way, ever in the shadow of historic wrongs. It makes him too self-conscious, cripples his authority. But then, his authority is precisely what the utopian temper renounces. After all, our professor belongs to a guilty past, and he must accept the authority of the young conscientious objectors if he is to prove his virtue. That's the rhetorical genius of the proposed questions and of all the Millennial cries for safety: "no hate," "end racism now,".... Take the emotional pleas out of these demands, and the power play becomes clear. For all their language of justice and care, their projection of self-defense and victimhood, equality and inclusion, we have here an assumption of prerogative. At bottom, the youths' lingo of sensitivity masks a naked menace. A banner carried by students at Yale University at the March 2015 "March for Resilience" captures perfectly the uneasy mixture of peace-and-harmony with in-your-face threat: "WE OUT HERE WEVE BEEN HERE WE AINT LEAVING WE ARE LOVED." (You can see a photo on Yale's website.)[45]

You see it, too, in the disproportionate fates of the parties in such situations. If a teacher lets it be known that he supports a biblical definition of marriage, LGBT students cannot claim to suffer any pain except the knowledge that their teacher questions the merits of their lifestyles. That's the worst they can allege they are suffering: the aggravation of a differing view on sexual matters. But if students complain to the administration of a hostile climate on campus, a lot worse can happen to the professor. These charges will find a ready ear (as we've seen many times), and the teacher may find his livelihood in jeopardy. The temporary discomfort of the students versus the permanent termination of the professor—those are the relative injuries, and they tell you who holds the reins.

The transformation has been astonishing: a putative self-defense via siege tactics, victims asking for protection turned into hunters seeking prey. Joseph Epstein calls it "The Tyranny of the 'Tolerant'";[46] others call it "cancel culture" and its perpetrators "crybullies." Mary Eberstadt has been especially eloquent on the emotive forcefulness, and Bari Weiss, Andrew Sullivan, and many more conservatives and liberals have detailed its workings and sometimes suffered its punishments.[47] Millennials lead the way. That came through in a July 2020 poll of registered voters by Morning Consult and Politico that included questions about cancel culture.[48] Asked whether cancel culture had gone too far, not far enough, or neither, 36 percent of respondents age eighteen to thirty-four answered "too far," only one-third of the age group—a dismayingly low figure. Older cohorts showed greater concern: 41 percent of thirty-five- to forty-four-year-olds believe it has gone too far, 47 percent of forty-five- to sixty-four-year-olds that it had done so, and 59 percent of those sixty-five and older. Worse, nearly one in six of the younger respondents (16 percent) claimed that cancellation hadn't yet claimed enough victims (the wording was "not far enough"), a bit higher than the next older age group (14 percent) and much higher than the other two (seven and five percent).

That "not far enough" number is even worse than it seems, for two reasons. First, 23 percent of eighteen-to-thirty-four-year-olds answered "neither"—that cancel culture had gone neither not far enough nor too far, implying that the current level of cancellation is just fine with them. So if we add together the rates for not-far-enough and currently-just-fine, Millennials who wish to restrain or reverse cancel culture are outnumbered by those who don't. We should note, as well, that another 25 percent of the age group answered "don't know/no opinion"—an apathy that favors the aggressors.

Given this breakdown, the advantage that the last group (the indifferent ones) gives to extremists helps explain the success of cancel culture. It's a pattern one sees all the time. In episodes of protest, an inspired minority can often influence the course of events far more than their numbers would suggest. There is the "chill" phenomenon, of course, whereby one case of censorship and punishment compels others to stay quiet for good, but there is more to the power of the minority than that. Squeaky wheels are the ones that get the grease. If, for example, three students complain of a teacher's prejudice while the other thirty-two students say nothing about it, the few complainers inevitably take priority. The "Law of Group Polarization"—the tendency of groups in which most members hold to a particular opinion to drift toward more extreme versions of that opinion as they discuss it—is an instance of the same phenomenon. The law was outlined in a 1999 paper by Chicago law professor Cass Sunstein, who examined certain deliberative bodies such as trial juries and found the phenomenon repeated again and again. In product liability cases, for instance, when an individual sues a company whose product resulted in an injury, if the jury generally regards the company as liable but ten members initially favor a modest award to the plaintiff while two push for a stiff award, in the deliberations to follow, the two will pull the ten far in their direction. The final judgment will end up much higher than the average figure as calculated from the beginning.[49] The psychology is perfectly comprehensible. The extreme members feel more strongly about their opinion than the others. That's the way extremists are. But the moderates basically agree with the extremists about (in this case) the culpability of the manufacturer. The difference lies in the intensity of feeling, and so the moderates don't regard concessions to extremists as a compromise of principle. They are more flexible, willing to defer to people more passionate about a principle they share.

Thus the 16 percent rate of young Americans who want cancel culture to move farther and faster is worse than it seems, particularly in light of the 23 percent who regard cancel culture as at just the right level and the 25 percent who don't know or don't care. If young social justice warriors find someone who has raised objections to homosexuality on Facebook or wrote once on Twitter that Americans of African descent are low-IQ, the extremists spring into action, coaxing peers to sign petitions, send emails, and make phone calls to the culprit's employer. The moderates may feel uncomfortable about getting someone fired, but they don't like homophobia and racism, either, and so they sign and send; the pressure of the extremists works, and the numbers of protesters swell. What starts as distaste over a politically incorrect opinion turns into a campaign of intimidation. The moderates can't resist joining in because the extremists paint the original crime in the lurid colors of historic oppression, which calls for a hammer response, and moderates don't want to argue over the severity of the original misdeed. In this hothouse zone, it's impossible to say, "C'mon, it was just a stupid remark; we all do it sometimes."

And so the extremists set the tone. Their "idealism" and commitment bring a fair number of their more easygoing peers on board. Another recent survey, the American Worldview Inventory 2020, shows the reach of such illiberalism. On the very virtue for which Millennials were hailed but a few years back, tolerance, the survey found a stark divergence by cohort: "findings show Millennials—by their own admission—as far less tolerant than other generations. In addition, they are more likely to want to exact revenge when wronged, are less likely to keep a promise, and overall have less respect for others and for human life in general."

As for the call for mutual respect commonly heard from Millennials, the survey concluded: "Millennials are also twice as likely as other people to say that the kind of people they always respect are those who hold the same religious and political views as they do. Despite their well-known advocacy of 'tolerance,' they emerged from the survey as the generation that is the least tolerant—by their own admission—of people who possess different views than they do."[50]

This intolerance touches upon other parts of the First Amendment besides freedom of speech. We noted above the Millennials' willingness to restrict "offensive" speech in the name of anti-hate. In this case, it is religious and political differences, too, that are under suspicion—something that strikes at the heart of the principles of the Founding: freedom of religion and freedom of assembly and association. To disrespect people of other religions and politics is a right possessed by anyone in a free society. The liberty to express that aversion is guaranteed by the words of the First Amendment. But along with the legal rights guaranteed by the First Amendment comes an attitude that calls for circumspection when it comes to judging the religious and political views of others. Americans have traditionally given their brethren a little private space for beliefs they consider wrong and feelings that may be bad. If your neighbor belongs to a church that opposes same-sex marriage and you disagree, you don't let it poison your relationship, as long as he doesn't push his belief on you. To allow the church membership, party affiliation, or the like of this or that person to grow so strong in your social judgments is to forget the common citizenship and common humanity presumed by the American situation.

Nearly twenty years ago another survey, commissioned by FIRE, yielded results that explained the Millennials' active disrespect of pluralism. When asked about what the First Amendment actually says, only 2 percent (!) of students knew that freedom of religion comes first. Fewer than one-third of students knew that religious freedom appears anywhere in the Amendment.

This is more than ignorance of the Constitution. It suggests that Millennials haven't learned the civic sense that undergirds the First Amendment, the attitude of tolerance and pluralism that the

Founders hoped to sustain and asked citizens to adopt. The First Amendment is more than a law; it's a sensibility, too, which was somewhat forced on Americans from the start. There was more religious diversity in colonial America than anywhere in the world—churches of many, many kinds, often existing in close quarters and requiring of everyone a thicker skin in liturgical matters. It worked very well compared to what had happened and still was happening in Europe. In the famous *Letters of an American Farmer*, a book much admired by George Washington and Ben Franklin, J. Hector St. John de Crèvecoeur couldn't stop marveling at the peaceful coexistence in the colonies of persons with sharply contrasting backgrounds and beliefs. Individuals and families from different countries speaking different languages and attending different churches lived side by side, mingled in business and social affairs, and rarely disputed, Crèvecoeur observed—and not because the law told them so. Tolerance was an American personality trait. Crèvecoeur wrote the book before the Revolutionary War broke out, and it was published seven years before the Constitution, but according to him many of the advantages we trace back to the Founding documents were already present in the temperament of the colonists, especially the tendency to accept fresh and often strange arrivals with their odd ways chief among them. The book was a hit with Europeans who wanted to hear about the Americans, those rowdy characters, their farms and towns, occupations, mores, marriages, wealth, and faiths, especially avid for vivid contrasts with themselves, and Crèvecoeur put tolerance and peaceableness near the top.

War is a perpetual fact of life in the Old World, he says, and so are sectarian tensions, but he observes, "Here, on the contrary, everything is modern, peaceful, and benign."[51] The American enjoys an open "system of felicity," one that provides "freedom of action, freedom of thought."[52] Europeans suffered the bloody Wars of Religion, and Catholics and Protestants there still mistrust and sometimes fight one another, but even though America has an even more varied mix of rival believers, a "general indulgence leaves every one to think for themselves in spiritual matters...our thoughts are left to God."[53] No Inquisition here, no need for Relief Acts (which, starting in the 1770s, granted Catholics in Great Britain some basic rights), and the scattered persecutions of the early colonies Crèvecoeur doesn't consider worth mentioning. America in 1775 is the most open and heterogeneous society in existence when it comes to worship. In a single village we find a Catholic at home worshipping in his distinctive fashion, Crèvecoeur continues, and "his prayers offend nobody." Next door, the Lutheran has his own services, and "he scandalizes nobody." Further along lives a "seceder" (one of a Presbyterian sect that split from the Church of Scotland in the mid-eighteenth century)—an ardent follower, yes, but what he does on his own time is "nobody's business." Finally comes a "Low Dutchman" (a member of the Dutch Reformed Church) who worships in his peculiar fashion while leaving the settlement of conflicts between him and his neighbors to "the Great Creator." Everyone goes his own way, stays true to his faith, and still gets along. The religious pride that produces oppression in Europe, the zeal that takes offense at the strange liturgies of others, the eagerness to deem a neighbor's doctrine a threat...they "evaporate" in the diffuse and opportune space of America.[54]

It couldn't have been easy. Human nature runs against tolerance, as an hour with six toddlers will prove. Crèvecoeur attributes this American triumph of tolerance over compulsion to local circumstances: plentiful land and common prosperity, vibrant middle-class commerce and no dukes and duchesses, out of the shadow of Europe's bitter past. Why care about what the fellow across the meadow is doing in his church when you have a nice harvest, and so does he, and there are a dozen other townspeople you know by name with their own peculiar wonts, your daughter needs a husband, and there aren't many in your own sect from whom to choose, you don't have to deal with a magistrate picking sides and imposing one denomination on everyone, a small family of unknown origin has just moved into the cottage over the hill, and a young man from Wales has shown up looking for work...? There were simply too much dynamism and mobility and room for Americans to fight over matters of conscience. The environment wasn't conducive to sectarian strife. Apart from upright manners and good work ethic, morality was a private affair.

Crèvecoeur and the Founders wouldn't like the Millennials' self-righteous disrespect. They would have seen instantly that such intolerance wouldn't work in America. People in earlier times had good reason to avoid religion and politics during social occasions. With so much diversity of background and belief, America needed Americans to live and let live, keep the sources of friction low, tend their own gardens, do and think what they wanted in private, and ease up in public. Once they dropped the do-your-own-thing posture, once Americans presumed to judge and dishonor what was going on in one another's heads, American diversity would become a liability. The mind-your-own-business attitude that Crèvecoeur praised would collapse, the tensions of the Old World would emerge where they didn't belong, social mistrust would spread, and the experiment in individual rights could fail.

That's a dire prospect for the country, and I imagine many readers of this book consider it an exaggeration. But it describes exactly where Millennials stand at the present time. They do not possess the facile acceptance of odd beliefs and practices (so long as they did not disrupt ordinary commerce in the public square) that their ancestors had. They do not enjoy the benefits of the softening assumption that what a neighbor thinks about God and man will not disturb the lives of others. They enter social life and business affairs more suspicious than that. In the 2014 "Millennials in Adulthood" report, Pew Research found that young Americans suffer from "low levels of social trust," much lower than those of older Americans. To the question "Generally speaking, would you say that most people can be trusted or that you can't be too careful in dealing with people?" only 19 percent of the young agreed with the first part, that most people can be trusted. That rate came in at less than half that of Boomers (40 percent). A complementary finding was that Millennials were significantly less attached to political and religious institutions than their elders, with 50 percent declaring themselves "political independents" and 29 percent having no religious affiliation (Boomers came in at 37 percent and 16 percent).[55]

A more recent study by Pew entitled "Trust and Distrust in America" showed no amelioration among the Millennial age group. Nearly half of them (46 percent) qualified as "low trusters" and only 11 percent as "high trusters" (thirty-to-forty-nine-year-olds scored 39 and 18 percent, respectively, and fifty-to-sixty-four-year-olds 31 and 25 percent). When asked if they trusted figures in various different areas of society, younger Americans likewise expressed much lower confidence. While 91 percent of Americans over fifty trusted the military, eighteen-to-twenty-nine-year-olds came in at 69 percent. Religious leaders earned the trust of 71 percent of people fifty and up, but only half of the younger crowd. Business leaders earned 50 percent trust from the old but only 34 percent from the young. If we return to the American Worldview Inventory cited above, we find another distinction between old and young. There, Millennials acknowledged more than any other age group that they were "committed to getting even" with those who did them some form of injury. The rate of difference was stark: "[I]n fact," the summary stated, Millennials were "28 percentage points more likely than Baby Boomers to hold a vengeful point of view."[56]

These findings make for quite a contrast with the portraits of confident, optimistic, talented, and educated youth that were pouring forth in the 2000s and early '10s. They invite the question of how a generation so idealistic and broad-minded, more schooled than any group before, cosmopolitan and committed to justice, socially conscious and forward-looking, leading America into the twenty-first century…ended up bitter, suspicious, disappointed, cancel-conscious, unforgiving, and vengeful. The whole thing makes sense, though. The optimism is still there—there will come a day when it doesn't matter whom you love!—but it's of a utopian kind, which doesn't respond well to disappointment. The higher it shoots, the more unjust seems its failure, the more unhappy its purveyors. Their ignorance sets them up for resentment. Why won't discrimination stop? Why must unhappiness continue? Why? They know of no cause other than the existence of bad people. It's their fault, the bad ones.

As we shall see in the next chapters, Millennials are aggrieved and hostile because the learning and experience that would have deepened their understanding of human nature and tempered their utopia didn't happen. They spent their formative years on other things—tools and toys, games and gossip, photos and memes, self-promotion, and one another—all of which saved them from the sad lessons of growing up, settling down, occupying a smaller place in space and time, and enjoying the scaled-down satisfactions of a realistically virtuous life.

CHAPTER THREE

An Anti-Formation

If you were sixteen, seventeen, eighteen years old in 2010, here is how you spent your day: There was school Monday through Friday, of course, running from nine to three, and a lot of you had part-time jobs—enough of you for the entire age group to average seven hours of "[w]orking and work-related" activities per week: one hour per day. Many of you put in time helping people inside and outside your household—a grandparent, perhaps, or a needy neighbor—making for an average of twenty minutes per day. Still others belonged to some kind of civic, religious, or youth organization, going to church or temple on the weekend, praying a little each night, volunteering or otherwise serving in some capacity (overall average labor per day: sixteen minutes). Add the necessities of cooking and eating, shopping, pet care, doing dishes and cleaning rooms, mowing the lawn, homework (of course), bathing and laundry, applying to colleges and preparing for the SAT or the ACT, getting to and from school and jobs, runs to the bank or DMV or gas station, and it sounds like a full day.

But we haven't gotten to the largest bloc of time in a teenage life, larger than "educational activities," which tally fewer than three and a half hours per day (because school days are averaged with no school on weekends and holidays, including summer vacation). There was a bigger component. Logging in at fully five hours and forty minutes per day: "leisure and sports."

Those numbers come from the 2010 version of the American Time Use Survey (ATUS), an annual project supervised by the Bureau of Labor Statistics. The statistics I've cited are for 15-to-19-year-olds. With an impressive sample of respondents (more than 13,000 in 2010) who are asked to keep a "time diary" and sit for interviews with data collectors, plus a nice breakdown of demographic traits and the many activities people report doing, the ATUS is a reliable measure of how Americans live their lives. Fresh results appear every year, showing trends among different groups. For instance, the remarkable 340 minutes of daily leisure for late teens in 2010 went up in 2011 to 359 minutes, a hair short of 6 hours. The ATUS goes further and divides leisure into 7 categories, showing what Americans like to do in their free time when they have the luxury of choice. Teenagers have to eat and sleep and go to school, but what do they do when they don't have parents and teachers and bosses ordering them around?

The most popular leisure activity for our average teen Millennial was a familiar one: "Watching TV," which accounted for two and a quarter hours on weekdays, two and a half hours on weekends and holidays.[1] (That figure matched television time in another survey from 2010, "Generation M[2]: Media in the Lives of 8- to 18-Year-Olds," a study conducted by the Kaiser Family Foundation, which clocked fifteen-to-eighteen-year-olds at two hours and twenty-five minutes of regular television viewing in a typical day.)[2]

Next in the ATUS that year came "playing games and computer use for leisure"—about 50 minutes on regular weekdays and an hour and 6 minutes on other days. This put more than half of the overall minutes of teen leisure on a screen. Another 350 minutes per week went to "socializing and communicating," which we may assume was partly carried out on a computer or a handheld device, through social media, or with a tool made for talking and texting, running the screen portion of leisure time even higher.[3] That inference is borne out by another survey from 2010, which we've seen already, "Teens and Mobile Phones" from Pew Research, which reported that 75 percent of 12-to-17-year-olds owned a cell phone that year—a huge rise from 2004, when less than half (45 percent) of them did.[4] In its study, Kaiser set the percentage of 15-to-18-year-olds with a cell phone at 85 percent and, boy, did they love to text. Kaiser had them talking on the phone for 43 minutes per day and texting (either sending or receiving) for an hour and 51 minutes.[5] Pew counted half of them sending more than 50 messages per day, ⅓ of the whole sending more than 100 per day.[6] We've already seen, too, that in 2010 Nielsen Global Media reported 13-to-17-year-olds who had a phone sending 3,339 text messages each month. Texting, in fact, came up as the top reason why teens wanted a cell phone at that time, beating "safety," the chief reason in 2008, by 8 percentage points. Falling just one point behind safety was a motivation that we should understand as nearly indistinguishable from texting itself: "Keeping in touch with friends."[7]

Moving back to the leisure portion of the ATUS and moving down the list of activities, we find "sports, exercise, and recreation" pulling three-quarters of an hour on weekdays and a few minutes more than an hour on weekend days. Next comes the opposite activity: no physical exertion at all, just "relaxing/thinking," at not quite one hour per week. Think of a seventeen-year-old lying in bed and staring at the ceiling for eight minutes.

The ATUS had an "other" category as well, which accounted for activities such as attending cultural events and traveling that weren't consistent enough to be placed on a per-day basis.

There was one final regular activity laid out in the survey, the one that is the focus of our interest: reading. It barely registered in an average teen's day. Reading print accounted for a meager seven minutes on weekdays and six minutes on off days.[8] (Kaiser raised the reading-for-pleasure time to thirty-three minutes for fifteen-to-eighteen-year-olds, though it did note that reading is "the only media activity that decreases as children grow older."[9])

The numbers didn't square with a common motif of the time, that of the goal-setting, worldly, adept, career-fixated Millennial in 2010 battling to get ahead, to achieve the ideal work-life balance, and to unite personal accomplishment with bettering the world. Six hours of free time per day? No way—not according to the many popular accounts of motivated, high-energy kids, such as "The Net Generation Goes to College," a 2005 story in the *Chronicle of Higher Education* that presented savvy academic observers insisting that, as they proceeded to college, Millennials would "alter the way professors teach, the way classrooms are constructed, and the way colleges deliver degrees," because, as one librarian stated, "they want to learn only what they have to learn, and they want to learn it in a style that is best for them."[10] I scanned those portraits of determined, energetic, multitasking teens and early twenty-somethings around the time I wrote *The Dumbest Generation*, reading about how much homework they had to complete every day in that moment of heavy accountability (the days of No Child Left Behind and Common Core), learning of their massive turnout in the 2008 election and the vast organizing and volunteering they did, too, while they headed to college in record numbers, and I wondered if I was getting them all wrong. The low daily hours for "educational activities"—a grand total of three hours and forty minutes of in-school and out-of-school study—in particular didn't sound right. "The time our children spend doing homework has skyrocketed in recent years," proclaimed the promotional copy for *The Case against Homework*, a popular 2006 book that wasn't the only jeremiad against the "serious toll on American families" that the nightly burden was taking.[11] A story in the *Washington Post* the same year recounted the debate under the straightforward title "As Homework Grows, So Do Arguments against It."[12]

I couldn't deny that Millennials had to compete and perform in ways that Boomers couldn't imagine when they were the same age, not when I looked at how selective top schools had become. I got into UCLA in 1977 with a high school GPA of barely a B, which admissions officers would laugh at in 2007. "It was the most selective spring in modern memory at America's elite schools, according to college admissions officers," reported the *New York Times* that year. Harvard had turned down 1,100 applicants with perfect 800 scores (!) on the math part of the SAT exam that season; Columbia took only 8.9 percent of all who applied.[13] In 2011, Andrew Ferguson devoted an entire book, a very funny one, to his son's admission process with the indicative title *Crazy U: One Dad's Crash Course in Getting His Kid into College*.[14] The rat race stressed them out, we were told, forming characters such as "AP Frank," one of the high school kids profiled in *The Overachievers: The Secret Lives of Driven Kids* (2006) whose academic pursuits—six AP courses in one year—amounted to a mania.[15] The chase was turning them into neurotics but also creating a cohort that was striving and innovating like no other before. "They're optimistic; they're confident," *Time* magazine declared in May 2013 under the headline "Millennials: The Next Greatest Generation?" adding another virtue as well: "[T]hey're pragmatic."[16] They work-work-work, and they're busy-busy-busy. "Nonstop: Today's Superhero Undergraduates Do 3,000 Things at 150 Percent," announced *Harvard Magazine* in a not untypical profile of one of them.[17] "[T]he average Millennial is driven," stated one youth writing at the Huffington Post. "Millennials are incredibly ambitious.... I often feel like I work two full time jobs, but only one of them pays."[18]

And yet, here is what high schoolers themselves said in 2006 when queried by the High School Survey of Student Engagement, a poll of eighty-one thousand students conducted by the Center for Evaluation and Education Policy at Indiana University. To the query about the number of hours of "reading/studying for class" during an average week, 12 percent of respondents answered "0"; 43 percent, "1 or less." You read that right: more than half of high school students in the United States at that time didn't really do any reading homework at all. As for written homework, 7 percent did none; 35 percent, one hour per week or less—not per day, but per week. At the top end, where we would find the supercharged Millennials falling, only 5 percent of high schoolers spent ten or more hours per week on written homework; a tiny 2 percent, ten or more hours on reading homework. In the six-to-ten-hour range, things didn't climb as much as we might expect: 12 percent of the kids doing writing homework; a still single-digit 7 percent doing reading homework.[19]

Another large poll from the same year, the *American Freshman* survey, an annual project of the Higher Education Research Institute at UCLA that dates back to 1966, confirmed those findings. Among the dozens of questions asked of first-year students in colleges was how many hours per week of homework they had logged in their last year in high school. Keep in mind that these were the better students—no dropouts and no vocational school or community college attendees, only the ones who had enrolled at four-year colleges. Nevertheless, the amount of homework involving any reading or writing came up remarkably low in 2006. Nearly two in five respondents (38.2 percent) completed fewer than three hours in an entire week—not even a half hour a night. Another 29 percent fell in the three-to-five-hour range, well short of one hour a night. Only

one-third of the students broke the six-hours-per-week threshold, and just one in seven clocked in at eleven hours or more.[20]

How do these numbers compare to those for previous cohorts? Well, in 1987, when the *American Freshman* survey started to ask about high school homework, the respondents performed much better. In that year, less than one quarter of them (23.7 percent) fell below the three-hour mark, while nearly half of them (47 percent) cleared the six-hours-per-week hurdle. That is, the Gen-Xers of 1987 worked harder than the Millennials of 2006, even though the latter group had higher academic ambitions: while 70.7 percent of 2006 freshmen intended on obtaining a postbaccalaureate degree of some kind (master's, doctorate, medical, law), only 62.5 percent of Gen-Xers in 1987 had. And as they proceeded through their college careers, the Millennials didn't up the homework effort, either. "Consistent with other studies," noted Arum and Roksa of undergraduates in *Academically Adrift* (cited in chapter one), "we find that students are not spending a great deal of time outside of the classroom on their coursework: on average, they report spending only 12 hours per week studying."[21]

So this was a day in the life in 2010 of the rising citizens of the United States. We had a small number of superkids—a very small number—who achieved 4.0 grade point averages and stratospheric test scores. They built daunting résumés and entered elite colleges, stressed and exhausted now and then, but climbing into the professions, imagining start-ups, organizing for justice, doing creative things with technology and media and art. They featured in lavish descriptions in the media, with the theme *Who Are These Amazing Millennials, Anyway?*, with a frequency well out of proportion to their actual numbers (probably because journalists who covered them lived and worked in elite worlds and didn't much encounter the average American teen). The vast majority of Millennials didn't fit the industrious profile at all. Step outside the top 5 to 8 percent,

and the educational effort dropped quickly. Very little homework, very few pages read or written. And the rest of those Millennials didn't make up the lost homework time with leisure habits that boosted intellectual accomplishment in other ways. That's what the negligible minutes of personal reading showed. Kids who did less homework had a lot of leisure time, whether they had part-time jobs or had to care for a sibling or volunteered on weekends. Lots of open hours: lots of shows to watch, games to play, friends to text. In the "Generation M²" report, Kaiser added TV content, computers, and video games together and came up with a daily consumption by fifteen-to-eighteen-year-olds of seven hours and nine minutes (note: if a youth had the TV on for thirty minutes while messaging with friends on the computer simultaneously, Kaiser counted that as one full hour of media).[22]

Those hours put the measly minutes devoted to print in dismal perspective, at least for those of us still wedded to books. The kids themselves were quite open about their carelessness. The High School Survey of Student Engagement I quoted above gave us reading homework tallies. It also asked how often high schoolers did "reading for self" in an average week. There, in free time, the rates were just as bad:

LEISURE READING HOURS

0	16%
1 or fewer	40%
2–5	30%
6–10	9%
10+	5%

Remember, this is reading per week, not reading per day. The results classified more than half of late teens as effectively nonreaders

and another one-third as casual readers (seventeen to forty-five minutes a day). Only one in seven counted as an avid reader, logging at least an hour a day, which—let's remember—constituted only around one-sixth of the entire free time that the kids in the age group enjoyed.[23] Obviously, for the large majority of the young, it wasn't only reading for homework that they avoided; it was reading itself.

Respondents said so in the very next table in the survey, which asked about the same activities but called for a judgment, not for time spent. The prompt was "importance of particular activities," and here is how the kids replied on both school reading and pleasure reading:

HOW IMPORTANT

ACTIVITIES	Not at all	A little	Somewhat important	Very important	Top priority
Reading/ studying for class	8%	19%	33%	32%	8%
Reading for self	16%	29%	33%	18%	4%[24]

Note the two columns on the left: "not at all" and "a little." The depressing rates of unconcern for required homework reading, 8 percent and 19 percent, we might chalk up to alienation or boredom with school itself. In the High School Survey, two-thirds of respondents said that for some period of every school day they were bored in class, 17 percent of them bored in every single class.[25] That makes the distaste for homework reading not hard to understand. The artsy student doesn't like her physics textbook, the jock doesn't want to read *A Tale of Two Cities*, and the future dropout hates them all. They didn't choose those books, some of them couldn't stand the teachers, and a lot of them didn't want to be anywhere near the building. To resent or dismiss homework wasn't startling.

But when it comes to "reading for self," individuals have all the discretion. They can read anything they want; distaste for school doesn't factor in. Indeed, students who detest school could satisfy their frustration by reading things that reflect troubles with courses and classmates, such as *The Catcher in the Rye* or the fabulously popular *Wimpy Kid* series. It would raise the importance of reading for self even as it lowered the importance of reading for school. But the numbers went in the other direction. Self-reading turned out to average as far less important than school reading, a sign that students recognized the personal value of reading much less than they did its academic value. Once again, as with reading-for-homework time, nearly half the kids (45 percent) responded with a shrug. Reading for leisure was not understood as a valuable habit they recognized they should have practiced but simply couldn't work up the energy or time for. No, reading itself just wasn't terribly important, wasn't meaningful.

The publisher Scholastic came up with worse numbers in its *2010 Kids and Family Reading Report* when it asked kids about how important "reading books for fun" was. Fully 24 percent of fifteen-to-seventeen-year-olds answered "not important," while 37 percent said, "not too important."[26] If we look back to the High School Survey, for another one-third, reading was only kinda-sorta important, even though nearly all of that group would be heading for college soon, where an ingrained habit of reading is key to surviving freshman year. (Staying in college is correlated with a student's ability to read and comprehend "complex texts," according to ACT.[27]) Barely one in five saw reading as crucial.[28] As you take in these dismaying stats, let's emphasize that "reading for self" wasn't just school assignments or Great Books or the classics. It didn't have to be a highfalutin endeavor.

Harry Potter and Stephen King and comic books could count. Youth stuff was just as valid as traditional stuff. The question didn't focus on textbooks or even necessarily on books. Magazine reading was included as well—*Sports Illustrated* or *Teen Vogue*—web pages, too, if the respondent conceived of them as reading material. Reading was reading, no matter what the level or the content.[29] Somehow, someway, nobody, not a parent or teacher, sibling or grandparent, coach or minister, had convinced these kids that reading is a primary path to knowledge and discernment, taste and maturity, or merely joy. If they didn't do it often enough, that was one thing. If they didn't believe they needed to do it at all, that was worse—a formula for a prolonged adolescence.

Perhaps the most distressing point in the findings was that the indifference to books and magazines, science fiction and sports bios, fantasy and fashion—not just to Shakespeare and World War II—ran well up the achievement ladder to youths going on to 4-year colleges. A year later the survey results were echoed in the 2008 *National Freshman Attitudes Report* issued by higher education consultant Noel-Levitz (sample size: 92,894), which had 2 out of 5 first-year college students acknowledging, "Books have never gotten me very excited." Slightly more of them (42.7 percent) admitted, "I don't enjoy reading serious books and articles, and I only do it when I have to." A paradoxical data point from the High School Survey made this lack of interest even more depressing. While TV and video games drew many more hours than reading in an average week, respondents rated those entertainments *less important* than reading. The same was true of "surfing/chatting online." In other words, kids chose screens over reading not because they found those diversions more significant.[30] They just liked them better, and despite their belief that reading was more important to their development, it still didn't have enough meaning in their minds to overcome that preference.

Let's cite one more source, the 2006 *American Freshman* survey, which also asked respondents about "reading for pleasure." It found that, in the previous year, one quarter (24.5 percent) of high school seniors who had been admitted to four-year colleges answered "none." Another one quarter did "less than one hour" of reading in a typical week, while still another quarter (24.5 percent) did one to two hours, roughly ten to twenty minutes a day. This was astonishing. How in the world could so many college students care so little about books? It's not only that these kids who would be landing just a few months later in freshman composition, U.S. History to 1877, and Psychology 101 apparently didn't realize that a mere fifteen minutes in bed at night with a novel, a bio of a president, or some pop psychology might do a lot to prepare them for the hustle of freshman year. There was the human element, too, not just the desire to do well in school, but the thrill of rousing stories and moving characters. Here they could find dramas wholly relevant to their experience and taste, such as *Election*, Tom Perotta's dark novel of a high school campaign for school president; the graphic novel series *Sin City*; the story of rapper 50 Cent chronicled in *From Pieces to Weight: Once Upon a Time in Southside Queens* (2006)…where were even those teen-friendly tales? Nowhere in most of these kids' worlds. The library, the bookstore, Amazon…not for them. Barely one in ten broke the one-hour-of-reading-per-day threshold.

That was one hour, I repeat, out of nearly six hours of leisure time per day. As noted above, the large majority of those entering freshmen—fully three quarters of them, in fact (74.9 percent)—intended to pursue a degree beyond the bachelor's, but they didn't seem to make the connection between leisure reading and academic success. If they thought that an hour a day with *Harry Potter* or *The Dark Knight Returns* would do nothing for them in history and English class, they were flat-out wrong, and apparently nobody told them otherwise. The division between reading a civics textbook for school and reading rapper bios or romance novels, it turns out, is a lot less sharp than most people think. The evidence confirms that while the content of fun reading may have no relation to school assignments whatsoever, the very exercise of reading any print material in a teen's free time correlates closely with reading comprehension in academic contexts. This finding consistently shows up in studies of general reading habits and test scores. Here, for instance, is what the National Assessment of Educational Progress (NAEP, the "Nation's Report Card," a project of the U.S. Department of Education) stated in its 2012 *Trends in Academic Progress* report under the bare heading "Students Who Frequently Read for Fun Score Higher": "At all three ages [nine, thirteen, and seventeen], students who reported reading for fun almost daily or once or twice a week scored higher than did students who reported reading for fun a few times a year or less."[31]

The differences were marked. In the 17-year-old group, "[a]lmost every day" readers amounted to 19 percent of the total, and they reached an average score of 302. "Never or hardly ever" reading sounds like an extreme category, but it was a larger portion of the whole, 27 percent, and that group scored fully 30 points lower. We should note, too, that "[a]lmost every day" didn't require long sessions of reading. The category didn't have a minimum cutoff. Ten minutes at a time for 5 days a week would qualify. Indeed, even short sessions with print proved consequential: those kids who read only once or twice a week produced significantly higher scores than non-readers. The low bar proves the benefit: merely a more-or-less regular reading habit, not necessarily an intense one, could carry over to considerably better academic performance.

Keep in mind that, like the other surveys, the NAEP didn't distinguish the quality of reading material. Here, too, comic books and *ESPN The Magazine* and the *Twilight* novels counted just as much as

Mark Twain and Robert Frost. This was something I confess I didn't recognize before I came across correlations of academic achievement and pleasure reading *of any kind* in this and previous NAEP long-term studies. Like many an English teacher, I set the bar higher: "reading" signified Dickens and Browning, not the *Left Behind* books and Marvel comics. I couldn't see how my students' love of *Harry Potter* would produce better results on the tests I gave them; if anything, I thought, the travails of Harry and Hermione would probably harm their engagement with Hawthorne and Dickinson. So I assumed, but that was a mistake. The distinction between high literature and middlebrow (or lower) choices is best saved for later, I realized, after youths have established a solid reading habit for a few years, no matter their preferred materials. That's what the NAEP data showed. Now that the Digital Age had arrived and books had to compete with a whole other order of screens and socializing, English teachers and other mentors couldn't afford to discriminate among books so nicely. If they wanted to maintain a youth readership, they had to push reading per se, print of any kind, and push it harder than ever, knowing that while running through all the *V for Vendetta* volumes wasn't quite as beneficial as tackling the works of William Faulkner or Willa Cather, it was much, much better than TV, texting, and Twitter when it came to school achievement.

It didn't happen; we didn't save them. In 2004, the National Endowment for the Arts issued its *Reading at Risk* report, cited in chapter one. It showed that only 43 percent of eighteen-to-twenty-four-year-olds had read any literature of any kind in any amount in the preceding twelve months. In 1992 the rate was 53.3 percent, which was already a disconcerting slide from 1982's 59.8 percent. A 2007 follow-up report by the Endowment, *To Read or Not to Read: A Question of National Consequence*, to which I contributed, found that 48 percent of eighteen-to-twenty-four-year-olds had read no book at all in the preceding twelve months. The no-book rate in 1992 was much lower, at 41 percent. In 1984, 31 percent of seventeen-year-olds read "almost every day" for fun; by 2004, the rate had slipped to 22 percent. That particular data point came from the very NAEP *Trends* report cited above (the Arts Endowment included NAEP's findings and those of many other research projects). It should be said, too, that a slightly older National Center for Education Statistics *Trends* study, *NAEP 2004 Trends in Academic Progress: Three Decades of Student Performance in Reading and Mathematics*, showed that the loss of reading for fun was not due to increases in homework.[32] This was an excuse for nonreading occasionally offered in those years, as in an NPR story from 2014 that said, "Of course, some students say they love to read but have too much homework."[33] But the rationale didn't fly given the evidence of the NAEP studies. In 1984, when leisure reading was higher, seventeen-year-olds actually did *more* homework than they did in 2004. In that year, 40 percent of them completed one or more hours per day; in 2004, only 33 percent did so, although the students in that 2004 group were assigned a slightly higher page count. The starker change was in the reading-for-fun stats. To repeat: in 1984, only 9 percent of seventeen-year-olds admitted that they read "never or hardly ever," but in 2004, the rate more than doubled to 19 percent. In 1984, 31 percent read "almost every day"; in 2004, only 22 percent. In sum, leisure reading went down at the same time that homework went down. Homework was no excuse.

Let's situate the reading trend within the big picture that NAEP draws, as its full name, the National Assessment of Educational Progress, implies: What do we see in "educational progress" from year to year and decade to decade? From 1984 to 2004, reading scores for seventeen-year-olds declined by four points, in spite of all the government action and public and private funds dedicated over the years to raising them. That's the bottom line for the state and federal agencies charged with handling the schools, the outcome against which reading habits are measured. Educators want to see improvement, and so do politicians who tie their competence as leaders on education to gains in test scores, graduation rates, and college readiness. Recall candidate George H. W. Bush in January 1988, speaking at a high school in Manchester, New Hampshire: "I want to be the education president. I want to lead a renaissance of quality in our schools." What do we have a Department of Education for, why are property taxes so high, if we can't boost the learning of our kids? The year 1984 is a significant one relative to this question, a good starting point for marking the decline of reading and the rise of concerns over outcomes, even though it came after a stunning collapse of reading scores on standardized tests in the '60s and '70s. For the 1984 scores followed the 1983 publication of *A Nation at Risk: The Imperative for Education Reform*, one of the most influential government reports of the twentieth century, an alarm sounded by a commission appointed by U.S. secretary of education Terrel Bell that raised the standing of assessment results issued by the Federal government to critical status and remains today an origin story for the accountability movement. The infamous opening of the second paragraph in the document set the tone: "If an unfriendly foreign power had attempted to impose on America the mediocre educational performance that exists today, we might well have viewed it as an act of war. As it stands, we have allowed this to happen to ourselves."[34]

Government commissions don't usually talk this way, not with so much dread and certitude of failure. Those lines were quoted everywhere, and although it had its critics, the general thrust of the report as a red alert about the state of the schools made its mark. The urgency caught on, and a nonstop focus on test scores commenced that hasn't waned. Accountability called for measurement, not feel-good tales of teachers who really, really cared about the kids, like the sentimental '80s favorite *Dead Poets Society*. A better film of the time was *Stand and Deliver*, in part because the pedagogy of the inspiring teacher aimed at a wholly unsentimental goal: to get his students to score well on the AP Calculus test. The dramatic climax in the movie was just that: pass or fail, and it's easy to see why. Test results are a quick and compact way of determining the quality of education—indeed, the quality of the young. They put pressure on mayors and governors, touch the anxieties of parents hoping that their kids will impress admissions officers at the kids' first-choice colleges, and reassure funders from the business and foundation arena who demand hard evidence of what their dollars have yielded. As one education reporter told me in 2005, "If I can't hang a story on an outcome, it's not a story."

The pressure to raise scores increased through the Bush I and Clinton presidencies (Clinton signed the Goals 2000: Educate America Act in March 1994), culminating in No Child Left Behind in 2001 under Bush II, which tied federal support of school districts to state assessments that met NAEP standards. I was working at that time at the Arts Endowment under Chairman Dana Gioia, and I recall arts educators with whom we regularly collaborated upset and frustrated by the legislation, which put so much emphasis on math and reading that it threatened arts and music programs in their schools. They were right to worry. If school districts had to produce what was called "Adequate Yearly Progress" or else, and if AYP was proven solely by better scores in math and reading, then school officials would allocate resources accordingly. The yardstick was set, and the aims were freighted with all the apprehensions of the *Nation at Risk* outlook. To leave *no* child behind was always an impossible goal, of course. But it rendered neatly the utopian anxiety to move forward, to keep moving, to get better and better, and to make sure every child joined the advance—every single one, without exception.

How curious, then, and how destructive to the plan, that all the efforts fell upon in-school activity. We must break out of mediocrity, the reformers cried, and the classroom is where we do it, the only place we do it. We face "determined, well-educated, and strongly motivated competitors," as *A Nation at Risk* warned, mentioning Japan, Germany, and South Korea, and survival starts with learning, "the indispensable investment required for success in the 'information age' we are entering."[35] Reading scores had to rise; schooling was key, and so we saw large projects to craft learning standards from kindergarten to senior year, billions poured into national and state assessments, President Clinton's "Accountability Fund" for low-performing schools, President George W. Bush's "Reading First" program, and so forth. What we didn't see were any campaigns to raise the leisure reading rates of high school students, certainly nothing with the scope of school initiatives. This was a fateful oversight given the "fun" factor in reading comprehension skills. Nor was there much fretting over the teen drift away from books. Oh, there were periodic outcries about video games and violence, a little distress here and there over the media saturation of youth culture, plus worthy pushes of reading such as Oprah's tremendously popular Book Club, which started in 1996 and managed to insert Dickens, Tolstoy, Faulkner, and Steinbeck amidst the contemporary lit choices. But those rare initiatives couldn't slow the growth of screen time, and a contest over how kids spend leisure hours appeared to politicians as just the kind of culture skirmish that they didn't want to fight after the bruising Culture Wars of the late '80s and early '90s. Anyway, how could government get involved in what teens did once they closed the doors to their rooms? Not only that, but to campaign for books was to campaign against screens, and governors couldn't do that when they were busy with programs to wire classrooms and show that they were fully committed to the most up-to-date machinery. They didn't want to face angry parents crying, "How come School X has a fancy one-to-one laptop program and ours doesn't?" By 2000, in fact, the education establishment didn't see screens as harmful to learning. On the contrary, they were the answer. Governor Angus King of Maine told *Wired* magazine in early 2002, as the state rolled out its program to equip all seventh and eighth graders with laptops, the first statewide program in the country, "I think we're going to demonstrate the power of one-to-one computer access that's going to transform education. The economic future will belong to the technologically adept."[36]

This was never going to work, though. The exclusive focus on the classroom doomed the whole accountability movement, at least in the area of reading. Apart from a short gain in the early '90s, these programs and laws and initiatives and projects didn't come close to doing what the designers and politicians hoped and said they would do. In spite of all the money and dedication, novel curricula and glistening computers, and enormous gifts such as Mark Zuckerberg's $100 million to Newark schools in 2010, reading scores in the twenty-first century weren't any better than scores when the nation was "at risk" in the '80s. Six years ago, a meta-analytical study of research into computers in class found decisive improvements, which a story in *Education Week* summarized: "1-to-1 Laptop Initiatives Boost Student Scores, Study Found."[37] But "in reading achievement," as the study itself admitted, with one exception, "students in the laptop program scored no differently than their comparison group.[38] Another project, Common Core, which came along nine years after No Child Left Behind and was bolstered by $150 million from the Gates Foundation and overseen by the chief education officials of the states, didn't produce higher reading scores, either. (I contributed to

Common Core, helping craft literary reading standards in later grades, but realized afterwards that in the area of reading the reform wouldn't succeed.)[39]

A quick glance at the reading-for-fun numbers reveals why. The evidence was right in front of us. It showed that leisure reading had to play a role if test scores were to rise. If schools put more labor and money into reading instruction but kids increasingly did less reading on their own, the plan would falter. More tutelage in reading for kids who, more and more, found reading both in and out of school unimportant would yield diminishing returns. If reading were just a school subject, if it had no personal meaning for the youth, the instruction wouldn't stick. In other words, declining reading scores were a problem that extended beyond classrooms and homework time. They pointed toward teens in their bedrooms surrounded by TVs, desktops, cell phones, and game consoles or on the sidewalk with eyes glued to a tiny screen, never entering a public library, fascinated by text messages from friends, but not by Pip or Jem and Scout. Reformers and politicians were asking schools and teachers to solve a problem that originated and persisted in the whole life experience of the young, not just in their academics. To read or not to read was, indeed, *A Question of National Consequence*, and it applied to the forty hours a week of leisure time as much as it did to the twenty-five hours per week of class time. Bad attitudes toward books did more damage than scanty reading homework did. The former led to the latter, and it would lower reading comprehension skills and hurt college readiness.

It is tempting to focus on school achievement during those heady ed-reform decades, with easy calculations of test scores, money earmarked and spent, and hours devoted to homework and to leisure reading that correlates with skill levels. What isn't so clear, now that the fourth graders of 2000 have all grown up, is the broader impact of nonreading, the bare human cost to a youth who skipped books during adolescence. What did it do? It did what an aliterate existence could be expected to do. It deprived the young of the knowledge and acumen that men and women rightly possess, the exposure to human nature up and down the scale of good and evil, beauteous and vulgar, smart and stupid, to strange times and far-away places, acts of heroism and disloyalty, the most eloquent words and sublime sounds and perceptive images. Government reform and the accountability movement ignored a reality in plain sight: the average day for a seventeen-year-old Millennial in 2010 was an intellectual wasteland, an immersion in other things, in games and gossip, photos and messages, shows and songs that would do nothing to help him grow up, to acquire the tragic sense that is essential to shaping prudent hopes of what life can be and to the realization that what they believe and enjoy in adolescence is best forsaken by age twenty-two.

After the publication of the *To Read or Not to Read* study cited above, the *Guardian* published a scornful commentary under the heading "Dawn of the Digital Natives" by science writer Steven Johnson.[40] Johnson was (and is) a sharp observer of intellectual trends in American culture, the author of *Everything Bad Is Good for You: How Today's Popular Culture Is Making Us Smarter,* and he didn't hesitate to condemn the report. Although its release had led to widespread concern ("Newspapers dutifully editorialized about America's literacy crisis," Johnson remarked), in truth *To Read or Not to Read* amounted to a standard "'our kids in peril' story—right up there with threats of MySpace predators," a predictable entry in "yet another 'Johnny can't read' mini-panic." The whole enterprise, he implied, was simply hand-wringing by bibliophiles who didn't understand and thus felt threatened by the new literacies of the Digital Natives. Let's move on.

The alarmist nature of the project was easy to see from its flawed methodology, Johnson argued, including its restrictive definition of reading. While he conceded that the authors of the study made a convincing case for the decline of book reading among the young, the percentage of eighteen-to-twenty-four-year-olds picking up a book for fun having fallen 12 percent since 1992, Johnson found an astonishing oversight in the data we had compiled: there was no recognition of screen reading. The report was packed with statistics, but, Johnson said, "in almost every study it cites, screen-based reading is excluded from the data," a "preposterous omission." Johnson compared this exclusion to "doing a literacy survey circa 1500 and only counting the amount of time people spent reading scrolls." If we do include screen time, he countered, we find a dynamic literacy of an entirely different kind unfolding, one that leaves the Arts Endowment study and its print bias in the dustbin of history.

He had more to say. True, Johnson admitted, we read "smaller bites on the screen, often switching back and forth between applications." But that's not necessarily a bad thing, only a variation of the old way, and it could prove to have unforeseen advantages. Johnson backed that speculation with a snippet from a study by the British Library that cast this jumpy reading practice as promising: "[N]ew forms of 'reading' are emerging as users 'power browse.'" Furthermore, he went on, screen reading is a more "interactive" exercise, encouraging less passivity and more critical response, as shown by the explosion of web writing—"we are writing more, and writing in public for strangers: novel readers may have declined by [10 percent], but the number of bloggers has gone from zero to 25 million." Additionally, Johnson found a contradiction in the statistics that brought down the whole gloomy edifice of the report. While test scores for older kids had indeed fallen, those for younger ones had gained, Chairman Gioia himself stating, "[T]here has been measurable progress in recent years in reading ability at the elementary school level." Nine-year-olds had jumped seven points in reading since 1999, a fast rise that predicted a better future as they got older. Meanwhile, seventeen-year-olds had dropped five points, but that was since 1988, a fairly minor decline that was "[n]ot exactly cause for national alarm." What the results called for was more patience and less the-sky-is-falling doom and gloom—that was the upshot.

Johnson's commentary was a brisk takedown, levelling several common criticisms of our report. Many others at the time derided and pooh-poohed those of us who feared what the Internet would do to literary culture and the education of the youth, but with less intelligence than Johnson. I remember a panel at a private high school in San Antonio that had brought four of us in to speak to the student body about growing up in the Digital Age. After I did my turn warning the kids against a screen-soaked life, a young academic rose to dismiss my take as a "moral panic" no different from Socrates' objecting to the advent of writing or mid-twentieth-century critics' objecting to comic books. Perhaps it impressed the seniors and juniors in the audience as a scholarly rebuff, but I had heard and read these exact points a dozen times before in the preceding months. I wanted to exclaim, "Do you think I haven't read the *Phaedrus*? Do you think I'm not familiar with what Irving Howe, Dwight Macdonald, and Clement Greenberg said about mass culture?" But that would sound defensive. My usual rejoinder at those moments was to remark, "It is mighty strange to hail the Internet as comparable to the invention of writing and the breakthrough of Gutenberg, a veritable revolution in word and thought, and then to be vexed by skeptics raising doubts about its impact."

Johnson's criticism delved into the numbers and the facts, however, and it merited an answer. I discussed it with Sunil Iyengar, who headed the Endowment's research office at the time (I had left in 2005), and we wrote a statement that appeared in the *Guardian* a few weeks later under the prosaic title, "There's Good Reason to Worry about Declining Rates of Reading." First, we made corrections. As you can see from the surveys cited in this chapter, many studies included in *To Read or Not to Read* did *not* exclude reading books and articles, poems and plays, on a screen. The questions asked by the surveys were generic and usually did not explore how and where one did the reading. Also, Johnson had pointed to the score improvements for nine-year-olds as if they portended increases to come, but those gratifying results signified nothing about the future. The pattern had held for a long time: elementary school–age test scores had gone up, but when those elementary school students became high school seniors, twelfth-grade scores had not. As kids proceeded through middle school and high schools, the advances had disappeared.[41] Finally, when Iyengar and I looked at the British Library study that Johnson cited as affirming innovative forms of digital study, we came across this bitter summation of screen reading: "From undergraduates to professors, people exhibit a strong tendency towards shallow, horizontal, 'flicking' behaviour in digital libraries. Power browsing and viewing appear to be the norm for all. . . . Society is dumbing down."[42]

That's what we found in 2008, which we took as a solid refutation of the shrugs of Johnson and others. But we had to admit that things could change quickly. The digital habitat was volatile; new tools surfaced every month; Twitter was just then taking off. Fans of Facebook and Wikipedia could always point to the extraordinary potential for the web to become a spirited intellectual arena as young users became more experienced and cultivated better and best practices. We might very well have credited Johnson with predicting a future that would, indeed, diverge from the past as digitally enhanced Millennials headed toward adulthood and grew bored with callow habits. But today, at a date more than a decade onward, we might ask what actually happened in the following years. As these high-performing nine-year-olds matured and put the new tools and games and media that came their way to use, what reading aptitude did they acquire?

Johnson rightly noted the copious writing that teens did in the virtual environment; the numbers I have cited so far on texting and social media back him up. In 2012, 2013, and 2014, youths did more writing than at any time in human history.[43] The ability to write, comment, rate, opine, observe, evaluate, and create was, to be sure, the core feature of Web 2.0, the name for the search engines and websites that enabled users to contribute to their content and function.[44] Instead of merely reading a webpage in the Web 1.0 way, which digital commentators regarded as a passive activity, users in this next phase of the Digital Age could talk back, as in Amazon's product review sections and Wikipedia's editing capacities. Votaries of Web 2.0 such as Johnson treated this empowerment of users as a decided advance, especially in relation to the couch-potato nature of TV viewing. Surely we would see writing scores rise as Millennials grew up in so inviting and composition-heavy a habitat. Fortunately, the SAT decided at that very moment in 2005 to add an essay section to the test, which would constitute a reliable way to pick up the enhanced verbal skills. The addition would give educators a new yardstick of progress, every year charting how increasingly digitized teens would perform as academic writers.

Here is how the results fell out for the following ten years:

Year	SAT Writing Score
2006	497
2007	493
2008	493
2009	492
2010	491
2011	489
2012	488
2013	488
2014	487
2015	484
2016	482[45]

Scores fell every year except for two, 2008 and 2013, when they were flat. That's a decline hard to explain away, in that it transpired during the very years of grossly expanded leisure scribbling. How could all that writing generate a fall (instead of a rise) in writing ability, especially as much of it was done in an active Web 2.0 mode? It was so much better than the old, rote way of learning to compose by copying out passages from prose masters, right? Plentiful writing online should have produced better writers in the same way that daily workouts produce healthier bodies. Instead, the opposite happened. Why? How? There had to be some other factor in play that interrupted the transfer of social media writing into competent analytical writing solicited by the SAT. Either that, or more writing of the kind teens typically did on their screens would never carry over to academic writing, perhaps because the genres were too distinct (good writing isn't necessarily transferable—an eloquent columnist may be a terrible novelist). Whatever the cause, the dwindling performance on the SAT was a big sticking point for the 2010 cheerleaders. It put the value of texting and similar activities in a different light, or, at the very least, it should have curbed the enthusiasm.

We stop at 2016 in the chart above because the SAT decided to drop the essay requirement that year, I imagine because the bad news was starting to hurt the brand and push high schoolers aiming for college to SAT's competitor, the ACT exam. (The writing section is now optional, though high achievers applying to top schools often take it.) When we examine ACT scores starting a few years after the SAT began to require an essay, however, the news doesn't improve. ACT has a measure it calls "college readiness," which shows a student's capacity to perform well in a specific first-year college course. There are four areas of college readiness that ACT calculates: math, science, reading, and English. Reading is tied to social studies–type classes, while English is tied to freshman composition courses, the latter category being the most relevant to writing competence. The ACT defines "readiness" as the likelihood (above 50 percent) that a student will earn a grade of B or higher or the strong likelihood (above 75 percent) of earning a C or higher in freshman comp at a typical college.[46]

Noting the rampant grade inflation in higher education in recent decades—a 2016 study found that 42 percent of all grades in both four- and two-year colleges are As[47]—we should interpret "readiness" as a low hurdle. It really doesn't take much work to get a C in a college humanities class. Nevertheless, it still proved difficult for an increasingly large portion of college-bound kids. Here is the trend in the percentage of ACT test-takers who succeeded in meeting the benchmark from 2009 forward.

Year	College Readiness—English
2009	67%
2010	66%
2011	66%
2012	67%
2013	64%
2014	64%
2015	64%
2016	61%
2017	61%
2018	60%
2019	59%[48]

Not as steep a drop as the scores on the SAT essay section, but still going in the wrong direction, consistently so. Drip, drip, drip; the average keeps falling, eight percentage points in ten years, tens of thousands more kids in 2019 falling down than in 2009.

How, then, taking into account the evidence of the two college-entry exams, can we say that the shift from print to screens has enhanced young people's writing abilities? In the past, apologists for these declines have attributed them to the larger pool of test-takers, and the SAT population from 2006 to 2016 did indeed grow from, roughly, 1.5 million to 1.65 million, while the ACT grew by an impressive half-million from 2011 to 2016 (1.6 million to 2.1 million). More Millennials aimed for college than their elders did, the argument went, and so the slip was inevitable. They only looked worse than Boomers and Gen-Xers because less-talented students in those previous cohorts didn't take the test.

But given the claims made for Millennial talents and ambitions, along with the explosion of writing in a Digital Age, we should have seen better outcomes than these. With so many more Millennials shooting for college than older Americans did, we presume that they worked harder in high school and polished the skills they knew would be tested. Not only that, but from 2016 to 2019, the numbers of individuals taking the ACT test actually dropped, and the trend in declining scores didn't stop.

The same thing happened with reading scores during these years, not just writing scores. When we track SAT results before our existing window, from the mid-'90s to the mid-'00s, we actually see some notable positive movement, 1994's average score of 499 climbing to an average score of 508 in 2005. But look at what happened after that, with the scores of high school seniors who were born late enough for digital devices and habits to have touched them at tender elementary school ages and flooded their teen years.

Year	SAT Reading Score
2005	508
2006	503
2007	501
2008	500
2009	499
2010	500
2011	497
2012	496
2013	496
2014	497
2015	495
2016	494[49]

After all the emphasis on reading in No Child Left Behind and in Common Core, this is a sorry record, another dramatic fall. (I stop at 2016, as I did before, because the following year the SAT revised the test and the scoring.) In two of those years we had a slight rise, the rest a drop or a flatline.

As for the percentage of test-takers who were deemed "college ready" in reading, here is what ACT shows.

Year	College Readiness—Reading
2009	53%
2010	52%
2011	52%
2012	52%
2013	44%
2014	44%
2015	46%
2016	44%
2017	47%
2018	46%
2019	45%[50]

Once more, an overall decline. There were only two years of gains, 2015 and 2017. The huge drop in 2013, eight percentage points (!), occurred because ACT adjusted its readiness benchmark that year. It gave the following reason for the change: "Routine monitoring of their predictive validity indicated a need to update the Reading and Science benchmarks." In other words, evidence showed that previous rates of readiness hadn't held up: many test-takers deemed "ready" in, say, 2009, did *not* earn the decent grades that the ACT's benchmark predicted they would when they got to college in 2010. That is, years 2009 to 2012 likely overestimated the number of college-bound seniors capable of college work, and so the ACT had to adjust the benchmark.[51]

Another major reading test given to twelfth graders in these years, the NAEP exam, covered all high school students, not just those heading to college, and there too the results proved disappointing. While the average score climbed two points from 2005 to 2009, as Twitter and Facebook and iPhones and texting spread—or, we might say, as high school seniors who had now logged many years with an iPhone and social media sat for the test—average scores lost one point in 2015 and another two points in 2019. In that latter year, in fact, the lowest performers, the tenth- and twenty-fifth-percentile groups, achieved the lowest reading scores ever in the history of NAEP, going back to 1974. The score of the lowest-performing group among that year's test-takers fell twenty points short of the tenth percentile's score in 1992, while the second-lowest group's score fell thirteen points short of the twenty-fifth percentile's score in 1992.[52] (Recall the finding, noted in chapter one above, that kids from lower-income households, who tend to score lower on tests, spend more time on screens than do kids from higher-income households.)[53]

Meanwhile, as reading scores lagged among high schoolers, Millennials began to age out of adolescence. As they graduated from high school, went to work or entered college, proceeded through their twenties and thought of settling down, their reading habits didn't improve. If we go back to the American Time Use Survey in more recent years and look at older cohorts, we see that in 2019 twenty-five-to-thirty-four-year-olds clocked a paltry seven minutes of reading per day. They weren't kids any more, but that didn't make books, magazines, and newspapers any more appealing. They didn't have to read boring textbooks for classes at this stage of life, and in spite of jobs, household tasks, money worries, marriage, and children of their own, they still enjoyed substantial leisure time—four and a quarter hours per day—but reading for fun or enrichment was no more enticing to them than it had been when they were seventeen.[54] The burdens of their lives had changed, but their leisure preferences hadn't, at least as far as books were concerned. The ordinary challenges of adulthood pressed upon them, and print offered them no fresh guidance or relief, nor did they expect that at a pause in their duties, when they might sit down and relax, books would deliver any joy.

Four years ago, the American Historical Association issued a troubling report on a recent trend in higher education. In 2008, it said, 34,642 college students in the United States majored in history. In 2017, the number had plummeted to 24,266, an astonishing drop for a long-standing, central area of study. "Even as university enrollments have grown," author Benjamin M. Schmidt stated, "history has seen its raw numbers erode heavily." From 2011 to 2017, the number of graduates with a history degree fell more than 30 percent, the worst performance of any of the 49 fields included in the report. Computer science, physics, chemistry, and 29 other fields, mostly scientific, showed gains, while among the subjects that lost majors, 6 of the bottom 7 were in the humanities (area studies, one of the poor performers, I count as a social science). Philosophy, English, and foreign languages all slid by more than 20 percent.[55]

The news didn't surprise anyone who had paid attention to enrollment patterns over the preceding twenty years. Stories about the "declining humanities" seemed to appear every week. Tales of programs shutting down, funding cuts, "adjunctivization" (the conversion of regular faculty to part-time faculty, which was especially common in English and the languages), moribund academic conventions, a horrible job market for recent Ph.D.s, sliding undergraduate enrollments... they were so commonplace in the 2010s that the only unexpected, scary thing about each one was the volume of the collapse. In late 2010, the president of SUNY-Albany announced that five departments would be closed: French, Italian, Russian, classics, and theater.[56] A story at Inside Higher Ed in early 2015 reported that the

English department at University of Maryland–College Park had lost 40 percent of its majors in three years.[57] I think the worst I saw was this from the *Chronicle of Higher Education* in early 2019: "Colleges Lose a 'Stunning' 651 Foreign-Language Programs in 3 years."[58]

I and other conservatives and traditionalists blamed that collapse in part on the leftist bias and identity politics of humanities professors. How many students who might have been disposed to major in history were put off by a teacher who could announce, "The Whitesplaining of History Is Over," the title of an essay in the *Chronicle of Higher Education* that began, "When the academy was the exclusive playground of white men, it produced theories of race, gender, and Western cultural superiority that underwrote imperialism abroad and inequality at home."[59] If you were a nineteen-year-old white guy, would you want that teacher grading your papers?

The American Historical Association report, on the other hand, blamed the declines mostly on financial pressures, stating, "The timing of the trend strongly suggests that students have changed their expectations of college majors in the aftermath of the economic shift of 2008." Given the high cost of college and the stumbling economy in those years, it argued, students sought majors that seemed to promise immediate and well-paying employment after graduation, namely, the science fields and business, not the soft and fuzzy humanities.[60] "What're you gonna do with that degree?" is a question harder for philosophy and English majors to answer than for psych and chemistry majors. Evidence from the *American Freshman* survey backs this up. When asked for "very important" reasons for going to college, students chose monetary hopes over intellectual goals by a wide margin. In the 2013 version of the survey, the reply "to be able to make more money" beat "to gain a general education and appreciation of ideas" 73.3 percent to 69.6 percent (respondents could list more than one reason as "very important"). "To be able to get a better job" beat "to become a more cultured person" nearly two to one—86.3 percent to 45.9 percent.[61] In 1976, when the survey first started asking that question, the rankings were the opposite, with "general education and appreciation of ideas" drawing about the same amount, 67.5 percent, but "make more money" much lower, at 49.9 percent.

This trend in attitude explains why the business fields, which exploded in the 1980s, now award more bachelor's degrees than all the arts and humanities fields combined. But it doesn't explain why the humanities have fallen so far in recent years. During the first decade of the millennium, according to the National Center for Education Statistics, the number of arts and humanities bachelor's degrees jumped mightily. We went from 214,107 degrees in 2000–01 to 288,446 in 2010–11. But look at what happened after that: In 2014–15, the total dropped slightly, to 280,956, and three years later there was a greater slide, to 268,554. That may not look significant, but keep in mind that during those years of absolute decline, the overall number of bachelor's degrees was rising dramatically, from 1.48 million in 2005–06 to 1.98 million in 2017–18. The percentage distribution of degrees conferred gives a clearer picture of the magnitude of the slide. In 2005–06, the arts and humanities claimed 17.6 percent of all bachelor's degrees; in 2017–18, they accounted for only 13.6 percent of them.[62] That gave impetus to dozens of articles such as "The Humanities as We Know Them Are Doomed. Now What?"[63]

To attribute that direction to a more career-oriented approach to higher education on the part of Millennials is to miss the fact that the career orientation was already well-established among college students by the 1990s. The "very important reasons for going to college" data in the *American Freshman* survey for those years show that quite well. In 1994, for instance, 75.6 percent of freshmen chose "to get a better job," while only 40.9 percent cited "make me a more cultured person."[64] And yet in the following year, arts and humanities still drew 16.6 percent of all degrees, well above the current rate.[65]

There is another variable to consider, then, one that was generally ignored by professors, administrators, and higher education experts and journalists as they registered the fall of the humanities—and also by reformers and politicians out to improve reading scores for high school students. It's the factor we've been stressing—leisure reading—which should have been recognized instantly as an obvious component in an undergraduate's choice of field of study. A kid who likes to read may choose biology or business just as readily as English or history. A strong reading habit may run in many directions, to novels or to *Scientific American*. But we can say with confidence that a youth who doesn't like to read in his free time, who avoids books altogether, will tend to avoid book-based majors that require a lot of reading. He could choose economics, but not English. A non-reader browsing the course catalog as he selects next semester's courses won't go anywhere near "Comparative Literature 201: Tolstoy and Dostoevsky."

That expectation is confirmed by the survey evidence. You might assume that anyone going to college does a good bit of reading on his own. Not so. In 1994, the *American Freshman* survey started to ask respondents how much "reading for pleasure" they had done in a typical week in the preceding year, allowing respondents to choose answers ranging from "none" to "over 20 [hours]." Nearly one fifth of them in 1994 answered "none."[66] Not one word of print; nothing. Only an active aversion to reading could cause that degree of anti-habit. The rate sounds almost unbelievable, and one would like to know how many of those aliterate college students dropped out of school before the end of spring term. Six years later, though, the rate had worsened, to one in four freshmen (24.7 percent). And then, in 2013, it leapt even higher, to nearly one in three (31.8 percent). In 2015, it hit 32.6 percent. If we add to the "none" group those at "less than one hour," we get 45 percent in 1994, 52.2 percent in 2000, 56.7 percent in 2013, and 58.2 percent in 2015.[67] This means that the pool of habitual readers from which the humanities draw majors got smaller every year, even as the overall size of the entering classes grew. There's the reason for the sliding humanities—not future earnings anticipated by students after graduation, but leisure tastes formed in the past, before the adolescents ever got to campus.

Hence the formation of Millennials in school and out of school, an anti-formation, really, marked by a sweeping shift from print to screens, books to sites, and history, literature, religion, art, science, and politics to games and videos and youth culture. This was, in fact, a slap in the face to teachers who'd devoted their lives to books and civilization, but as I have said, liberal intellectuals and academics didn't want to chastise kids for their choices. That would stigmatize the critics as conservatives or grouches—designations abhorrent to most academics. But the nonreading habits of rising adults didn't leave left-leaning mentors unscathed. As we see from the numbers, it left them with fewer readers for their op-eds and magazine articles, fewer students in their classes, more Americans uninterested in what the teachers and commentators had to say. The mentors had to respond. On campus, the humanities departments were bleeding. The professors couldn't devise a way to make seventeen-year-olds start reading *The New Republic* and scholarship in *New Literary History*, but at least they could work up revisions to the curriculum.

A broader liberal arts education, one that would ensure an informed, discerning, articulate college graduate with some exposure to humanities subjects—that was an obvious and workable beginning. In late 2016, Nicholas Lemann wrote an article for the *Chronicle of Higher Education* that straight-off identified the necessity of that course correction. It was called "The Case for a New Kind of Core," and Lemann himself had just the right profile to make that case:

someone familiar with secondary and higher education, academia and the cultural sphere, able to address how a new curriculum in the classroom would fix problems that had started outside the classroom. He was half academic and half journalist, a staff writer at the *New Yorker* and former dean of the prestigious Columbia University Graduate School of Journalism (and still a professor there). He also had experience with high school kids and their transfer to college, having authored, in 1999, *The Big Test: The Secret History of the American Meritocracy*, a saga of standardized tests, particularly the SAT, and their social impact on the country.

In the article, Lemann regretted the "continued erosion of the role of the liberal arts within undergraduate education," and he implicitly chided his colleagues for failing to communicate to students "a stronger argument...for an undergraduate education that isn't overwhelmingly oriented toward employment skills." He didn't mention the leisure habits of the young, but he did register "the diminution of the liberal arts in recent years," which he blamed on two things: one, a career-focus on the part of students, who end up "taking courses designed to prepare them for specific jobs," and two, weak general education requirements that enable them to skip the more humanistic courses. In other words, the kids don't want to study Impressionism, and the educators help them avoid it. We can't censure the kids, either, he continued, since they hear the practical emphasis from so many quarters, including the Obama Administration, whose College Scorecard project rates schools by how much money their attendees earn in the years after graduation. Broad liberal arts courses such as "Survey of English Literature from Chaucer to Dryden" strike them as a hindrance, and professors immersed in their research don't like them, either, because those courses are "labor-intensive and intellectually constricting." Hence the university now reinforces anti-intellectual tendencies, acting more like a business than an academy, and the liberal arts are slipping away. That was Lemann's complaint.

"The key to reversing their decline," he urged, "is to move in the direction of a core curriculum." Few institutions have one, and the effects are showing, Lemann observed—and he was right to do so. For a long time now, I have witnessed general education—that is, the courses that all four-year students have to take outside their major—become a loose and random process. Most schools lay out broad categories for students to fill: "humanities," "physical science," "diversity," and so forth, or they organize the categories with a more cognitive taxonomy such as Stanford's "Thinking Matters Requirement" and "Ways of Thinking/Ways of Doing Requirement."[68] Typically, students meet those requirements by selecting from a large number of courses that have been approved by the faculty and administration. This is the elective approach, a Chinese menu of offerings, with some version of freshman composition often the only common class. "The Ways of Thinking/Ways of Doing Requirement" at Stanford, for instance, is subdivided into eight categories, each one containing dozens of courses that may fulfill the requirement, and the selections have but a distant relation to one another. Under "Social Inquiry," we find the following options:

- AIDS, Literacy, and Land
- CAPITALS: How Cities Shape Cultures, States, and People
- Introduction to Comparative Studies in Race and Ethnicity
- Media, Culture, and Society
- Technology and National Security
- World History of Science

These are just examples of Social Inquiry courses suggested by Stanford on its Ways of Thinking/Ways of Doing web page. Many other courses qualify (Stanford is on a quarter system, so students there take more courses than those at semester schools). As you can see from Stanford's system (and that of nearly every other four-year school), there is no core, no coherence, only a jumble of courses that students regard as ways to fill in a checklist. With so many scattered options, they don't see the courses they end up taking as cumulative or complementary, a totality that enters their minds and forms them into "a citizen worthy of a free society and a free university." Convenience and personal taste guide them, not a sense of their own formation. They don't envision general education classes as supplying a body of knowledge that all educated Americans must master. Those classes are, instead, an interesting this and an appealing that, things in which to dabble or just to get out of the way. The elective system encourages that attitude. Stanford promises students "tremendous flexibility to select topics that appeal to [them]," which means that Stanford cannot prescribe any particular topics or knowledge that all students must acquire. Instead, these requirements "will help [them] to develop a broad set of essential intellectual and social competencies"—Stanford names them "Engaging Diversity," "Ethical Reasoning," "Scientific Method" . . . in sum, forms of critical thinking and social awareness that can be applied as easily to the design of a department store as to the design of Wagner's *Ring*. These abstract tools of thinking and socializing are the only unifying elements in the curriculum, and students may reach those capacities via a host of unrelated pathways.

As you just read the paragraph above, that "citizen worthy of a free society" line might have puzzled you. It doesn't seem to fit with this elective model. The word "worthy" sounds a bit too moralistic and formative, while the epithet "free society" has an air of classical liberalism that doesn't jibe with the social motif of the current requirements. That's because the quotation comes from another Stanford document from another time, some sixty years ago. I came across it a few years back when I attended an event at Berkeley and added a side trip to Stanford to visit the archives and pore over old university catalogs. I often did that while giving guest lectures at various schools in the 2010s, strolling into libraries and asking research librarians for old materials from the school, often getting a quizzical look in response. "Do you have catalogs and course listings from 1965?" I would ask, and I noted their amusement at a research query that obviously they'd never heard before. It was part of an ongoing inquiry I was making into how general education requirements had changed over the years, which I took as evidence of how the faculty understood their purposes at different times.

This time I had made arrangements in advance, and the staff had five or six years of volumes waiting when I arrived. Stanford, I found, called its general education in those pre-Vietnam days the "General Studies Program," inaugurated in 1956. The description of it in the catalog included the "design a worthy citizen for a free society" rationale, and it did indeed hark back to a whole other academic universe. In this presentation of what Stanford students would learn, there was no deference to undergraduate preference. Students had very little choice in their first two years of study back then. Everyone had to take a full year of freshman English (Composition and Literature). The first quarter would "train the student to write lucid, orderly, and logical prose." The second quarter would provide "some introduction to forms of literary expression." Finally, the third course would emphasize "reading and analysis of forms of literary expression." The focus on literature in the second and third courses would have surprised a freshman comp teacher in 2016. By then, you see, literature was not an essential ingredient of freshman English. During my time as a graduate student and assistant professor in the '80s and '90s, an anti-literature movement swept the composition field, pushing teachers to abandon the belletristic and largely Dead White Male canon of the old-fashioned English 101 syllabus, of which the '50s-era Stanford sequence was a perfect example. Leading figures in the field of rhetoric and composition pushed the reform vigorously, many of them wanting to distinguish their field from English, others enthusiastic about designing a new pedagogy that was based on a communications model and ranged across non-literary genres, still others wanting to widen the conception of rhetoric and writing well beyond the confines of Keats and Hemingway. It was also a way to shift course content toward contemporary matters and social themes of race, class, gender, sexuality. That afternoon I spent in the Stanford library was a pleasing nostalgia for me, the insistence on literary expression (which would surely include some classics), on writing presented without a framework of politics or identity, a nice escape from "relevance."

The next section of the requirements appeared even more out of date. It was History 10, 11, and 12, "History of Western Civilization," a full year of Homer, the Roman Empire, the Renaissance, the Enlightenment... The text in the catalog didn't much elaborate on this three-course demand, no justification or explanation. It didn't have to—not in an era when immersion in the epochs of the West was synonymous with liberal education. The confidence the school had in this sequence contrasted so sharply with the suspicion of Western Civilization that spread in the '80s (and now equates it with white supremacy) that I read the description three times just for the novelty of it. In another section of the catalog, on the pages concerning the department of history, the department expressed absolutely no doubts or recriminations: "The course in the History of Western

Civilization, which surveys the development of the Western world from its earliest times to the present, is required by the University of all students as a necessary part of a liberal education and supplies a foundation for the other work in the Department."

The most important words in that long sentence are "all," "necessary," and "foundation." No compromise, no exceptions, no apologies. It had to be done; you couldn't progress toward junior and senior years without it. And by "it" they didn't mean higher-order thinking skills such as learning to "think historically" or to "interrogate" the very notion of "the West" or to uncover the ideological underpinnings of the canon formation that cast Homer, Sophocles, Virgil & Co. as "classics." The outcome of History of Western Civilization wasn't to be a cognitive skill, a "Way of Thinking/Way of Doing." It was, precisely, *The Odyssey*, Caesar and Christ, Michelangelo and Romanticism and the French Revolution. No dithering over whether we should force every student to read Shakespeare and describe the Reformation—of course we should! They must digest the details of *The Prince* and Bernini's *Apollo and Daphne*, memorize the facts, the concrete specifics of the stuff on the syllabus, not polish their skills of "Social Inquiry" and "Formal Reasoning" (two of the "intellectual capacities" in the later Stanford system). The goal of the pedagogy was knowledge, not "Ways of Knowing." A liberal education without a year of Western Civ was a defective one, the historians at Stanford could declare without a whisper of doubt.

How satisfying it was to hear this note of certainty, which has been absent from the humanities ever since I started teaching in 1989. The humanists at Stanford circa 1960 understood what should have been obvious to the humanities professors of the 2010s watching their departments slip steadily toward the margins of higher education. They knew where the attractions lie, for no nineteen-year-old ever majored in a humanities field out of the motivation "I really want to become a critical thinker." No one chose French because she expected it to advance her "Ways of Doing." Majoring in French would, in fact, cultivate her "Doings," yes, but that benefit would hardly serve as an incentive before she started. The ambition of one "Way of Thinking" or another would just as easily lure a freshman to neuroscience as to English. If a humanities department promised to instill such mental skills, fine. But that promise wouldn't draw a twenty-year-old in. If he did choose English, he would come because of Emily Dickinson and Oscar Wilde and Virginia Woolf, the actual poems and novels and memoirs, the real things that offered him inspiration. And he would be all the more inspired if the professors presented those writers and artists, thinkers and musicians, with the air of "necessity" and "foundation" as the old requirements had. "You must read this," they had to say, "or you will be an insufficiently educated, tasteful, and interesting adult."

How unusual it was in 2016 to encounter such an assured proclamation of mission. I apologize for repeating that point, but it felt too good to forget. Ever since that 1960 moment, of course, the trend has run in the other direction, toward less confidence, less prescription, less identification of essential materials, of a core. By 1980, I would say, the traditionalist perspective was already a loser in advanced professional circles, and the stigma drifted downward and outward through the professorate steadily through the decade. Most humanities professors remained focused on traditional topics, Shakespeare and the rest, but they learned not to push them on others. Best to do your thing and let others do their things and let the students pick and choose. As I watched it happen, I couldn't believe that full professors with respected books to their credit couldn't stand athwart the waves of '80s relativism and cry, "Stop!" Culture Wars figureheads William Bennett, Lynne Cheney, and Allan Bloom all earned loud cheers in the public square when they pointed out the "politicization" going on, but they didn't slow its course in the humanities. One school after another lowered its standards and eased up on reading lists. I didn't like those conservative critics at the time, didn't like their politics, but their resolve put to shame the pusillanimity of the literature professors who were willing to go along: "Yeah, sure, go ahead; drop that literature requirement." They were Republicans—ugh!—but at least they weren't spineless, like the mentors whose relaxation had acquired the status of rigid dogma by 1985. Anyone who stood up to affirm a core, a strict set of requirements—especially a Western one—had to live thence onward with the reputation of having a backward character, hidebound and narrow-minded. When in 1987 E. D. Hirsch's *Cultural Literacy* appeared and spent six extraordinary months on the *New York Times* best seller list, the professorate denounced him as a reactionary, a "Eurocentrist," a Dead-White-Male advocate, in what Hirsch later characterized as "a torrent of abuse from the academy."[69] Perhaps his critics didn't know that Hirsch was (and still is) a lifelong liberal Democrat and that his model of education was designed to provide underprivileged kids the same acculturation that middle- and upper-class kids were receiving and that would enable them to score well on tests and hit the college grounds running. But that didn't matter. The book ended with something unforgiveable, an appendix entitled "What Literate Americans Know." The appendix had some introductory notes by Hirsch and two colleagues at the University of Virginia before the real substance unfolded: an unadorned list of terms, names, dates, titles, quotations, and idioms that anyone with cultural literacy should recognize. They were staples of educated discourse in America, Hirsch maintained, and familiarity with them would help individuals make their way through the culture, enabling them to understand, for instance, the mention of "Star Chamber" in a newspaper op-ed, a politician invoking "city on a hill," and other unexplained references in public discourse. Hirsch saw that this cultural knowledge had a stratifying effect, putting well-educated people in the know and poorly educated people in exile, and he conceived the "cultural literacy" list as a way to even things up. Here was a bare-bones core of items that could guide a curriculum for the schools from grade to grade and prepare the disadvantaged for upward progress. The edition I own includes an "Updated and Expanded" list of five thousand entries running in two columns down sixty-four pages. Hirsch called the organization he started with the earnings from *Cultural Literacy* the Core Knowledge Foundation; its purpose is to provide elementary and middle schools that very curriculum (disclosure: I have served on the board of the foundation for many years).

The problem wasn't only that the list appeared way too narrow, too Eurocentric, to the multiculturalists who were at the time in the middle of their conquest of the humanities. Yes, they could single out what appeared to be cultural bias on the list—the Alamo but no Wounded Knee; Jefferson Davis but not Miles Davis—but what disturbed people most of all was the identification of any particular content that *every* educated person had to imbibe, any tradition at all held up as authoritative. Who's to say what "literate Americans" must study? That was the question of the moment, expressing the ascendant anti-authoritarianism that presumed to lead the way toward openness and diversity. Why *deus ex machina*, Dido, and John Dillinger (all on the list) and not Sally Hemmings, Tahiti, and Pancho Villa (not on the list)?

These were the kinds of challenges thrown at Hirsch. Though they had become clichés by 1990, they were nonetheless quite effective in discrediting defenders of a core curriculum and downgrading requirements such as the old Western Civ courses at Stanford. Hirsch didn't understand his critics' motives. Why were people attacking a program that would meet their political purposes? He explained them this way in the essay cited above, which he gave to me for a volume I coedited with Adam Bellow in 2015:

> In the name of destroying cultural hegemony, the academy was preventing K–12 education from delivering the knowledge that Americans need to fulfil their democratic citizenship and that disadvantaged students need to close the achievement gap and climb the class ladder. Academic critics were so angry at the very idea of cultural literacy—that is, a body of knowledge common to informed individuals, made use of continually in their criticism—that they did not even try to follow the scientific evidence showing how essential that knowledge is to basic and advanced literacy.[70]

In other words, the attack on a core as "hegemonic" deprived the very kids whom the attackers presumed to represent of the intellectual equipment they needed to prosper and grow. It prevented the class mobility that educators professed to want to ensure for the underprivileged. Hirsch conceived his curriculum as progressive, but his critics judged it stultifyingly conservative. They measured it by the content of the list of core items, not by the fate of kids who don't learn those items.

Put it this way: Two kids go to college and sit next to each other in a freshman course in U.S. Government that meets a distribution requirement. One student attended a high school whose curriculum had her reading lots of classic works, ancient history, and European history from the Renaissance forward. She grew up in a nice suburb in a household with books and newspapers lying around. She recognizes a lot of the items on Hirsch's list. The other kid attended a low-income school that had pushed the curriculum toward contemporary works of literature and recent history, perhaps out of notions of "cultural relevance." He earned grades high enough to win him entry to college, but his instruction in traditional areas of history and literature and art was sketchy. Meanwhile, at home the student watched a lot of TV. His parents didn't read much to him when he was a child and didn't encourage him to read on his own when he was in high school. Much of Hirsch's list would perplex him.

Now, what happens when, in a class meeting early in the semester, the teacher starts talking about the Founders and the Roman Empire? The subject comes up in a session on the debates in Philadelphia and in the Federalist Papers over the drafting of the Constitution. "Why are the Federalist Papers written by a guy with a Roman name?" a student asks. Professor X, assuming that all the freshmen have heard of the Roman Empire, probably won't feel the need to explain what it was. He'll jump right to the lessons about the dangers of popular rule and tyranny that the Founders took from Roman history. He won't expect the students to have read Plutarch, but he will expect a little familiarity with Caesar, the Roman Senate, Apollo, and perhaps Christians and the lions. The first student may not remember a great deal about Rome and the emperors, but she has enough background exposure to hear some echoes and follow along. Our other student never heard of Cato and Antony, Virgil or the Colosseum. He didn't read Shakespeare's *Julius Caesar* in tenth grade or *Vacation under the Volcano* the summer he was ten (an entry in Mary Pope Osborne's *Magic Treehouse* series that sends the protagonists back to Pompeii the day before the eruption). He's baffled and lost, probably nervous, and a little embarrassed, too. The teacher doesn't notice, however, as he encounters the group only a couple of hours a week and meets just a few of them in office hours. If a student disappears halfway through the semester . . . well, that's one less paper to grade. College doesn't allow for the close guidance of high school, and few freshmen see their teachers as involved mentors. Our second freshman nonetheless knows full well his disadvantage, and chances are it will show up at grading time.

Knowledge of the facts in *Cultural Literacy* would act as an equalizer: "Roman Empire" is on it. That was Hirsch's contention. Inequality of income and home environment could be compensated for by a cultural-literacy curriculum. Poorer kids don't get the allusions and references to books and events, titles and characters that better-off kids pick up at home, and that deprivation prevents their uplift. Educators couldn't change these kids' private lives, Hirsch understood, but they could ensure that underprivileged students learn to identify Achilles and describe D-Day as well as the others, if only their schools had the right curricula. A richer diet of English, social studies, science, and art that followed Hirsch's list would show up in higher SAT scores.

But that argument couldn't overcome the disgust of the educators in 1987 at Hirsch's case for the necessary "core" element of cultural literacy. "As far as I could tell," Hirsch sighs, "the book was excluded from all syllabi in education schools, mentioned only as something evil to be avoided."[71] Academics in charge of curriculum in those years adhered to a strict dogma when it came to humanities education: *core* is a bad word, and so is *all*. Teachers would have to proceed without an imposed focus on any particular content. No prescribed works or facts of events.

But this created a practical problem: educators would still have to run the institution and determine what overall value it provided. A degree from Williams College had to signify a value of some kind, eight semesters that added up to ... well, something distinct. As multiculturalists proceeded to break up the core, multiplying the cultures kids could study, opening up the canon, diversifying the reading lists, and increasing student choice, most professors nevertheless understood that they had to maintain some form of coherence in general education. Yes, in May 1969 the Brown University faculty famously approved what became known as the Open Curriculum, which left general ed wholly up to each undergraduate's discretion, with no required courses, but few other schools followed suit. And for good reason: the complete absence of a formative telos in an undergraduate's experience in four or five years on campus (apart from the major, which makes up only about one-third of the courses a student must take) not only raised questions about the educational worth of a school whose sticker price had climbed to forty to fifty thousand dollars per year. It also implied troubling things about the value of the teachers themselves. For, apart from realizing that such a student-centered approach guaranteed a whole lot of bad decisions by nineteen-year-olds, professors felt uncomfortable with the idea that their own classes played no constitutive part in a student's overall development. Professors like to think that their influence will endure, that what students learn in their respective classrooms will shape their learning in future classrooms, that there is some dynamic relationship between what they teach, what other teachers teach, and the fully-formed mind of the student at graduation time. They want the impact of Poli-Sci 201 and Italian Cinema to last more than one term. There should be some overall design in which each course plays an essential role, not just an episodic journey from class to unrelated class.

But how to institute that unity when diversity disallows any unifying content such as "Western Civilization"? Where could design lie, when the materials had to be multicultural and students to be granted freedom of choice? The answer was obvious: precisely the thinking skills that Stanford and almost every other major school lay out in their general education descriptions. When Harvard finalized its revised general education curriculum in 2009, it organized courses into "eight broad categories of learning," including "aesthetic and interpretive understanding" and "ethical reasoning," along with a few hopelessly vague topics ("culture and belief," "societies of the world"). As for immersion in a particular tradition that all students must explore, there was a perfunctory bow in that direction that only underscored the inconsequence of what was being required: "At least one course, the requirements say, must involve a substantial study of the past."[72] The wondrous result claimed for this twenty-first-century education was a student with "new intellectual capacities," as Stanford assures us in its description: a judicious, critical temperament. The "Basic Education Requirements" of the University of Texas at Austin, to take another example, lay out some strong expectations that cross many areas of history, government, math, science, and humanities, but when they summarize the results for an individual who has completed the program, we see the same abstract skills and aptitudes: "communicate clearly and accurately," "have a critical understanding of the society," "be able to analyze ethical issues," "understand aspects of mathematics," and so on.[73] Certain "Signature Courses" are also part of the core at UT, but they, too, highlight "new ways of learning through a myriad of subjects and topics." The emphasis has shifted from "what you will know" to "what you will be able to do." The analytical mind, the critical thinker—that's the be-all and end-all for general education. The contrast with the old way is clear. Mid-twentieth-century academia idealized a college graduate as one who recalls Socrates and Galileo and Beethoven's Ninth. The twenty-first-century college identifies her as one with habits of critique. We have evolved from knowledge to dispositions, materials to skills. This is coherence without content, an attempt to resolve the contrary demands of diversity and direction with a new spin on *e pluribus unum*: out of many unrelated college courses, one analytical mind.

This model was never going to make youths read more literature and learn more history and appreciate more art. It made no appeals to greatness or brilliance or beauty; it didn't stand strong for anything concrete, nothing specific. Because it didn't affirm any specific content as crucial, the way of getting at that content wasn't really crucial, either. That was the implication. If one history was pretty much just as good as any other, maybe history itself wasn't that important. If Great Books weren't so necessary, was reading anything at all so crucial? I can't imagine that college students wouldn't draw the larger conclusion about the value of reading itself and apply that conclusion to their own leisure choices. If Shakespeare was just an option among many others, if Grant's *Memoirs* was merely a matter of taste, as the intellectual-skills model implied, higher education wouldn't slow the migration to screens or blunt the natural adolescent predilection for the present in the slightest. Only a vigorous defense of books by the professors and forthright predictions of futility and confusion in adulthood if the students didn't read, bolstered by a curriculum that forced them back to precontemporary print, would break the anti-intellectual habits of the young. But my colleagues couldn't do it. They had lost confidence in their own materials and were unable to insist on the traditions. The Shakespearean scholar would not tell her pupils that they must close their windows and open *As You Like It* or suffer the consequences of a shabby sensibility. The old way had held to the traditions and thereby invited young Americans to behold themselves as inheritors of it. The new way invited youths to see themselves as inheritors of... nothing. The authority of the past, and of the professors, too, vanished under the dictates of diversity and student empowerment. But this didn't liberate the young. The process played out quite differently: "Authority has been discarded by the adults, and this can mean only one thing: that the adult refuses to assume responsibility for the world into which they have brought the children."[74]

That's Hannah Arendt, again, in the essay "The Crisis in Education" (published in *Partisan Review* in 1958 but written a few years before). Every education reformer today should read it. Arendt had witnessed child-centered education spreading in the schools through the influence of John Dewey and others, and she found the notion that it showed greater sensitivity to the growth and trials of childhood entirely absurd and, in fact, destructive. In the freedom and initiative granted to students by an open curriculum, she predicted a terrible fate. Dewey and other progressive educators believed that the modern world was unstable, making "old" knowledge ever more obsolete and rewarding adaptive, flexible minds. So a sensitive and caring pedagogue would focus more on inculcating those modern habits, not on teaching dead writings. The key to forming those minds was to minimize the rote learning of the past and coax the young toward independence in a process of "learning by doing." We see here the seeds of collaborative learning, students' "taking ownership" of their education, active learning, and other key ideas of education theory. They are, indeed, the very language of the field, but Arendt saw them in a whole different light. They were, to her, a grand abdication. The older generation, she wrote, has a responsibility to present to rising adults a world, a society, a reality that has been created and that they shall inherit. The young need that assurance, even if they don't like that world and reject it. Some kind of order and structure and history are necessary to their well-being, and they need the elders to uphold it with conviction. But in the student-centered pedagogy, the mentors withdraw. They may believe that they are empowering the young, but Arendt knew that the opposite was happening. Here is how she put it (as if the progressive teacher is speaking): "In this world we are not very securely at home; how to move about in it, what to know, what skills to master, are mysteries to us too. You must try to make out as best you can; in any case you are not entitled to call us to account. We are innocent, we wash our hands of you."[75]

That was sixty years ago, but the indictment still applies. It translates smoothly into the current humanities professor's shrugging, "I teach baroque art, but, hey, you can take it or leave it." Or, as a distinguished literary scholar stated once on a panel at a regional meeting of the Modern Language Association after I had laid out for the audience the dismaying results of *Reading at Risk*: "Look, I don't care if everybody stops reading literature. Yeah, it's my bread and butter, but cultures change. People do different things."

As Arendt understood, the issue is the teacher's responsibility. It's not only that our twenty-first-century humanities professor doesn't have the stomach to profess her own subject matter with the certainty that the older mentors possessed. It's also that the new mentors misconstrue their own position relative to their juniors. In 1966 Princeton University approved an experimental course that brought the rosy faith that "children flourish when they are allowed freedom" into the highest reaches of higher education. The instructor would be history professor Martin Duberman, recently tenured and interested in modeling a classroom on an "anti-authoritarian basis," drawing on his experience with group therapy. He recorded the trial in "An Experiment in Education," an essay in *Daedalus* (Winter 1968) that detailed his intentions and student responses.[76] No "transmission of factual information" would be solicited in the two sections of this course, he recalled, and no grades would be given, either. Duberman wanted more student "self-exploration" than usually happened, and existing pedagogies tended to interrupt that kind of growth. The current system trained young people to seek "the approval of others...to manipulate others in the way one has been manipulated," he grumbled.[77] Grades "turn potentially creative individuals into data-processing machines...inculcating docility and compliance." Everything that made students passive and inferior had to go. Let's have no titles in class, as well, Duberman proposed, everyone going by first names, including the professor.

The course topic was American Radicalism, and the syllabus would adjust week by week to what students "felt would be most logical and useful."[78] Duberman created a long reading list from which students could pick the selections that looked intriguing and ignore the rest. "Nothing, I made clear in that first session, was required: neither reading, nor attendance, nor 'performance'"[79]—no exams or papers. The pedagogical warrant for this laxity is what we've heard already: in the education of the young, there is no quintessential content, no book or artwork or philosophy or event that is indispensable. As Duberman explained, "the notion that certain bits and pieces of knowledge are 'essential'...is dangerous nonsense."[80] The teacher, then, has no standing to require anything, only to suggest. Let the kids take the lead. At one point, he told students they could bring beer.

It didn't go well. Some students complained of the combative nature of the discussions, others of the unseriousness of the course. When Duberman brought an expert in to discuss pragmatism, as the discussion progressed, he observed, "[O]ur ineptness...became increasingly embarrassing."[81] Class conversations drifted into current affairs and left the historical material behind. One student in the afternoon section, "Sherm," kept trying to restore "some form of authoritarian structure," mainly by attempting to keep discussants on topic and move the colloquy forward, but he usually failed.[82] Students applauded the absence of grades and tests, but all save one doubted that they did as much work as they would have with an exam looming. "Natural curiosity" wasn't enough. The "formlessness" and "lack of direction" bothered others, and many objected to the high "bull-shit quotient" of what came out of the mouths of their peers.[83]

It sounds pretty bad, but Duberman interpreted these responses as only partly negative. The discomforts were inevitable, he reasoned, since the course broke so many academic rules the Princeton students had internalized. The dissatisfactions and revulsions many experienced stemmed from their failure to assume responsibility for their own learning. Pain was a sign of improvement, or at least of potential gain. They still wanted the professor to "do it for them," yes—and that was precisely the attitude he aimed to disrupt. As for whether the students walked away with much knowledge of radical movements in America, everything indicates a traditional course would have yielded a lot more. That, however, was the wrong standard by which to judge. Duberman had another goal for the youths: "self-knowledge through group interaction." Just as therapy involves facing disturbing truths about oneself and others, so did American Radicalism. "If History 308 did partake of psychotherapy," he concluded, "I would, therefore, not only welcome the news, but consider it the best possible vindication."[84]

The most damning piece of evidence comes not from what students said, however, but what they didn't say. Strangely, Duberman mentions nothing about students' enjoying the material. No one, apparently, left the room enamored of William Lloyd Garrison or Eugene V. Debs. Duberman barely mentions course contents—not a single book title. None of the students gushed, "I want to read more of this, lots more." The only subject matter enthusiasm that surfaces comes, not surprisingly, from some students who decided to get tough and form a radical "movement for change" at the university itself. Princeton needed reform! The group met outside of class late at night, drafted a "Statement of Principles" regarding higher education, and circulated copies around campus. But the project didn't last. Fewer kids came to late-night meetings as the semester wore on; the statement was ignored; "the movement brought no concrete results." The students didn't learn very much radical history, nor did they become active radicals.

Arendt predicted this outcome. When a teacher denies his own authority, she maintained, when he cannot single out any writings that students must read, he shortchanges the knowledge and competence he wields. He goes down in value, too, just as much as the background subject matter, for the teacher doesn't just explain the materials students study. He embodies them. He *is* the books, the science, the art. That's what lodges him in front of the class, the body of knowledge that he has worked hard to master. When he steps away, when he becomes the "guide on the side," he takes the knowledge with him, away from the center and the focus of the class. That's the regrettable consequence. When Duberman made the course content optional, he robbed it of "necessity." "Radicalism in America" could have been a rousing tale of riots and marches, daring ideas and daring men and women, Pinkos and Reds, strikers and strikebreakers and Pinkertons, Birchers and the FBI. Duberman could have outlined the history, assigned the readings, imparted his expertise, and tested the enrollees. Students would have left with a story in their heads, remembered long after the course had ended. Instead, his tour through "American Radicalism" became a thin pretext for "self-discovery." Duberman and so many other educators, then and now, replaced the ideas, words, and works of the dead with the liberation of the living—and were darn proud of doing so. The kids, however, weren't so improved by the experience. If a year later someone had asked any of his students to reconstruct an argument made by a populist radical of the late nineteenth century, I am certain that they wouldn't have come up with much of a reply.

The current method of general education—a smattering of unrelated courses that is supposed to result in a graduating critical thinker—doesn't do much better than Duberman's experiment when it comes to actual learning. The curriculum doesn't demand a full scope of background knowledge, a core cultural literacy of any kind, nor does it even succeed in promoting the favored thinking skills. When Arum and Roksa examined scores of 2,322 students on the Collegiate Learning Assessment, a measure of reasoning and problem solving, over the course of their college careers, they found precisely the "limited learning" that appears in the subtitle to *Academically Adrift*. They summarized the most hard-hitting finding in the study: "[M]any students are only minimally improving their skills in critical thinking, complex reasoning, and writing during their journeys through higher education."[85]

The loss of a core and the slide into incoherence foretold that disappointment long before. That's why when Lemann's essay with the title "The Case for a New Kind of Core" passed my desk I grabbed at it. But I wasn't impressed for long. After the opening paragraphs on the problem of students' fleeing the humanities and the potential of a new core to stop the flight, Lemann finally gets to specifics and announces this underwhelming encapsulation: "[M]y proposal is for a methods-based, rather than a canon-based, curriculum."

When I read that line, I blinked. Huh? This is new? When Lemann says he has no "confidence" in identifying "a limited number of books, or a specific body of knowledge, that are so universally important that everyone should have mastered them," he situates himself firmly in the 99 percent of American academics who already take that position. Without that confidence, but nonetheless sure that nineteen-year-olds need a tighter framework than currently exists, he suggests a core based on certain "methods" that will endow students with "a suite of intellectual skills . . . a tool kit that would help a student become a more empowered user of the university." That's all this new core amounts to in the end: the same old skilled mind of before. The wording couldn't be much more pedestrian, the vision more dated. Indeed, the headings under which Lemann's required courses would be classed are even more empty than the ones we've seen so far: "Information Acquisition," "Cause and Effect" (a variant on scientific method), "Interpretation," "Numeracy," "Perspective," "The Language of Form," "Thinking in Time" ("historical thinking"), "Argument." Lemann is right to say that entering students need "a high level of direction," much more than the current mishmash provides, and the eight courses he requires boost the workload of typical general ed requirements, but this model is no more coherent, cumulative, or memorable than the others out there. His new core would "put methods above subject-matter knowledge in the highest place of honor"—exactly the wrong thing to do.

How could academics have failed so badly? The cliché of skills-not-knowledge has persisted for so long, surviving as a thoughtless dogma among the teachers since they themselves were students, that they overlook how clueless and irresponsible it is. That an intelligent, well-meaning, worldly figure who has at hand all the disastrous evidence of the abandonment of the humanities should advise such a fruitless been-there-done-that approach betrays the blindness that afflicts the entire profession. The walls are crumbling, enrollments are down, programs are closing…and the professors still can't bring themselves to revive Western Civilization, or Eastern Civilization, or the Great American Novel, or any great overarching lineage and proceed to make every single student pass through it. They know they're in trouble, but the mentors still can't manage any urgency about the precious value of Shakespeare, Debussy, and the rest. It's stupid, and it's pathetic. High school students don't read, college students don't read, Millennials in their twenties and thirties don't read, and teachers and intellectuals won't mount a national enterprise, mobilize a public awareness campaign, or craft a curriculum that pushes and prods young Americans back to print.

Kids go to college with great expectations—eager to have fun, of course—but ready for grown-up matters, too, the contents of authentic manhood and womanhood. They don't read much on their own, but they're alive to what is significant and true. Social life with friends continues, yes, but that doesn't prove they don't crave relationships with an elder or two who will help them distinguish the meaningful from the inane, the superior from the middling. A teacher who enters the room as a force of tradition, willing to deem this book or that event essential for all intelligent adults only bores or annoys some of them, to be sure, but it inspires others. He lets them know what is great and momentous. He gives the agreeable ones worthy objects to fit to their evolving sensibilities, and he gives to the disagreeable ones a meaningful understanding of the past against which to rebel. His syllabus tells them what really counts, and his attitude toward those materials affects their own convictions, positive or negative, about larger things. Think of this in terms of the developmental psychology of an eighteen-year-old. What message does a teacher of core knowledge send, and what message does a no-core-knowledge teacher send? A silent communication takes place, whether my colleagues intend it or not. In fact, I don't think humanities teachers realize the inference freshmen draw when they discover that the authorities in charge of general education at State U can't single out one book, one time period, one hero or country or war or peace or faith or philosophy that they absolutely must learn about in their march toward graduation.

Skills-and-methods people apparently trust that their model charts a sophisticated path for willing minds. But imagine the high school senior freshly admitted to a number of competitive universities in the spring and searching the catalog for courses for fall semester of her freshman year. The curricula of Stanford and similar universities strike her as bloodless bureaucratic schemata. Nothing exciting there at all. She has to dig further into particular courses that fill in the blanks. There on one syllabus or another she finds books and artworks, episodes and social phenomena that might spark her interest. But the excitement is particularized, so to speak, pertinent to just that class, not to the whole design. "General education" at State U doesn't signify anything general to her.

On the other hand, imagine our high schooler in 1959 scanning Stanford's catalog and facing History of Western Civilization right up front. It's daunting, cosmic. We go from small pictures to Big Picture, random choice to universal requirements, from a curriculum that covers a slice of time and place to one that traces the ages. It's not a specialized class on a neat topic. It's two-and-a-half millennia of Western Civilization, Odysseus and Hamlet and Queen Victoria, Marathon and Agincourt and Waterloo. The difference registers well beyond the selection of classes. What the mentors presented to these teens about to leave home and submit to a new authority in 1959 was not just a set of course requirements. It was a conception of the past, of the world. A metaphysical impression rose in each youth as she assembled her upcoming course schedule.

Our 2016 high school senior on her way to higher education sees that there is no particular knowledge she must acquire, nothing that happened in the past that is so vital that everybody must acknowledge it, no works of such standout genius that everyone must experience them. That leads to a natural conclusion: the universe is a casual place, the past no more mysterious and compelling than her present social media; all the creations of human beings over the centuries fall on a level plane. Our 1959 senior met her requirements as if she were stepping into an epochal condition—and she was. This is the best; this is the greatest; this changed everything that came after. That's what the old way tells her. The past is meaningful, very meaningful. You exist amidst the reverberations of might and sublimity. The world into which you have been thrown resonates and glows. Your life can do the same.

What a horrible thing it was to exclude Big Pictures and Grand Narratives, Great Books and Masterpieces, from the rearing of the young. What a hoax to frame this deprivation as progress, as liberation. If they didn't like Western Civilization, why couldn't they have drafted some alternative legacy to transmit to the next generation—for instance, "The Three Abrahamic Faiths: Judaism, Christianity, Islam," anything with scope and continuity and a claim to greatness and significance and posterity? Why leave young people with no meaningful horizon, nothing more than a technocratic aptitude for "critical thinking"? As we've seen, kids heading to college in 2016 needed mentors more than ever. As younger teenagers they had read a lot less than previous cohorts had, and, outfitted with laptops and iPhones, they were more deeply immersed in youth culture and peer pressure than ever before. In 2010, when they were thirteen, the mentors in their lives had spied them at their screens, heard them typing and clicking, and let it go on, as the data on screen time and book time at the beginning of this chapter prove. The academics' handling of freshmen is merely one case of a broad cultural attitude toward adolescents that swept all the mentors of the time, in class and out of class. They knew the rules of the twenty-first century: Don't bark at the kids for skipping books. Don't trash their cell phones and media. Don't be a grump. A parent who in 2010 insisted on a little daily book reading and grown-up exposure to news, good music, art, and politics was going against the grain of the Digital Age. A teacher who exhorted, "You must read what Dido says to Aeneas as he prepares to leave—stop texting!" stood out as a throwback. Lemann himself states that "core-curriculum discussions are difficult and unpopular," and so he softens his challenge to what may be accomplished within the limits of the "current consensus," assuring his readers that he's just "trying to start a conversation."

That's an anxiety we should dispense with in 2022. Ten years ago, fifteen years ago, American teens were swept by a tidal wave of technology, and it killed reading habits that were already fragile. The high schools and colleges didn't rise to the threat and reassert the sublimity of the greats and the necessity of culture. A genuinely revolutionary deterioration took place, greater than any ever seen before, and the mentors stood silent and passive. They lacked the certitude needed to slow and reverse it. If reading scores had risen in the 2010s, if we had any evidence that Millennials possessed more knowledge and better skills than their forebears, if they did more reading homework and wrote more elegant prose, we couldn't blame the mentors for anything, and I would have to shut up. But the decline is a fact: the SAT and ACT scores don't lie, and the number of English and history bachelor's degrees awarded by Stanford went from ninety-eight and seventy-five in 2000 to forty-seven and thirty-five in 2020, respectively.[86] Millennials in adulthood aren't upping their humanities experience after graduation, either. Their reading skills fell below those of their predecessors, and they don't care. They don't want to read. The intellectual equipment and predilection that a reading life in adolescence and a core curriculum in high school and college would have supplied they don't have. What happens to a fifteen-year-old who doesn't read when she hits age twenty-six? She becomes the delicate and dangerous utopian sketched in chapter one.

What have we done to them? We have made the past a repository of irrelevant and unknown strivings. They aren't interested. As for the present, it's a battleground of dreams nursed in adolescence pitted against rent, job, car, breakups, and aging. The knowledge of the Passion and of Appomattox, the ruminations of Elizabeth Bishop and

Nick Adams, the music of Satie and Brubeck, Thomas More in the Tower and the Invisible Man in his basement...those touchstones would have negotiated a modest peace in their hearts and souls, but they aren't available. Our unread Millennials went to college and believe in diversity, they have online friends who tender support, they work pretty hard and play pretty hard, but they're not as worldly and adept and articulate as they think they are. Older coworkers and neighbors aren't as impressed with them as their buddies are, and it doesn't seem right. People aren't what they're supposed to be, they believe. Their ideals keep losing out to circumstance. Something that should have happened over and over long ago didn't happen; their seniors didn't make it happen. They didn't watch *Citizen Kane* or *Wild Strawberries*, didn't stare at *Nude Descending a Staircase*, didn't listen to *La Traviata* or "Blue 7," didn't read *Candide* or "Ode to a Nightin gale" or *Seize the Day*...

CHAPTER FOUR

The Psychological Novel

"Why are they so upset?"

This time I wasn't talking to the student in my office during the Milo episode at Emory, the one who answered with the everyone-deserves-to-be-happy dream. Instead, months after that conversation, I was posing the same question to a longtime friend from graduate school, now a professor of rhetoric at University of Winnipeg. He was older than the other grad students at UCLA in the '80s and had a different focus. While we applied the writings of Jacques Derrida, Michel Foucault, and Jacques Lacan to literary works, he delved into social psychology, understanding literature as rhetoric and rhetoric as verbal behavior, a way for individuals to understand and relate to others, including by manipulating them. It made him an outlier in the program—stimulating to talk to, a nice break from our increasingly clichéd patter of literary theory.

Bob and I had earned doctorates and taken jobs around 1990 in far-apart places but had reestablished contact a year or two earlier and spoke every few months about things happening in academia. I enjoyed the view from Canada of Black Lives Matter, the Trump phenomenon, feminist professors, and student unrest offered by him from an entertainingly canny rhetorical-behavioral perspective. He always had a fresh angle on things, and the news of his death in September 2020 would have me feeling like a precious well had gone dry, leaving the world a less replenishing place.

"Why are they so emotional, Bob? Why does a joke set them off?"

This may have been just after the election of Donald Trump, which had ramped up the hurt and outrage on dozens of campuses, caused some street riots, a few flag burnings, many grave gatherings, and lots of sputtering students incredulous and fearful at the outcome. I was sure Bob would have an acute psycho-political insight. He would somehow translate the hot-tempered fragility of the kids into a commanding interpretation of ego defenses and socializing tactics. But that's not what he said.

"Well," he drawled, "they haven't read enough literature."

He paused, and so did I. Usually, he would expound at length, but this diagnosis he let sit by itself. It was unexpected. What does literature have to do with students in the streets? He could have chosen so many other aspects of the phenomenon to comment on. For example: *These youths are so bathed in politically correct notions from kindergarten forward that any counter to them only sounds an alert in their heads*, I imagined him saying. *They don't know how to meet ideological difference with evidence and argument instead of anxiety and name-calling. They're not used to it.*

Or, he could have offered a meritocratic analysis. *The kids at selective colleges* (where so many protests had taken place) *have had to compete for limited spaces at one of the Ivies or a top state school since they were fourteen. The stakes they attach to every grade and standardized test have turned them into thin-skinned alarmists. Outside of class, they want assurance and safe space, not challenge.*

Or, we might have agreed that bad pedagogy was the cause. *Elementary and secondary school teachers and administrators have promoted self-esteem and identity-affirmation to the point that the students take any clash of ideas personally. A debate is not an intellectual contest or even a political one; it is an existential threat.*

Or, he could have blamed the professors whose leftist bias encouraged students to regard conservative people as abominable. *The rise of Donald Trump didn't hit them as a political defeat. It was a moral scandal, and such things deserve righteous indignation—the more emotional and voluminous, the better.*

But no, my friend pointed to poor literary formation. The distance between novels, poems, and plays, on one hand, and the ostensible object of the demonstrations, on the other—be it Trump, a controversial visiting speaker, or a racially charged encounter with the police—didn't slow him at all. This was one I had never heard before. Haidt and Lukianoff, expounding on their "coddling" thesis, hadn't mentioned anything about Edith Wharton and Henry James. Young Americans have been coached to see themselves as brittle, the authors had argued, "to react to words, books, and visiting speakers with fear and anger because they had been taught to exaggerate danger [and] amplify their first emotional responses," leaving them in a state of *"vindictive protectiveness."*[1] How would Charles Dickens change that? David Horowitz's Academic Bill of Rights campaign in the previous decade had rightly pinpointed the dangers of an ever-more-aggressive political correctness, but it didn't call for more Goethe, more John Donne—only more freedom of expression. College presidents who met with irate students and heard their demands didn't reply, "Let's start a reading group!" To identify aliteracy as a cause of turbulence was a stretch, to say the least. Perhaps we could believe that a little reading on the Reign of Terror and life behind the Iron Curtain could warn the protesters of the hazards of radical passions, but Victorian novels and Restoration Comedy? When a group of students at University of the Arts disrupted a lecture by Camille Paglia, denouncing her (supposed) transphobia and pulling a fire alarm,[2] they sounded like spoiled brats who wanted their car keys back, not adults with insufficient exposure to Romantic poetry. A 2017 survey of eighteen-to-thirty-four-year-olds by GenForward found that 41 percent of respondents believed that colleges should be able to limit the wearing of costumes that stereotype racial and ethnic groups.[3] Can we really believe that a few weeks with T. S. Eliot and James Baldwin would lower the rate? I knew well how far literary reading had fallen among the young, but would "Elegy Written in a Country Churchyard" compel a junior not to join a Twitter mob all of her friends had joined? Would Ovid make them leave that Confederate statue alone?

No matter—Bob's diagnosis was set: the actions and attitudes of the angry young followed clearly from their literary deficiencies. Yes, the undergraduates at Evergreen State who took over the campus and put the president through a good old-fashioned struggle session (lacking only the physical assault element)[4] claimed to be victims of racist conditions, but in truth their problem was a weak literary reading habit. The tumult of 2015–17 didn't originate with Donald Trump on that escalator or a swastika painted in a hallway. It stemmed from the times these protesters lay in their rooms, went to the beach, relaxed at Starbuck's, and sat on the bus with no short stories in hand. That was my friend's explanation.

We kept talking, and he turned the point around to his old focus, the nonliterary, behavioral grounds for prizing the literature these querulous kids didn't read when they should have. "Mark," he said when I asked him how fiction would constrain them, "a good novel is very good psychology." Again, he paused, not because he thought he'd passed along some esoteric wisdom. On the contrary, his point was too homespun to require explanation; he had nothing to add. He didn't mean anything complicated by that remark, only that good novels land interesting characters in situations of conflict, and good authors give them psychological depth. The characters have motives, and you have to figure them out. Read the books, and you treat the characters as real people having actual thoughts and doing real things. I immediately agreed. His point was too commonsensical to dispute. That was my experience, too. It took me back to when I was an undergraduate, when I read a lot of novels for my own reasons before I became an English major (I bounced around from subject to subject for three years until I made a choice). I was the same way earlier in high school, when I skipped homework because I would rather read existentialism and crime stories and sports bios, the heroes in those books seeming a lot better to me than what my teachers thought was important. Reading was personal. I wanted to see what would happen to Philip Marlowe and Jim Bouton and Roquentin, Sartre's hero in *Nausea*, how they would behave when the pressures hit. And once I started teaching, I found that most kids cared about the books I assigned for the same reason. Should Isabel Archer leave her husband? Why does Raskolnikov kill? Where will Huck ever feel at home? I may have asked them to analyze and interpret, but their actual experience of *Portrait of a Lady*, *Crime and Punishment*, and *Huck Finn* steered them into more immediate responses that included some rudimentary probing of the protagonists, of their thoughts, moods, memories, and feelings.

Of course, then, I agreed with Bob. No argument here; that was basic—too basic, in fact, to have impressed me previously as a vindication of literary reading. That's why I hesitated. I had expected to hear something more exalted—the obligation to conserve the tradition, for instance, to "maintain the sublime in the old sense," as Ezra Pound said. Or the elevation of public taste, a better vocabulary than the "like…like…like" idiom that has spread from Valley Girls in the '80s to guests on NPR and young members of Congress. Or the replacement of hectic diversions on the screen with quiet meditations over Tolstoy's Prince Andrei on the battlefield, bleeding and defeated, staring at the sky as his hero and conqueror Napoleon speaks to him, but now in a new zone of experience: "To him at that moment all the interests that occupied Napoleon seemed so insignificant, his hero himself seemed so petty to him, with his petty vanity and joy in victory, compared with that lofty, just, and kindly sky which he had seen and understood, that he was unable to answer him."[5]

Now *that's* what literature is for.

Bob had a lesser demand of literature, however, a more commonplace experience. If I looked up at my bookshelves, I could find theories of reading in terms that were not for amateurs: textuality, deconstruction, signifier/signified, *écriture*...not the bare, unselfconscious act of imagination. But that was Bob's point, and it was easy to follow. Literature helps you get to know what people are like. Novels get you out of your own thoughts and into other people's heads. The fiction needn't be terribly profound nor the experience of the reader earthshaking. The process he had singled out didn't require any special training in English or a high verbal IQ, just a steady reading habit. A C-student in high school who reads pulp fiction can experience it along with the AP English Language and Literature kid, if at a lower level of penetration. The acquaintance with far-off lives still goes on, whether with Molly Bloom in Joyce's *Ulysses* or with a ferocious soldier in Wellesley's army in 1809 Spain in Bernard Cornwell's popular *Sharpe* series. Follow a lot of these characters, enter vicariously into their circumstances, do it consistently for a few years, and you find that you've received a psychological coaching. You couldn't help it; the bare comprehension of what you read would force it to happen. A freshman at Mt. Holyoke in 2015 has no direct knowledge of the trenches in World War I, but watching Paul and the others in *All Quiet on the Western Front* visit a dying comrade and figure how to tell him that he won't need his nice boots anymore and that they will fit Müller's feet quite well would put her into a frame of mind closer to them.

I was convinced. Or rather, I was reminded. What I hadn't respected in thirty years of teaching literature I speedily acknowledged as central to why people read literature in the first place and what it does for all of us. Again, it took me back to high school and to the books that had grabbed me because I could identify, or wanted to identify, with the characters, from *Ball Four* to *The Martian Chronicles* and *The Sound and the Fury*. It also provided an answer as to why my colleagues had failed so plainly to respond to the collapse of the humanities in higher education and of literary reading among the populace. They had been disciplined not to; *I* had been disciplined not to. The basic psychological instruction of novel reading was a topic for amateurs, not the highly trained. As I experienced in the course of my doctoral study in the '80s, academia had turned reading into too analytical an act for the professionals to appreciate the intimate involvement of a lay reader with a hero. That kind of identification was too uncritical to qualify as critical reading or critical thinking. It lacked aesthetic distance, and that was the sign of an unwary intelligence. In the *Reading at Risk* report, Chairman Gioia had hailed the "transformative power of literature," which I subsequently heard professors deride as a foolish mystification. They didn't seem to be aware of the many novelists who receive letters from readers that begin, "Your book changed my life." In a response to *To Read or Not to Read* in the *New York Times*, Professor Leah Price offered a nice little putdown: "We're not the first generation to invest reading with miraculous powers," before concluding with a remarkable levelling of the novel: "The file, the list, the label, the memo: these are the genres that will keep reading alive. Whatever happens to the novel, we'll always need a rule book."[6] Price teaches at Harvard.

I remember reading that commentary when it appeared and rubbing my eyes at the sight of professors of literature at the very best institutions who were diminishing their own subject matter with such blithe knowingness. Price wasn't the only one to give a cosmopolitan shrug to the decline of literary reading. It was, in fact, a piece of disciplinary wisdom to regard an emphasis on "the literary" as a mode of "privileging" that was suspect and unwarranted. Ever since the '80s, it has been more sophisticated for literature professors to talk about "texts," not literature, and *The Terminator* was just as "textual" as *The Tempest. What is wrong with them?* I wondered. A chemistry professor wouldn't downgrade the marvel of electron orbits and ionic bonding. My father was a math teacher (not a Ph.D.) who put "pure math" at the pinnacle of thought. No decadence there—not in the sciences—only in the humanities, and it weakened them in the marketplace of campus disciplines. I'd been frustrated over and over by literature teachers willing to lighten literary demands in general education, as you can see by comparing that year-long sequence of literary coursework in Stanford's old General Studies requirements to the prevailing system at colleges today that often has no expressly literary requirements at all. That's a sign of literature and language professors who couldn't stand up for their own objects, and here they were doing it again when researchers had produced troubling empirical evidence that their own materials were losing value in the culture at large. Say something! Defend it! They couldn't, though. Any prescriptions were understood as a throwback to an authoritarian past. Not so many decades ago, not just Stanford but most universities had a literature requirement that went along with the freshman writing requirement—at UCLA in 1978 I had to take a composition course and an introduction to literature course—but that's pretty much gone now. In a 1993 essay in *College English*, prominent composition specialist Erika Lindemann noted that people across the university considered the emphasis on literature in the writing classroom down-right "arrogant" and argued that literary reading prepares students poorly for any classes they take outside the English department.[7] Why be so parochial, so narrowly literary? That was the complaint. The same year, a book entitled *Against Literature* appeared that, in the words of the promotional copy, argued "for a negation of the literary that would allow nonliterary forms of cultural practice to displace literature's hegemony."[8] Why should literature possess such privilege? The question has been answered. The English professionals of the twenty-first century know better. We don't judge; we don't discriminate; it's all good: novels and text messages, stories and memos. A pleasing equality of texts obtains everywhere except at those few Great Books schools such as University of Dallas and conservative religious high schools such as members of the Institute for Catholic Liberal Education. In many states' high school standards, in fact, "Media Literacy" stands right alongside "Literature."

To advocate the literary objects most of us have spent our working hours interpreting and professing is contrary to professional wisdom. That's one reason I readily went along with Bob. Against Price's equality of texts, a dogma of twenty-first-century Digital Age humanities, my friend had pointed to a basic advantage of literature that literature teachers facing a society whose literary culture was eroding should have seized and amplified every day. The most casual amateur reader of novels would read Price's commentary in the *Times* and shake his head at its obvious blindness. From where could such a levelling have come? Not one of the alternative texts Price mentioned—"[t]he file, the list, the label, the memo ... [the] rule book"—does the psychological work a novel does. In fact, neither do volumes of history, politics, or social science, though they may cover the same times and places as do the fictional versions—not unless they contain vivid portraits of persons and concrete situations, and very few of them do. When it comes to this particular brand of psychological enlightenment, none of them comes close to *As I Lay Dying*, or Flannery O'Connor's stories, or *Murder on the Orient Express*, for that matter.

Now, this conversation over the phone one afternoon a few years back wasn't just a couple of old-fashioned, soft-and-fuzzy English teachers getting carried away with their literary loves. We have hard evidence for the psychological value of literature. Recent findings in neuroscientific studies prove it. In her 2018 study *Reader, Come Home: The Reading Brain in a Digital World*, cited in chapter one above, neuroscientist Maryanne Wolf compiles some remarkable research into what happens in the brain when a person reads a novel or short story. In one study entitled "Your Brain on Jane Austen," Wolf reports, researchers "found that when we read a piece of fiction 'closely,' we activate regions of the brain that are aligned to what the characters are both feeling and doing."[9] Another one found that the somatosensory cortex, the portion of the brain that registers touch, lights up when someone reads a metaphor of texture, while "motor neurons are activated when we read about movement."[10] The act of imagination while reading, it turns out, entails a lot more than pleasure. We have a fuller cognitive reaction. Another study goes so far as to conclude that, in Wolf's paraphrase, "when we read fiction, the brain actively simulates the consciousness of another person." Again, this is more than sympathy for or identification with characters. It is an imaginative reconstruction of the characters' experience. As Wolf explains, in reference to Anna Karenina's suicide, "as you read that passage in Tolstoy's novel, *you leaped, too*. In all likelihood, the same neurons you deploy when you move your legs and trunk were also activated when you read that Anna jumped before the train.[11]

You see the cognitive benefit. The exercise of reading broadens and deepens your mind, whether you intend it or not. You *have* to go into Frank Chambers's callous and lustful head when, in *The*

Postman Always Rings Twice, he kisses Cora for the first time. You can't understand what's going on without doing so. You may not like it there, just as you don't want to love Big Brother as Winston Smith does at the end or sit by as Prince Andrei, returned home, loses the will to live, but there you are, stuck in another circumstance, another consciousness. Ten years of this and you've roamed through variants of love and hate, tried out courage and cowardice, helped some and betrayed others. You realize that the dictionary meaning of betrayal is one thing, a dozen words long, while the contemplation and execution of a specific betrayal by a particular, individual character is something else, a simmering mix of impulses and duplicities and plottings, more complicated and less scrutable, and, most importantly, more genuine and real. You read the dictionary meaning of betrayal and understand it. You read a case of betrayal in a novel that renders acts and thoughts and feelings of betrayer and betrayed, and you don't just understand betrayal—you experience it. The experience is imaginative, yes, not actual, but the process deepens and enriches the meaning, the context, motives, and consequences of the act. What should you think of a betrayer who feels wronged and justified, or who believes himself betrayed before ever deliberating revenge? You have to answer the question as you read. You don't wish to betray anyone, you don't have the motive, but you now have exposure to someone who does; you feel that motive, too—concretely so. If you keep reading, the replication of his consciousness continues in spite of your moral resistance. It's the old *Lolita* problem, where we enter the intentions and rationalizations of Nabokov's child molester so smoothly and rationally that we end up comprehending him to the point of mitigating his abuses.

This is a very good exercise for a young mind. Adolescents need to meet a wider range of personalities than their daily contacts provide. The human spectrum contains varieties of impulse they cannot imagine on their own, and they must learn them. The instruction sometimes will be relevant—for instance, Poe's "Man of the Crowd," whose twisted craving for company might offer a whole new angle on the peer pressure they experience every day. But relevance to one's own life isn't necessary; indeed, the enlightenment provided by literature usually won't be so applicable to young people's immediate experience. If it is too often relevant, in fact, the reading is too sparse. The adolescent must expand; his reading must branch out. It must go on for a long time, too, until after many years in the close company of D'Arcy and Dr. Watson, Ántonia and Tom Joad in the back of your mind, you begin to look at other people with a richer consciousness of alien motive. More knowledge of human nature, a savvier judgment of intent—that was the virtue Bob had in mind. Not form or language, genre or philology, theory or interpretation, just character traits, conscious and unconscious, the psychology of fictive beings. He had no problem taking Heathcliff as a real person, though our academic premises told us to judge that equation a naïve one. He didn't feel the need to apologize, and I knew what he meant.

To be sure, those questions aren't the kind a college teacher at a research university typically poses to students or makes the object of his scholarship. The discipline calls for more advanced analyses, theory and politics and identity, not character motivation, but I had been away from academia long enough to realize that those very human issues are the ones that grip lay readers the most. (Aside from working for three years in the federal government at the National Endowment for the Arts, I had gone to half-time at Emory by then and was full-time as an editor at *First Things* magazine in New York.) One of the first lessons I learned in the first literary criticism class I took was not to commit the error of A. C. Bradley, who in his *Shakespearean Tragedy* (1904) treated Hamlet, Othello, Lear, Macbeth, and lesser characters as real people leading real lives. Bradley speculated about what their days were like beyond what the action on stage revealed, as if he knew them well, really knew them as flesh-and-blood individuals to whom he related as he did his own acquaintances. It was quaint but rather foolish, those of us entering the profession had to understand. Instead, you had to take the "linguistic turn," treat the characters in more structural, symbolic, representational, and generic terms (depending on which critical school you had adopted). The prime joy unprofessional readers derived from novels—the chance to get to know Daisy Miller and Gatsby and Sam Spade, to figure them out, feel what they feel, and track them through life—you dropped as an uncritical posture, the stance of the man in the street.

No wonder, then, that the professional mentors who should have urged, "Read! Read! Read!" didn't do so. Leah Price's *New York Times* commentary faulted us at the Arts Endowment precisely for distinguishing literary reading as something special. She wrote, "what the N.E.A. calls 'reading for literary experience' has never been more than one use among many." *Fahrenheit 451*, *The Da Vinci Code*, lists, labels, memos . . . it's all reading. *"Let's not aggrandize novels beyond their due,"* says the cosmopolitan academic—though the excessive literariness Price admonished was a lot less common among scholars than she implied. In fact, the 2011 NAEP Reading Framework for twelfth graders stated that passages on the exam would be 70 percent informational and only 30 percent literary,[12] and Common Core followed suit. The accountability movement was hardly prioritizing literary over nonliterary reading.

Orson Welles liked to quote an observation by fellow filmmaker Jean Renoir in his prewar masterpiece *The Rules of the Game*: "*Tu comprends, sur cette Terre il y a quelque chose d'effroyable, c'est que tout le monde a ses raisons,*" which Welles translated, "You see, there is one awful thing in the world, and that is that everyone has his reasons."[13] (The English word *awful* doesn't quite catch the dreadful, frightful connotations of the French *effroyable*.) Welles repeated the line in an interview in which he discussed Hank Quinlan, the dishonest sheriff in his own film *Touch of Evil*: "There is no villain who doesn't have his reasons, and the bigger the villain the more interesting it becomes.... The more human you make the monster, the more interesting the story must be." Not that you excuse him, Welles made clear, just that you see him more fully. To enable his audience to do that, Welles explained that he had to make Quinlan a "real person."

Quinlan fabricates evidence against suspects and has for years; his methods run "against every good instinct we have in the democratic world," Welles remarked.[14] But villainy usually has reasons. Quinlan's is the murder of his wife long before, the killer never convicted because the evidence against him was deemed insufficient. There's the motive, the thing that humanizes the monster, which we don't discover until well into the film, when Quinlan says in a quick aside that he is always thinking about his wife—a factor that we haven't noticed before and that puts his machinations into a different light, though their effects are no less dastardly.

Thus the villain becomes more interesting in spite of our moral scruples, and no matter how many other characters are on screen, our attention never leaves him. We have to admit, too, that Quinlan's suspicions are correct. The prisoners he has framed are in fact guilty. Indeed, he sizes people up much better than does the ethical center of the film, Quinlan's antagonist, the Mexican official Vargas, played by Charlton Heston (who got Welles the job directing the film). Quinlan quickly pinpoints a suspect in a bombing that happened the night before, a young Mexican shoe clerk who is involved with the wealthy victim's daughter. Quinlan is sure he did the killing, but Vargas has doubts. As they interrogate the man in a cramped apartment and Heston appears to sympathize with him as he undergoes the third degree, Quinlan utters a curious line that stands out from the action as a nugget of shrewdness applying broadly to human behavior: "Just because he speaks a little guilty, that don't make him innocent, you know."[15]

Wait a minute, you think, *that doesn't make sense*. Oh, in lots of murder mysteries we have inverse cases in which an innocent-sounding man turns out to be guilty, and also cases of a guilty-sounding suspect who does emerge wholly innocent of the charges. But this is a little different. Quinlan seems to be talking less about the suspect and more about how we are to interpret the man's words. Some people, Quinlan implies, hear a guilty-sounding fellow speak and actually want to make that into a cause or proof of innocence. Or rather (he seems to suggest), some of us incline to believe in innocence as a general rule, and that inclination rises when a little guilt surfaces, and that's not very smart. That's Quinlan's point, and it tangles things up. Or rather, it untangles the issue: a guilty-seeming fellow sometimes *is* entirely guilty. The fact that an anxious or hostile guy has no good answers to a cop's questions quite rightly leads to the conclusion that he's not innocent. The implication is that common sense tells us that appearance and reality coincide more often than not, so stop overreading the man. Maybe this is Welles's playing on the detective genre, which overdoes the sketchy-guy-who's-really-guiltless plot. Or did Welles, who redid the script for the film after agreeing to direct, want to puncture the sentimental attitude that always assumes the fundamental goodness of everyone?

There is a further wrinkle to consider. Welles sets this little aperçu in a dramatic context that muddies our acceptance of it: it comes from the mouth of a man already morally compromised. Quinlan is physically repulsive, sloppy and lumbering, with puffy cheeks and sickly eyes, and we've just watched him smack the suspect across the face for speaking in Spanish instead of English. In every scene, the camera, light, perspective, tracking, and editing emphasize Quinlan's grotesque being. Are we to take lessons in guilt and innocence from this monster?

Of course we should, Welles makes clear, if his insight deserves it. The entire film presses the point. Quinlan is in the early stages of a murder investigation, and here he offers a maxim for the judging of evidence, of human testimony. At the same time, through the instrument of this crooked character who nonetheless utters ideas worth pondering, Welles, as the filmmaker, suggests a related maxim: the truth of a statement should be measured separately from the ego that announces it. Or rather, the film requires that we do two things: assess the statement as an independent proposition *and* relate it to the character of the character. Quinlan is a swine, but he has a better grasp of surface behavior and hidden motive than the rest of us do. His evil nature doesn't invalidate the truth-value of his words; we have to listen to him even as we reject him.

That's not easy to do. Do you sit in a meeting with six coworkers discussing a business strategy and give as much credence to the one you can't stand as you give to the five you respect? You need guidance and practice and lots of experience to reach that condition of suspending your distaste. The detachment necessary to weigh the words of a jerk accurately, to judge them as an impersonal proposition, not an odious man's expression, doesn't come naturally. The human heart doesn't like it. Renoir's carefully chosen word *effroyable* is exactly right. It shows that such suspension of the ad hominem requires you to accept a tragic condition that you would rather not accept. If only we could judge words by the moral state of the speaker, how much simpler would life be! If only the good were never wrong and the bad never right, how much better would the world become! Why must we complicate evil by allowing it "reasons"? Evil is evil, it's not human.

We don't listen to it; we stamp it out. And good is good; it never errs; it always sees clearly. You know where this is leading: to the land of Millennial utopia.

"God preserve us from all innocence," Querry tells Mother Agnes in Graham Greene's 1960 novel *A Burnt-Out Case*.[16] Like Quinlan's remark, this is a moral complication that steps out of the action and calls for pause. Habitual readers know that it's one of those loaded moments when a little extra instruction is going on. Querry's remark seems superfluous to the events, as if Greene were inserting, in a more explicit way, exactly the kind of psychological teaching or general rule about human behavior that comes up so often in good novels and plays and films. Not only that, but the comment doesn't make sense (God needs to save us from innocence?). If you're caught up in the action, if you want to know these characters as real people, you have to slow and reflect. If you haven't read the book, here's the situation:

Querry is a renowned architect who has fled the modern world and found work caring for the sick in a remote African leper colony managed by priests and nuns. He has designed famous churches and been celebrated in the press, but he's led a dishonest private life, loving and leaving vulnerable women, and those caddish ways now disgust him. He seeks only to serve in silence, unknown and unloved, and to serve the most debilitated and forgotten human beings. He told nobody back home where he planned to go, and nobody at the colony recognizes him. Maybe it's penance, maybe just a way to make up for his past; he doesn't say. He wishes merely to rise at dawn, clean beds and sweep floors and feed the sick all day, and sleep at night, which he does in peace until a sanctimonious middle-aged plant manager and his young, unschooled wife visit the colony, and the

man recognizes his face from past news stories and seeks a friend-
ship. Querry would rather avoid him.

Later, on a trip to town, Querry ends up giving the wife Marie a
ride so that she can visit a doctor and test for pregnancy. She's lonely
and unhappy, and he converses with her for hours that night in his
hotel room, where she admits her husband repels her. Querry spots
the signs of infatuation, but in his new life he has no sexual interest,
and she retires to her own bed. Days later, however, she shows up at
the colony with an accusation: she's pregnant, and Querry is the
father. The horrified nuns take her in. Only the camp doctor believes
Querry when he denies the story. The others glare at him, but the
mother superior does allow a private moment without anyone else
present in Marie's sickroom, where he asks, "Why have you told them
these lies?" The young woman admits to some bending of the truth,
but insists that she had, in a quite authentic way, slept with him and
conceived.

"What on earth are you talking about?"

"I didn't want him. The only way I could manage was to
shut my eyes and think it was you."

"I suppose I ought to thank you," Querry said, "for the
compliment."

"It was then that the baby must have started. So you see it
wasn't a lie I told them."

She smiles kindly at him, and he stares at her and says in appalled
wonderment, "You've burned the only home I have."[17]

This leads to Querry's final remark to Mother Agnes, who doesn't doubt a word Marie has spoken. He steps outside the room, expecting the nun to ask him to leave for good, immediately, and she does. Querry obeys, but warns her, "Be very careful yourselves of that little pack of dynamite in there." The nun, though, cannot comprehend how such an ingenuous child could possibly be dangerous:

"She's a poor innocent young thing..."

"Oh, innocent...I daresay you are right. God preserve us from all innocence. At least the guilty know what they are about."

A few minutes later, Marie's husband shows up to confront Querry, who is now preparing to leave. The husband has accepted her story, and when Querry laughs at the ridiculousness of it all, the man draws a gun and shoots him dead.

The exchange with Mother Agnes isn't long, only a minute or two. She never answers Querry's remark that "the guilty know." Moral philosophy doesn't interest her, only the shock that an innocent has been profaned by a man the colony took in without knowing enough about him. We understand what the mother superior doesn't—the flat-out lie that the innocent girl has told—so the nun's righteous anger only underscores Querry's warning. She believes 100 percent, and she's wrong 100 percent. Her wrong belief grants the innocence of the girl that much more force, from which only God can protect us. Querry's comment turns the ordinary view upside down: "Caution! Innocence at Work." Innocence, yes—and also dynamite.

When I read those lines the first time a few years ago, they stopped me in the same way Quinlan's did. They worked in a twofold way, as drama and as truth: in Querry's case, the drama of this childishly manipulative pregnant woman, plus the truth of the deadly blindness of human beings. Querry's epigram, and Quinlan's, too, fits the occasion in the story, but you can carry them beyond the film and the novel as practical wisdom. They are examples of the kind of tutelage that goes out of the plot and into your ethical toolkit. This one lodged in my head. The pathos of a guy who realizes he can't condemn this silly girl who has ruined his life because she really is innocent (in a perverse way) brought out a noteworthy truth, an insight that can explain why people do the otherwise inexplicable things they sometimes do. It was memorably ironic: Querry is innocent, too, but his innocence can't overcome her "innocence." It is her very innocence that enables her to destroy him. A guilty woman wouldn't be nearly so effective; she couldn't pull it off.

This is the psychological instruction of *A Burnt-Out Case*: innocence can do evil, it sure can. The case is worth studying. Needless to say, this is exactly the knowledge that the utopian Millennials lack, believing that love is always innocent ("It doesn't matter who you love") and that happiness is always innocent ("Everyone deserves to be happy") and that innocence is always innocent. Google orders its employees: "Don't Be Evil," but innocence doesn't guarantee good, as Greene makes clear. Marie loves Querry in her imbecilic way—that's what her heart declares. But she doesn't understand him, doesn't even know who he is, and has no empathy for his suffering at this moment. Her innocence is an obtuseness, an incognizance. Querry sees that, but the perception doesn't save him. It disempowers him. The novel doesn't set things aright; the truth doesn't come out. We are left with a tragic condition. Goodness can be stupid, destructively so. The guilty do bad deeds, but at least they recognize the sin. The innocent don't, and so they may very well do their bad deeds again. They have nothing to regret, nothing to confess. They're dangerous in a more frustrating way.

This is not a happy revelation; nobody enjoys it. *Touch of Evil* and *A Burnt-Out Case* are superb works of art, but their lessons are chastening. Querry dies and Quinlan dies, but their weary wisdom doesn't die with them. After you've met them and listened closely, innocence doesn't have quite the same status it did before, and a little sadness goes with the change. You feel a bit more grown up, and you now hear a whisper of tragedy. A youth taught that there should be no suffering in the world, not ever, and who detests the wisdom that says, "The poor will always be with us," doesn't want to hear it. Why watch movies and read books that bring you down? Is not even innocence, genuine innocence, free of the human stain? Is it really that hard to tell who is good and who is bad? Can I never feel fully confident in my own righteousness? Why must the world be like this?

Maybe it doesn't have to be this way at all. That's the interpretation our Millennial would like to draw from the climax outside Marie's sickroom. You can hear the wheels clicking in his mind as he takes in the scene and turns it in another direction. People make mistakes, he reasons; Marie's in a tough spot; she's young and Querry's middle-aged; the men in her life have ignored her; she needs some friends; maybe there is a certain higher truth that does call Querry the father of her child... we don't have to listen to this burnt-out case. He's selfless now among the lepers, but he has a lot to make up for from the past. He's no authority; what does he know about innocence? The universe he imagines is not the universe in which we wish to live, so drop it. That bilious assertion of his spoils the future, for if innocence, too, can "be evil," or at least do evil, if we still need God to help us triumph over depravity, then what are the prospects for making a better world? Bias, discrimination, malice, and injury will continue even if we don't intend them, Querry implies, and that's an idea that has to go. It's a personal affront, a direct challenge to the Millennial self-image. Remember, they were told when they were young that they are the most tolerant generation of all time, and the conviction stuck. They attribute even their intolerance to tolerant motives: *We're only intolerant of intolerance.* The ones who enlist in the cancel campaigns believe in their own guiltlessness. They have to, or they couldn't approve, for instance, the expulsion of an undergraduate who on his Facebook page satirized the banning of "cultural appropriation" at Halloween parties.[18] Or maybe they do feel guilty for a past crime—making fun of a fat peer in high school or laughing at *Blazing Saddles* and its many *n*-words—and here is a chance to prove they've reformed, that they're now "woke" and can become innocent once again.

Querry's comment brings their motives into question. They don't want to hear it. Marie's destructive innocence can't be acknowledged, for innocence is always good. Double and triple that for Quinlan. We certainly don't have to heed anything he says. Querry we may perhaps excuse for drawing an unpleasant moral conclusion from a devastating false charge. Quinlan, however, has no excuses. He lies, he schemes, and he's racist, too. Quinlan doesn't like Mexicans—a "half-breed" killed his wife, he divulges—and the moment today's twenty-five-year-old hears him grumble, "I don't speak Mexican," when Vargas and the suspect are conversing in Spanish, he will consign Quinlan to the basket of deplorables, from which there is no redemption, as Hillary Clinton famously said.

For Welles, however, Quinlan's racism isn't enough to invalidate everything else he says about people and things. Millennials can't follow him there. Twenty-first-century youth favor a less complex human nature, less mixing of innocence and guilt, an optimistic anthropology that will underwrite the purity of every love and happiness for all. Millennials can't tolerate the unpleasant beliefs we hear in Welles's film and Greene's novel. For them, the bigotry or pessimism of a Quinlan, a Querry, or any other character, imagined or real, is enough to cancel that person. Why? *Because they didn't read enough literature.* Too many hours of their adolescence were spent on a screen and not enough hours with fiction—that's the genesis of our closed-minded Millennials. They haven't undergone the literary formation that teaches one to interpret people cautiously, to withhold judgment until all the facts are in, to understand personality as multifaceted, a mix of positive and negative. They believe Quinlan's anti-Mexican bias makes him wrong all around, wrong about everything. Millennials find him easy to condemn because they have so little experience of human complexity. Read a great novel, read lots of them, many of them not so great, and keep up the habit for years, and they will be forced to change their social assumptions. In many of those novels, they will find, their initial impression of a character ends up evolving. Miss Betsey in *David Copperfield*, for example, appears at first to be a brusque, cold woman, but later she is revealed to be a staunch and loving aunt, though her manner doesn't really improve. Literary readers learn to expect such variation, and it carries over to their actual lives. The stories they read encourage a more hesitant and careful reading of real life characters. The young adult who doesn't read is more impatient, likes the snap judgment, and arrives early at a full verdict with full confidence.

And that lack of subtlety saves the Millennial from mental and psychological effort that would inevitably complicate his life. In the Graham Greene novel, Querry's despair invokes a belief we'd rather not entertain, but the fact that we admire other things he has done, including the time his deformed helper wandered into the jungle, perhaps to die, and Querry hunted him down and passed the night with him in a ditch, hugging the diseased man to keep him warm, forces us to take his insights seriously. Querry and Quinlan foul up the facile apportionment of good and evil upon which the utopia to come rests. If everything wrong with the world is simply the fault of a few villains, as the Millennial believes, all we have to do to make it right is remove the bad guys. The naïve expectation that signing that statement of demands, retweeting that tweet, or piling on the latest target of the cancel culture will cleanse the world of racism, sexism, and all the phobias to blame for our misery wouldn't be tenable if more young people had read novels and learned something about human nature and the world. In the Millennial's mind, a Facebook post containing the word *faggot* sufficiently proves the poster's total depravity. That's a leap no regular reader of novels is inclined to take. The story line of cancellation is too childish to please anyone who has tracked the adventures of Mark Helprin's hero in *A Soldier of the Great War*. The cancel narrative—*You said this one bad thing, so we shun you forever*—is too rigid and one-dimensional to suit a reader who is currently inside the head of Ross Macdonald's Lew Archer. What a tiresome drama the dangerous utopians keep staging ad nauseam: over and over again, righteous and pure judges face the solitary and penitent malefactor. It doesn't even have any spicy dialogue, only the same charges filed every time: *Racist! Sexist!* There isn't any actual conflict between the accuser and the accused. The bigot doesn't speak; why should he be allowed to speak? We shouldn't listen to him; no one should.

It's a problem of depth. To our nonreading Millennial, everyone is a "flat character." That's all the youth-oriented screen gives him, surface beings with overt designs and words with no resonance. Novelist E. M. Forster defined such flat characters in his 1927 Cambridge lectures, marking each as a type, a simplicity, a figure "constructed round a single idea or quality."[19] Polonius is a flat character, and so are Starbuck in *Moby-Dick* and Tom Buchanan in *Gatsby*. They have no depth, no inner life beyond the one or two impulses or traits that characterize them. Mother Agnes is flat because she never changes and nothing she says or does surprises us. A flat character such as Montag's wife in *Fahrenheit 451*, who embodies the tranquillized media existence of the future, "can be expressed in a single sentence," Forster says,[20] though he makes it clear that great novelists such as Dickens often use flat characters to sophisticated purposes. In the Orson Welles film, Quinlan's sidekick is Police Sergeant Menzies, whose "flat" loyalty to Quinlan and thoroughgoing honesty highlight his superior's corruption and exemplify the odd fascination Quinlan exerts over everyone around him. Menzies is wholly innocent of the framings he has unwittingly facilitated over the years, and that innocence doesn't produce a single insight in the entire story. Forster contrasts such flat characters to "round characters"—Moll Flanders and Ivan Karamazov and Becky Sharp in *Vanity Fair*—those creations who invite us into their heads. We don't have to figure out what Montag's wife in *Fahrenheit 451* is all about, to fathom her motives, but we do have to examine closely Captain Beatty, Montag's boss. And Captain Ahab, too, whose obsession with the white whale is a lot more complicated than Starbuck will ever comprehend. A round character "waxes and wanes and has facets like a human being," Forster explains,[21] so that your observation of him likely carries over to your perception of real human beings. Round characters possess "the incalculability of life."[22] They call for a more subtle response. Quinlan's anti-Mexicanism is not all there is to the man.

To look more deeply into the mind of someone you consider bad, to contain his evil to but one part of his character, to acknowledge it and still consider his "reasons"...it's too burdensome for youths raised on the certainties of racism, sexism, and various phobias and "normativities" that guide their judgment of others. The calculability of everyone is foundational to their dream. Millennials are busy; they have enough to do applying to grad schools, working odd hours, working out and hanging out, and managing the network. Why take the time to contemplate the mysterious recesses of a scoundrel's mind? They see no advantage in learning more about human evil, and their friends don't encourage it. Racism shouldn't be studied; racists should be expelled. "No man, no problem," as that master of management Joseph Stalin liked to say. Don't inquire into what homophobia is, just get rid of the 'phobes. That goes for their works, too: Wagner's *Tannhäuser*, which the Nazis loved, and *Intolerance*, the film that D. W. Griffith completed after *Birth of a Nation* and that bore a message opposite to the earlier film's race-baiting but can't redeem the artist sufficiently to make it worth their time. The loss of a few classics—or a lot of them—is a gain in domestic tranquility. A steady evasion of caustic people and places, a forgetting of bad ideas, soothes the pure heart. Hours spent with congenial things, with persons who draw no dark shadows, make for a happier existence.

Except that they don't. This isn't working out. As we've seen, Millennials are no more content than previous generations. They're more unhappy, not less, and the trouble they have with people of different beliefs and values, their rising intolerance and readiness to cancel, indicates that this superficial conception of human nature is a not-insignificant factor in their unhappy lives. I have observed young Americans in the process of contending with an assumed devil or with someone supposed to have complied with devilry, such as a hapless college president, and seen the anguish on their faces, the pain suffered by these crybullies, and wondered at the anarchic mix of outrage and frustration, aggression and fragility. The sight of a guilty party in power apologizing or resigning intoxicates them, yes, but the joy doesn't last for long. They have terminated the bad guy; racism and sexism and transphobia have lost one of their lieutenants, but the fact that badness ever prospered, that a patent rascal achieved status and position for a time, still pains them. The person may be gone—Milo banned from Twitter, biologist James Watson disinvited from NYU, and Donald Trump out of the White House—but the vices they represent live on. This and that racist goes down, but systemic racism lingers. The young people feel like they're punching a blob—because that's exactly what they're doing.

When the kids at Middlebury College rushed Charles Murray and his hosts, they didn't see him as an individual, a man with a history and an experience. No, they faced a racist, a depersonalized, undifferentiated embodiment of *racism*, a figure distinguished only by his fame and power. When on June 26, 2020, a bunch of protesters gathered around the Emancipation Monument that presented Lincoln symbolically freeing all the slaves, and a young man rose to declare, "We're going to tear that mother—— down!" he had no inkling of the inner lives of the persons in that statue, the president and the slave. All he registered was a White Man above a Black Man, and that condemned the whole thing (the fellow was a student at Harvard who had been profiled in *Harvard Magazine* a few weeks earlier as an impressive racial justice warrior, a man who, though only twenty-two years old, was "a culture critic and longtime advocate for communities of color").[23] Charles Murray had no real identity to the activist mobs, nor did Lincoln and the slave. The young man railing against the statue will never imagine what it was like in the Oval Office when the news arrived from Antietam of twenty thousand dead. The course of inquiry that led Murray to coauthor *The Bell Curve* didn't figure in the minds of the hooligans.

If they had, the youths wouldn't have been so angry. The depersonalization of these men emboldened them to yell and march. Murray fled, and lots of statues have come down, but after the victory and an hour of jubilation, what then? Murray was gone, but here and there one still heard a researcher veering into racial differences in intelligence. The remembrance of Lincoln didn't cease, and it's not going to cease. The world won't conform—and that's a frustration of which the dangerous utopians are too, too aware.

It's not the only one. There's another frustration, one they can't overcome because it originates from inside them, not in the world. It stems precisely from the deficiencies of their nonliterary life, their inability to grasp an antagonist as a whole person. Keep in mind what Millennials had to do before they marched across the quad, disrupted the lecture, signed petitions and painted banners, filed complaints and sent emails. They had to reduce the people they were targeting to figureheads, cardboard cutouts, flat characters. Only afterwards did they discover an unexpected truth: there is little satisfaction in defeating a caricature. They envisioned a foe made up of but one vile motive, but battling a cartoon villain like that had no human meaning, no heroism to it. They presumed to address a horrid condition—white supremacy—but it had no flesh and blood; they saw it in no detail; it was only a monster on campus and a "mother——" on the pedestal. And that superficial understanding of the threat they were facing down condemned them to dissatisfaction. They looked upon the acquiescent college president as a symbol of the institution, not a person, so a genuine human exchange was never possible. It's not simply that if they had known more about their targets they wouldn't have done what they did, though that's likely the case. I'm addressing the emotional side of the encounter: with a full-fledged person before them—be he villain or coward or racist or prevaricator or whatever, but nonetheless individualized and well-inspected—a more meaningful skirmish could have taken place. If they had understood more fully with whom they were dealing (including his own reasons for his position, however reasonable or unreasonable, bad or good), they would have felt better about what they were doing, and happier that they had done it.

Let me give an example, another rowdy event with a conversation attached. Several years ago, while driving home in Atlanta on a sunny afternoon, I stopped at a light on Clairmont Road at the entrance to the large Veterans Administration facility. To the right, on the grass and just off the sidewalk, was a scraggly fellow, middle-aged, long hair and beard, rocking from one foot to the other and holding a sign that read something like "THE VA KILLS!" (I can't remember the exact wording). Maybe a friend of his had died in the hospital or wait times to see a doctor had become perilous or he didn't qualify for care or a nurse had treated him poorly—I don't know, but there was a bad story somewhere, and he had to tell it. He might have been there all day and the day before, ticking off 250 drivers per hour looking his way and reading the sign. The red light lingered, five or six cars in front and behind me, and he took the moment to call out so everyone would look. That would be all; the light would change, and we would proceed up the road as he waited for the next group to line up. As red turned to green, however, another guy strolled up on the sidewalk, short and thick, fifty years old or so, just as disheveled, but with hulking manner. He halted, stared at the sign, then stepped forward and clocked the protester in the jaw.

I hit the gas, peeled to the right into the entrance, and stopped. The first man was on the ground, one arm grasping the sign, the other arm raised in defense as the second man hovered over him and yelled, poised to kick him. I lowered the passenger window.

"Leave him alone!"

He turned and growled at me, throwing a fist.

"No, no, sir, you can't do that," I went on, shooting for that middle ground between retreat and attack.

He stared, said nothing, glanced back at the victim, straightened up, stepped back, turned away, and stomped off toward the building. The first man clambered to his feet, shaken and humiliated, nodding thanks and stumbling back into position as I left. I spied him in my rearview mirror a little slumped now, rubbing his face, but the sign held up once more.

The whole thing lasted fewer than thirty seconds, and I didn't think there was much more to do or say. I was glad it was over and glad the aggressor hadn't turned on me. Perhaps I had caused him to back off, but I didn't dial 911, and I didn't get out of the car to check on the fellow's injuries. I might have wondered why none of the other drivers pulled over, but that's life in the modern city. One thing mystified me, though: What was the attacker thinking after I told him to stop? Not when he cursed at me, but the second time, when he hesitated, appeared uncertain, then stormed away—what passed through his mind? A few days later, I mentioned the episode to a friend, one with many years of martial arts experience and lots of fights in his youth. It was just a wacky tale to tell, but I did have a question.

"I don't get it," I told him. "The guy was really mad; why didn't he come after me as well?" He believed he had all the justification on his side, it seemed, and anyone who tried to stop him deserved the same treatment as he had meted out to the protester. He was indignant; the sign was an insult. The guy had to be smacked, and so did anyone who defended him. So I assumed. It wouldn't have shocked me if he had headed my way. The attacker was tough and seasoned, too, probably a vet, and wouldn't have found much intimidating about me, idling at the curb in my Volvo. Who the hell was I to intervene?

"Well, that's easy, Mark," my friend replied. "He knew he was doing something wrong."

I looked at him, and he shrugged as if there was nothing more to add.

"Really?" I said.

"Sure."

My more seasoned friend didn't pretend he'd said anything profound or secretive, only an obvious truth. That was it, the only fact to absorb, a simple matter of moral awareness: the guy knew he was wrong. My friend took it for granted that nobody could bash a poor soul on an ordinary day in an ordinary neighborhood in Atlanta and think it was okay. I hadn't thought about that. I had only seen the rage, but as soon as the words "knew he was doing something wrong" were uttered the moral logic became clear. The sign-carrier wasn't threatening anyone, just voicing a protest, and both the law and the code of civilization allow him to do that without taking a punch. The protester may have been a nut, and maybe the attacker treasured the caretakers inside and took the accusation personally, but that didn't authorize a right hook. I had imagined the attacker felt wholly in the right, but my friend was insisting the man couldn't possibly rationalize the attack. The assailant went all out for ten seconds, but that didn't mean he had no sense that he had crossed a line. All I saw was the punch, not the *What am I doing?* thoughts running through his head, and that was a mistake.

I didn't have anything to add to that. My friend's explanation fit the facts, and we moved on to talk about other things. Still, I felt corrected. The attacker was a brute, to be sure, and the sign-holder clearly incapable of defending himself, though the attacker might not have hit him again even if I hadn't stopped. It hadn't occurred to me that a man in the midst of pounding another would feel guilty, not if he'd been provoked. He had righteous anger; the sign had incensed him for some reason. If there was any guilt involved, surely it lay with the protester—in the eyes of the attacker.

That's what I saw, but my friend thought otherwise, adding a different moral angle. And he had a lot more experience with confrontations than I did. I reviewed the encounter in my head in a new light. My friend had to be right. Why else would the attacker have shifted from rage to scruple and retired so quickly? It wasn't I who checked him; it was the man's own decency, however latent. I now had an explanation as to why he had paused after I spoke, shaky for a second about what to do. As soon as something or someone drew his attention away from the target, he would have second thoughts. All I did was spark an inner restraint, a good angel on one shoulder telling the bad angel to hold off. It was time to interpret the assailant's actions with a little more patience and complexity, to see that he was not just a savage striking out at a damaged creature, but a moral agent—or rather, an agent of mixed motives, of angry impulses and bits of conscience. The fury won out for the moment, but the conscience didn't entirely go away. My friend's remark bid me look further into the assailant's character. I had imagined him as an ex-soldier, perhaps traumatized by combat—a few of his comrades wounded, addicted, or alcoholic—stopping by the center once a week for therapy or medication, now and then unable to control himself, a man without any moral determination. If he had any good scruples in his soul, he wouldn't have lashed out. The lesson now was this: he could be both.

This was a pleasing conclusion. That's why it stuck with me. An attack on the sidewalk at midday on a fellow citizen who wasn't harming anybody, merely voicing protest in his pathetic fashion, certainly could make you mutter, *What in the world are we coming to?* But the evidence of a little shame in the heart of the attacker called for the opposite response. It wasn't a matter of explaining away the assault; it was about seeing the assailant as a fuller individual, intemperate and violent and sputtering, but not without a moral sense, including the sense that others would and should judge him. He may have been one of those who struggle to stay afloat, the distraught and wretched, the underclass, the simmering vets...but he, too, divided right from wrong, though he couldn't always act accordingly. A guy waves a sign that maddens you—you shouldn't hit him for that, and you know it!

As I said, a pleasing conclusion, and not just morally pleasing. It's nice, yes, to find that people aren't as bad as you think they are, that malice has a counterweight, that no human heart is entirely malignant. But there was an added pleasure, too. I mean precisely what we've been talking about: the plumbing of motive, of people's "reasons." The very act of uncovering them produces a satisfaction all its own. This is the point: when my friend supplied a reason, it felt good. It made the attacker's inexplicable act of retreat sensible and limpid and rational, and that was reassuring in itself. To detect a "why," to divine a better reason than *The guy was a lunatic* brought a bit of relief. Not only because we had uncovered a moral factor lodging in the man's heart that tempered the rampage and proved he possessed the same sense of right and wrong that we did. There was also the sheer pleasure of knowing. That was my experience as we conversed about the attack: yes, it feels good to know what other people are about. Things happen; people make an impact with their deeds; we are implicated by and vulnerable to each other, and to understand what's going on behind their smiling, angry, loving, or hating faces is a comfort.

I've said that my friend had lots of fighting experience. He's a working-class guy with scars on his body; indeed, when I would roll hands with him as he schooled this neophyte in a little Wing Chun, his forearms made contact like baseball bats. He also, however, has a doctorate in Medieval Studies. His dissertation covered Arthurian literature up to Malory, which put him in the company of a whole lot of men and women acting on impulse and facing the moral consequences. Lancelot, Gawain, and the rest had to be read about in the course of his graduate studies, pondered and understood. In the literature he studied, the endless trial of desire versus virtue lies at the center of the interpretation of each character. My friend had the background, then, to comprehend the attack in terms beyond aggression and fear alone. The battles he had fought *and* the literary reading he had done helped him to empathize with hostile parties—not to sympathize with them, but to know their thoughts, to practice what psychologists call "cognitive empathy," the ability to reproduce in your own mind what passes through another's mind.

Again, this isn't sympathy. Cognitive empathy proceeds with sympathetic persons and antipathetic persons alike, imagining the inner lives of people you despise or fear, not just the ones you love and admire. It is an unnatural achievement, a habit that must be learned and sharpened and exercised. Children don't have the equipment to do it, and contact with friends in later life doesn't tend to develop it (because you know your friends too well). It goes against the innate tendency to huddle with your own and to dodge strangers. But if you wish to mingle in a diverse world, to stand up straight in a roomful of non-friends, your natural instinct to shrink from a threatening or unsavory character must be overcome—not in every case, of course, but certainly when a more thorough knowledge of him would be useful. The temptation to dismiss him with a hasty verdict must be resisted. Literary reading is the training for this cognitive empathy.

Which brings us to a final cause of the Millennials' nonreading: too much literature would expose them to human realities they prefer to ignore. In their sanguine idea of a better world wherein exploitation has ended and power serves only the good, where human beings treat everyone with a chaste equality in the kind of fellowship you see at the end of each unwatchable episode of the '90s show *Friends*, there is no place for the darker powers of sex and seduction, for savagery in human relations, for sobering disappointments and senseless deceits and primal fears. Original Sin they consider as hopelessly obsolete as a AAA map; if this world is "a vale of tears," that's entirely due to the failure of prior generations. They won't accept that children can be fiendish, that lovers may turn on one another with a hate that might frighten a drill sergeant, that gold can pervert the kindest natures...but literature shows it all. The atavistic upsurges in Frank Norris's *McTeague*, the survival of bloody ritual in Shirley Jackson's "The Lottery," the ruthless child-society of *Lord of the Flies*...they would only disrupt the utopian dream. Too many great tragic heroines—Euripides' Medea, Shakespeare's Cleopatra or Lady Macbeth, Racine's Phèdre—are "a conduit of the irrational," Camille Paglia says, "opening the genre to intrusions of the barbaric force."[24]

Alice Hindman is one of the solitary characters in Sherwood Anderson's influential 1919 novel *Wineshurg, Ohio*, a perceptive portrait of small-town life. The young man who seduced her at age sixteen and promised to marry her has moved to Chicago and forgotten her. Ten years of pining and regretting have left her a clerk in a store, uninterested in men, quiet and awkward, knowing "that her beauty and freshness of youth had passed."[25] She counts her money, rearranges the things in her room, and otherwise practices the "devices common to lonely people."[26] One night, however, as she retires to her hushed room for the thousandth time, her mother and stepfather gone for the evening, a mad fancy possesses her, and she undresses and runs out into the rain, "full of youth and courage,"[27] searching for another lonely soul to embrace. "What do I care who it is?" the fit commands her. "He is alone[,] and I will go to him." A man appears in the dimness on the sidewalk, and she calls out, but he's old; he can't make her out, and he's hard of hearing, too.

"What? What say?" he answers.

His fumbling words break the spell. His voice is so ordinary and anti-romantic that it acts like a snap of daytime reality that halts her ecstasy. She drops flat to the ground, hiding her nakedness as he passes on, unseeing and confused. She can't rise—she's too appalled at herself—and she crawls on the grass back to the porch. Shaking and weeping in bed she reflects, "What is the matter with me? I will do something dreadful if I am not careful." That comes in the final sentence. Nothing more happens save the pathetic resolve "to face bravely the fact that many people must live and die alone, even in Winesburg."[28]

Millennials don't want to hear that kind of story. They don't want to learn that adulthood doesn't always work out, that people can't always climb out of their frustrations, that loneliness must be endured and the hopes of adolescence abandoned, that the isolation of someone like Alice is largely her own fault...no, this isn't right, none of it. There's too much resignation; the view is too pessimistic. Life can't be so down and desperate. Millennials have social media, which means they never have to be alone. Alice nurses fantasies of her beau's returning long after it's obvious he never will, and Millennials are way too worldly for that kind of delusion. They know better than to let love sweep them off their feet. And what's with that crazy thing about running naked in the yard in the rain? LOL—get a grip! Alice and other characters in Anderson's novel are creatures of longing and unfulfillment. Beneath the surface of this bourgeois Ohio town society are midnight energies looking for release, but Millennials awaken and move in the daylight of innocence. The book's a drag.

Every high school student ought to read it, but today hardly any of them do. It used to sit in eleventh grade English, right in the center of the Great American Novel, but that tradition ended decades ago. The tales of Alice and the others would, indeed, have made the Millennials happier adults by exposing them to a richer collection of motives and experiences and personalities. It would have enhanced their cognitive empathy, which in turn would have reduced the friction when Millennials had to interact with individuals different from themselves at work and in public. The deep knowledge of others that such novels instill, the capacity to enter the characters' minds, the recognition of impulses outside your personal experience…these insights might kill the utopian dream, and that's a very good thing, because the dream isn't making them happy. It makes them bitter, ever irritated at the people who continue to stand in the way of the perfect world they envision.

Is there any type more joyless than the social justice warrior? I would be that way, too, if I had faith in a sublunary existence free of bias, selfishness, deception, and self-deception. But I grew up before the iPhone came along, when novelists and poets were still significant voices in popular culture. I read lots of American classics in high school, and in college took English 10A-B-C, which covered the sweep of English literature from *Beowulf* to W. H. Auden (the major at UCLA required it). I had an older sister who loved Victorian novels and majored in English at University of Maryland (though she ended up an epidemiologist), I had an identical twin brother who ate up the half-dark and half-funny works of Jim Thompson and Donald West-lake (though he ended up an actuary), and early on I came to look forward to moments late at night in bed, the day over and troubles of school and home laid to rest until morning, everything quiet except the teen anxieties bouncing inside my chest but waning as I reached to the nightstand, opened the page, and started reading:

> On my right hand there were lines of fishing-stakes resembling a mysterious system of half-submerged bamboo fences, incomprehensible in its division of the domain of tropical fishes, and crazy of aspect as if abandoned for ever by some nomad tribe of fishermen now gone to the other end of the ocean; for there was no sign of human habitation as far as the eye could reach….[29]

CHAPTER FIVE

Multiculturalism or Malcolm X?

Visiting the offices of the Intercollegiate Studies Institute a few years ago, I spotted a photograph on the wall showing a remarkable scene in progress. The black-and-white picture, dated November 14, 1962, is a wide-angle view—a very wide view, because of what the camera has to frame. What you see is the interior of a full-scale basketball arena, the lens managing to cover nearly the whole space. We are a ways up in the stands, well above the court, where the basketball hoops have been set aside and rows of chairs are lined up to face a platform and a podium. All the seats on the floor and well up into the bleachers are occupied—more than ten thousand people, I would guess. At the podium stands a white-haired man alone. The image is sharp enough that you can identify the closer faces in the crowd, all of them staring at the old man down below. The members of the audience appear young, bright, alert, and joyous: girls in sweaters and skirts, guys in sports coats and button-down shirts. We are at the University of Detroit sixty years ago watching Robert Frost read his poems.

I mentioned the photo in a 2019 essay in the online magazine The Agonist entitled "Nations Need a National Literature," using it as an example of the standing that writers used to have in American society.[1] In another episode of note, when T. S. Eliot travelled to University of Minnesota in 1956, more than thirteen thousand students packed Williams Arena to see and hear him, and this time the dignitary wasn't even reading one of his famous poems that might have been on the syllabi of a dozen classes at the school. The text was "The Frontiers of Criticism," a study broaching the definition of literary criticism and the pluses and minuses of different critical approaches—topics far from the daily concerns of Midwestern twenty-year-olds, yet there they were at the event.

I mentioned, too, a little 1964 mass-market volume of John Updike's short stories from the 1950s that I own entitled *The Same Door*. The cover brandishes a note advertising "16 short stories by the most talked-about young writer in America," while the back shows four other Updike volumes characterized as "Brilliant Bestsellers by the Most Significant Writer of Our Generation." I went further back in time and quoted the *New York Times* in the days after Mark Twain died in April 1910, one reporter stating, in only one of the many, many stories celebrating the author, "It has seemed almost impossible to realize an America without him." The discussion following Twain's death went on for days, with numerous remembrances and testimonials. The *Times* even tracked down the childhood buddy who served as the model for Huck Finn. I also quoted Ezra Pound on Walt Whitman ("He *is* America") and a *New York Times* reviewer of Edith Wharton's *The Age of Innocence*, who affirmed, "Mrs. Wharton is a writer who brings glory on the name of America." The review had an indicative title: "As Mrs. Wharton Sees Us."[2] At the very same time, Sinclair Lewis opened *Main Street* with a coda on the fictional setting of the novel that began, "This is America—a town of a few thousand, in a region of wheat and corn and dairies and little groves"—quite an exaggeration on the part of a mere storyteller, one would think, but it seems readers and critics swallowed the claim without blinking. Lewis was the first American writer to win the Nobel Prize.

The purpose of my essay was to recall this happy era of American literary culture, when writers had a national import and could summon large audiences. For a time, at least, society accepted writers as unique "representers," men and women telling us Americans who we were and where we were going, and nobody thought it presumptuous for writers to do so. Edith Wharton didn't have a Ph.D. or a faculty post, nor did she conduct social science fieldwork in cities or rural areas. All she did was paint characters and craft plots, and yet that gave her a perspective on her fellow Americans—"how Mrs. Wharton sees us"—that we had to respect. Pound knocked Whitman for his baggy verse—"I read him (in many parts) with acute pain"— but acknowledged him nonetheless as a national giant: "I see him America's poet." Whitman needed an editor, Pound said, a craftsman like Pound himself (who would edit *The Waste Land* for T. S. Eliot a dozen years later and earn the dedication "For Ezra Pound / *il miglior fabbro*"), but to embody a nation was still an Olympian achievement. It led Pound to compare Whitman to Dante.[3]

But that was another time. In 2022 you could book three award-winning *New Yorker*–published poets for a reading on a Friday afternoon at a large public or small private university, and you would be lucky to draw an audience of 150. If you opened a review of a volume of contemporary poetry with the bold assertion "This is America!" you might get an indulgent smile from your readers, at best. The representative assumption, the willingness to accept a writer as summing up or explaining or reflecting the American people as a whole, the notion that a wordsmith at home in Milledgeville, Georgia, or working in a hospital in Paterson, New Jersey, catches the national zeitgeist...such ideas disappeared a long time ago. Novelists and poets as the voice of America? A quaint notion—or a ludicrous one.

The culture is too fragmented; the printed word lost out to TV and YouTube and games; poets retreated into the academy; "diversity" won't let anyone represent things and persons outside his identity group.... Whatever the causes, it's a terrible development, especially because literary experience educates the mind to more intelligent interactions, as this book has argued. The whole society suffers if it is true that, as critic F. R. Leavis once put it, "thinking about political and social matters ought to be done by minds of some literary education and done in an intellectual climate informed by a vital literary culture."[4] Unfortunately, 90 percent of the discourse of politicians in this digital moment backs his assertion. Adam Bellow once told me that while his father didn't talk very much about politics and current events, he never stopped regretting the decline of literary culture in America since the days when writers popped up on the cover of *Time* and spoke with authority on the state of the nation. Mr. Bellow's regret wasn't just a professional complaint, as we can see all too well in the twenty-first century. The fall of the writer signaled the decay of civic life.

Oh, for the days when if you hadn't read and liked or disliked a particular novel, such as Norman Mailer's *The Naked and the Dead* from 1948, you felt as if you weren't up to date on something that mattered to society at large! Or when a work of literature appeared and was heralded instantly as the voice of a rising generation, such as Fitzgerald's *This Side of Paradise* (1920) or Kerouac's *On the Road* (1957). I think the last time the first one happened was with Tom Wolfe's *Bonfire of the Vanities* in 1987, and the second one was with Douglas Coupland's 1991 novel *Generation X: Tales for an Accelerated Culture*. When novels could do that kind of symbolic work, young people got the message that the world they would soon join had wholeness and meaning and significance to and for *them*, even if that meaning was a bit cynical and dismal (as in both the Wolfe and the Coupland). At this moment, when most Americans find that novels and poems represent America no better than Facebook and *Mad Men*, I think of that photograph of Frost at Detroit and mark not the high stature of the poet in the midcentury or the shoddy American public square and its puerile oratory in the twenty-first century. Rather, it's the experience of the kids in the stands that matters, then and now. Back in 1962, why were they there, crowding the cheap seats to hear an old guy with quivering hands mutter blank verse he had written before television and rock 'n' roll? Few of them aimed to become poets, and most of them likely remembered only a smattering of Frost's lyrics. The kids loved JFK (University of Detroit was a Catholic institution), and JFK had invited Frost to speak at his inauguration, but that couldn't account for the near universal attendance of the student body.

They had to go because they had to go. If they didn't, they would miss out on an experience that they expected to become an integral step in their education. They were young Americans, and this hour of verse would make them better Americans, better adults, a little more seasoned and aware. That was the understanding the moment the students heard that the poet would do a campus visit. The students had read and savored the lines, "Whose woods these are I think I know," and "Snow falling and night falling fast, oh, fast," and "I have been one acquainted with the night / I have walked out in rain—and back in rain," and it must have been fun to attach the words they had read in their anthologies to a real person. But *ten thousand* people? No, the presence of Robert Frost in the building had to have had an import beyond diversion or amusement. Frost stood for something bigger than a bunch of nice poems, and they knew what it was. It was this: he brought history to campus, the full meaning of a national legacy to young Americans who hadn't lived so long and were expected in their undergraduate days and nights to bond with that legacy as part of their passage to adulthood.

Consider the situation. Frost was eighty-eight years old and would die a few months later. His death would only deepen his significance when these undergraduates heard of it the next semester. Only a writer larger than life and transcending the present could attract a youth crowd as big as The Beatles would a couple of years later. Seeing him in the flesh would be something to tell their parents and friends back home. His fame reached back in time to another American age, to things they had heard about and imagined—Modernism, carriages and small farms, the Depression—things that produced *this* age. This was no ordinary celebrity. Frost was a living symbol of what the old curriculum of Stanford presented to freshmen in the very first months of their college careers: a world that preceded them, rich in purpose and value, greatness and genius, beauty and truth, there to endow them with a sense of the past, tradition sinking into their heads. That's what the photograph revealed: tender young sensibilities meeting a legend. The kids were nineteen, twenty, twenty-one, barely away from their parents, halfway into the world and figuring out what that world had to offer them. Society was not simply a landscape to discover, like the terrain around Saginaw Bay. No, it was the world their elders had created that awaited them. Frost was a distinguished representative of it. The resolutions "Good fences make good neighbors" and "I have promises to keep" and "For once, then, something" told them that the society beyond the campus, the nation in which they would have to live their lives, did have a worthy lineage. Hearing Frost read, the students took one more step out of adolescence and into the culture of their forebears.

We must not underestimate the value of this encounter to a maturing soul, psychological as much as intellectual. I remember once, in the late '80s, visiting my mother in Palm Springs for a few days and one afternoon stumbling upon a jazz concert in the park. It was open to the public, casually organized, not too crowded, and

I strode right in. People in their sixties and seventies sat on the grass and in lawn chairs, strolling back and forth from their spots to the concessions building while a band performed onstage. At the time I was just leaving behind the rock 'n' roll and New Wave music of my early twenties and getting into jazz (my dissertation advisor was a Miles Davis and Horace Silver nut). The timing couldn't have been better. *This is fantastic*, I thought, as I found an empty picnic table at the side of the platform. I listened and looked more closely at the players. Wait a minute, that's Dizzy Gillespie! You couldn't mistake the cheeks. Yes, that was him, here on a Palm Springs lawn, of all places, where you didn't even need a ticket. No one was dancing, no one clapping and calling his name, but there he was performing, like any other musician. I looked around and saw nothing else to signal that extraordinary fact. The blue sky, the palm trees, the meandering people, mountains in the distance... they were the same as always. The music was nice, a small group in a smooth groove, if I recall, not on a hard beat or hitting high crescendos. The identity of the one man had changed everything, though—his identity and the past he bore in his person. I felt it immediately; the sight struck me just as the sight of Frost must have hit the kids in the stands, as a bit of history shooting into my trifling little life. Dizzy Gillespie was more than just an aged man blowing great sounds on a horn. He had played with Charlie Parker, toured the globe for the State Department, written "A Night in Tunisia," and now he was fifty feet away and playing for real.

It got better. After ten minutes the musicians took a break, and Gillespie wandered off to the side, came forward to the picnic table, sat at the other end opposite me, laid out a sandwich, and started to eat. He nodded at me, and I nodded back, hoping not to do anything to annoy him. He seemed content, with an easy air, while I was imagining a thousand legendary occasions buried in his memory. The other people in the crowd didn't seem to notice; nobody sidled up for an autograph. Didn't they know what was happening here? Maybe they had already lived through too much history to be impressed in the way I was, but for me it was confirmation. The encounter had a reinforcing effect, though I couldn't recognize it at that moment because Gillespie's presence was too overwhelming. I see it now through the lens of a lifetime of teaching. Here was a figure of historic dimension presented to a twenty-something who had none, and it was great. He carried the weight of time—and did so with a smile. It gave me a feeling of destiny, not my own, really, but destiny "out there." For an hour, at least, the time and place were not routine and uninspiring. I wanted to go home and listen to "After Hours" with him and Sonny Rollins and Sonny Stitt, and to read more novels, too, and some history and philosophy, and draw a little more of the greatness that he carried all the time.

It's the kind of meeting that should happen to twenty-year-olds as often as possible. Gillespie, Frost, Eliot at Minnesota . . . they made the past reverberate, and every youth deserves such encounters with the legends. When they brush by, the air thickens, your reflexes slow, and the course of time takes a pause. I have a friend whose father was a famous intellectual and scholar, and he used to take my friend with him now and then to international events. My friend told me recently that in 1971, when he was twelve years old, during a symposium in a palazzo in Venice, the father drew him forward to an old man sitting in a chair with some notes in his lap. They hesitated a few feet away. "Pardon me, Maestro," the father said, "but let me introduce my son." A smile and a nod, and my friend meekly nodded back. They turned and walked away, as the father muttered, "You just met Ezra Pound." He remembers it vividly. He's Jewish, and he knows what Pound said of the Jews during the War, but those hands wrote "The apparition of these faces in the crowd" and piloted more than anyone else the progress of Modernism, one of the standout explosions of literary talent in all of European history. Moral or immoral, villains or victims, such figures bring to life romance and greatness and mystery. I cannot stress too much how salvific they are to a young sensibility tied to an iPhone and never off Instagram, who inhabits a universe with no enchanted objects, a history with no climaxes and turning points, just regular ups and downs, a tradition with no masterpieces, only a heap of entertainments. These young people don't know that experience can be so much better, that they don't have to settle for crude consumptions, not when there is an immortal in Palm Springs with his horn, a poet in the sports arena with his manuscript, or any of the items on a Western Civ syllabus. A young man stopped in front of my townhouse the other day blasting his pop music with the top down, and I said to him, "Do you know that if you drove through your neighborhood playing Beethoven that loud you would be a renowned figure, instead of a guy just like a million other guys your age?" He gave me a puzzled look that implied, *You some kind of a nut?* and drove off, but one can hope that the notion stayed with him. There is greatness to be enjoyed, he should be told over and over; there are talents to revere; the past contains wonders.

Believing that certainly helped me. I was a nervous graduate student with no money and no religion, unmarried and jumping from one crummy apartment to another every few months. A connection to fine and timeless things gave me a grounding and a heightening to offset the loneliness and toil. The acquaintance with a superior past long gone yet still available, with an unknown woman in nighttime hours in Amherst 1860 who showed that writing verse by candlelight could become a dramatic endeavor that would change the course of literary history, or with a mind that could conceive something as far-reaching as the ontic-ontological difference or as stately as the design of the Mall in D.C. . . . they lightened the fear that my own flickering time on earth would pass without consequence. There was nothing special about my need, but it felt special every time Gillespie or Coltrane, Parker or Monk, Dickinson or Heidegger satisfied it. Encounters with the greats gave me strength, and the men at the Alamo, the last paragraph of *The Education of Henry Adams*, and the girl waving at the end of *La Dolce Vita* kept me going.

The 1619 Project of the *New York Times* gets this emotional need exactly right in one sense—and miserably wrong in another. The good news is that its designers recognized the precious service offered to the youth of today by a meaningful past. They fashioned a history with the needy sensibilities of young Americans foremost in mind (though they assumed different racial groups had different needs). They understood that a world whose long foreground is missing or obscured leaves rising adults uncertain and oblivious. It helps young people to know that the practical reality of human affairs has been envisioned and built and developed by real people in specific circumstances and that the best ones deserve our fidelity, the worst ones our cognitive empathy. That gives them role models and adds layers of significance to the neighborhoods and nation they inhabit, the places they study and work, in the same way that rock formations show layers of geologic time as you dig downward. When in November 1977 my brother and I sprinted into UCLA's Pauley Pavilion for the first time to snatch seats on the floor, the banners in the rafters and the ghosts of Hazzard and Goodrich, Wicks and Alcindor and Walton made the ensuing game that much more significant. The stakes went up. A background packed with symbols and heroes, historic deeds and intriguing personalities, great art and books, landmark projects such as the Brooklyn Bridge and mythical moments such as Custer's Last Stand and John Wooden's last game...they nurtured the unsure teen.

The bad news of the 1619 Project, however, killed all of it: the condemnation of the American past as horribly and unremittingly racist. It's as if the designers understood the value of historical memory but laid out a version of history that would only make the youths studying it feel worse, not better. For, setting aside the accuracy of the 1619 Project's condemnation of all of American history, we have to ask how the kids whose schools have adopted a 1619 curriculum (the materials have spread widely already) are supposed to feel about that shameful past—and what kind of present it offers them. The debate over the historical facts may continue, but the impact matters, too. Will this conception of the American past inspire kids to learn more history, to adopt role models from two hundred years ago, to admire the Founding and memorize the Preamble to the Constitution and the Gettysburg Address, and to love their country, the place they call their own? Failing that, does it give them any alternative tradition, a positive genealogy they can embrace in this nation otherwise hostile to their existence? Or, rather, does it instruct the kids to reject the past altogether and lose the benefits of having any cultural inheritance at all? The 1619 educators want kids to learn the historical truth—let us grant them that noble intention—but the kids will quite naturally think to themselves, *Why bother to assimilate an ignoble background?* A past with only a bad meaning ends up neglected. That's human nature. The reformers who set out to correct the record and show that the musty stuff about the "Land of Opportunity" and the "American Dream" is a phantom, that the truth is much gloomier, forgot that fact. The 1619 designers made the same pedagogical mistake as previous revisionist historians from Howard Zinn forward: they saw things from their own learned perspective, not from the perspective of the pupils. The people who created the 1619 Project had a moral incentive to study the past, to feel history in their bones. But now that they have corrected the (putatively) false versions of history, now that the darker realities have exploded George Washington and the cherry tree and all that, what happens to the appeal of history to young Americans? It inevitably fades. The moral imperative—"You must know the racism, the exploitation…"—only works with the ones who find the guilty American past a pleasing occasion for their own thoughts, and those are and ever will be few. The rest will form no intimate relationship with the past. In the 1619 outlook the only personages worth taking note of are the protesters and martyrs, the anti-racists, figures contrary to the dominant white supremacist position, a countertradition too small and conflictual to meet the psychic needs of adolescents that we've outlined here. (Even before the implementation of 1619 curricula, more than half of twelfth graders scored "Below basic," the equivalent of an F, on the NAEP U.S. History exam.)[5]

Eighteen-year-olds want to believe that they are entering a world worth entering, one that has a past worth remembering and past heroes worth honoring and villains worth scrutinizing. They feel, if mostly unconsciously, a close relationship between what they believe of the past and how the present appears to them. If there is no past that deserves their attention, if they are given only yesteryears fraught with shame, heroes with clay feet and clay hearts, too, the present becomes a barren habitat. It doesn't answer their deepest longings for home. The tough circumstances in which they find themselves at age twenty-eight are just that—circumstances with no framework, no etiology. What happens in their lives has no further reason than "shit happens." Only the future can provide the ideals that invest their hours with purpose and design, easing the pain of a bad grade, a breakup, or a job loss with the promise of a utopian tomorrow. That's where the meaning is. The college that recruited the young man of color with joyful pictures of laughing youths on the quad, chosen with exquisite attention to diversity, has just returned his Organic Chemistry midterm to him with a D+, blowing his dreams of medical school. They promised him success, guaranteed that he would thrive at "State U, where all dreams come true," so don't hand him any bunk about Abe Lincoln walking miles to and from school each day. He resorts to another history, flat and impersonal and indistinct, but wholly serviceable for the purpose of explaining away his pain: the systemic racism of this college. He doesn't know the details, but so what? This "history" instantly gives his disappointment a new meaning, one powered by feelings of betrayal. He has a new goal: racial justice and social change and a better future, which he will pursue hereafter with the passion of a forever-retained humiliation. He is primed for utopia.

In 1968, a committee at Stanford University had this to say about general education at the school: "The University cannot in any event impress upon its students the total content of present knowledge, and it is impossible to choose what exactly it is that every student should know."[6] Those despairing words come from a review, conducted by a faculty steering committee, of the entire academic enterprise of the university, ranging from administrative governance to study abroad to advising to graduate and undergraduate education. The final report had ten parts and contained sixteen curricular recommendations and fourteen operational ones. You can see from the statement above that the faculty had forthrightly abandoned the old general-ed layout and Western Civ sequence, an attitude adjustment from "This is what all of you must learn" to "we cannot say," along with the implication for incoming freshmen: "It's up to you." After ten years of the General Studies Program, a rift had opened between what the system implied and what the professors believed. The authors of the review were candid, stating with an undertone of contempt, "A prescriptive academic program is founded on pretensions of eternal truth that we do not share."[7] They claimed they wanted to hold off out of respect for the undergraduates, whom they "hope[d]" had enough "curiosity and independence of mind to suspect any 'eternal' truths, any 'infallible' methods, any 'indispensable' knowledge."[8] (Note the sneer quotes.) Indeed, for withholding their judgment and lightening their prescriptions, the professors gave themselves a nice pat on the back: "This freedom to choose what knowledge and what disciplines to learn may be Stanford's greatest gift to the student."[9]

You got that? In *not* passing along a necessary tradition, in *not* choosing certain essential texts, in *not* requiring a set battery of courses, Stanford will actually offer a better education than the university did when it followed the General Studies model. This was no abdication, in other words; it was liberation. In the second part of the report, the authors wasted no time before panning the ancien régime: "Our present arrangements place far too much reliance on prescription; the General Studies Program is simply the most obvious case in point."[10] The old model is rigid and superficial, the authors asserted, and they accused it of "unreality" as well, observing that renowned Western Civilizations programs at University of Chicago and Columbia University were "dead or dying."[11] (Those predictions didn't come true.) The Western Civilization sequence should be dropped, they recommended, and a looser generic requirement put in its place: "An exposure, in the freshman year, to some aspect of historical studies."[12] From a full-year immersion in Homer-to-Freud to "exposure" to an "aspect" of history—that was the urge, uttered without a trace of shame. Nevertheless, the report did its job. By 1970, General Studies was out.

But if the 1968 professors believed that a freer, more student-determined curriculum would draw more undergraduates to the humanities, if they assumed that the old-fashioned, inflexible History 10-11-12 and the three-course English hurdle had actually discouraged kids from pursuing the majors, and that by making history and English less prescriptive they would make those subjects morc appealing to students, they were flat-out wrong. The students disagreed, as the results of the change showed unambiguously. In the following ten years, the popularity of history, English, and the rest of the humanities took a nosedive. From 1969 to 1979, annual humanities majors at Stanford fell from 1,062 to 624. The size of the overall undergraduate population didn't much change, but the share of graduates choosing the humanities dropped from 25 percent to 15 percent. Course enrollments plunged similarly: 24,550 in 1969 to 15,255 in 1979.[13] Those Stanford humanities professors who had been eager to end the supposedly authoritarian control of the freshmen, who had abhorred those narrow compulsory classes, who had proclaimed their respect for the desires of students to take charge of their own formation, and who perhaps expected students to flock to the classes of the sympathetic teachers, were, it turned out, voting against the exposure of Stanford students to *themselves*, to their own teaching. Ironically, the more they aimed to appreciate student choice, the less the students chose *them*.

Those numbers I have quoted were reported by Carolyn Lougee in a 1981 article in *Women's Studies Quarterly* entitled "Women, History, and the Humanities: An Argument in Favor of the General Studies Curriculum." Lougee was a history professor at Stanford, a feminist committed to diversity and the integration of more women into all the disciplines (one year later she would become Dean of Undergraduate Studies). Nevertheless, she deplored the "precipitous decline of undergraduate studies in the humanities." Moreover, she tied that decline to the loss of mandated general education coursework. The trend couldn't be ignored, she believed; the numbers couldn't be explained away. What the 1968 professors had cast as an unappetizing, obsolete burden that Stanford undergrads had to shoulder before declaring their majors had in reality been something quite different: an inspiration to further study. The imperative

English and history courses proved a pipeline into those fields; when they were closed down, the students disappeared from later humanities classes.

And so, Lougee explained in the article, in the preceding months she and others had led a curriculum revision that restored the old Western Civ requirement, though in modified form. Under the label "Western Culture Program," the course they had developed would be taught in small discussion groups, and it would incorporate more interdisciplinary variety. Yes, Lougee acknowledged, every section would stick to "the same core list of Great Books from Homer to Freud," and "women are few and far between" on the syllabus, but she promised fellow academics that teachers could approach the works from a feminist perspective and add women's materials along the way. Inserting a uniform, broad civilizational course that all students must take would serve the greater goal of maintaining "the study of the humanities as central to the undergraduate curriculum." The new Western Culture requirement was "a marvelous course in many ways," she assured her feminist readers. The program began at Stanford in 1982.[14]

Longtime observers of higher education know that it didn't last. What happened after that is perhaps the most famous episode in the Culture Wars of the late '80s and early '90s, at least as that war unfolded in the academic theater. In spite of the collapsing humanities numbers in the '70s, younger professors at Stanford increasingly didn't like the still Eurocentric-and-white-male-dominated syllabus of Western Culture courses. Minority students, too, were unhappy. By 1986, the Black Students' Union, a Chicano student organization known as MECHa, the Stanford American Indian Organization, the Asian American Student Organization, and Students United for Democracy in Education openly opposed the course. The rest of the student body didn't agree with them, it should be noted, more than

two-thirds of undergraduates giving the Western Culture requirement high ratings, as an article by Isaac Barchas, a student on a committee formed to debate the merits of the course, would later report.[15]
But accusations of racism were loud and bitter, and few professors
and administrators wanted to be seen arguing with undergraduates
of color. When Jesse Jackson came to campus on Martin Luther King
Jr. Day in 1987, activist students and many professors, too—some of
them inspired by his 1984 campaign for the White House—were
ready to aim his Rainbow Coalition at the local problem. Five hundred of them gathered in the plaza at the center of campus to hear
this charismatic speaker, who was gearing up for another run for the
U.S. presidency in 1988. As Jackson finished his exhortation and the
students departed, they sounded the chant that would be repeated
in a thousand news stories: "Hey hey, ho ho, Western Culture's got
to go!" One year later, Western Culture was, indeed, gone.

The events that day—and a year later, when the faculty voted for
new requirements—made national headlines, and a full account
appears in a remarkable study by Stanley Kurtz, published by the
National Association of Scholars in early 2020 under the title *The Lost
History of Western Civilization*.[16] Kurtz recounts the long history of
Western Civilization in educational practice going back to the eigh-
teenth century, and he explodes the leftist thesis that Western Civ was
concocted around World War I as a tactic to assimilate non-WASP
immigrants. Kurtz details how many of the revisionists on the faculty
relied on this spurious thesis in their attacks on Western Culture and
also frames the Stanford controversy over this course requirement as
an important harbinger of the vitriolic multiculturalism of our own
time. Previous calls for diversity and multicultural education, he says,
were offered in positive terms,[17] and anyone around at that time knows
what he means. Over and over, throughout my grad school years in
the '80s, I heard requests to "open up the canon" in precisely those

celebratory notes. The recognition of women and minorities would mean no denigration of Shakespeare and Chopin, we were promised—not at all. Multiculturalism merely meant giving students a fuller, richer understanding of the past. We weren't getting rid of Shakespeare; we were adding Aphra Behn. The rediscovery of Zora Neale Hurston didn't harm Henry James; it complemented him. This wasn't a power play; there would be no displacement involved. The new, more inclusive curriculum would be a more accurate rendition of what came before. The Dead White Male syllabus distorted the past; the multicultural syllabus would fix it, like an optometrist updating a prescription. The revision was historiographical, not political. It was considered a professional advance. Students who passed through a multicultural curriculum rather than a Western Civ program would be more worldly, more literate, more educated.

The Stanford affair was animated by no such benign goals, according to Kurtz. Rather, it brought a new malice to the academic Culture Wars: "Western civilization was attacked straightforwardly at Stanford in the late 1980s as racist, sexist, and imperialist."[18] The campus newspaper quoted a leader of the Black Students' Union saying that Western Culture had a clear subtext: "Niggers go home"[19]—a charge that made Western Culture no longer an academic matter. If that was the allegation, the debate was over. There could be no deliberations once the protesters raised their identity into a precious object that the University was continuing to injure and damage. How were defenders of Western Culture supposed to respond? You don't contest feelings of rejection. You don't tell an insulted sophomore, "Buck up!" A handful of conservative professors might reject this early instance of crybullying, but liberal professors, even those who still harbored a somewhat traditionalist outlook, didn't know what to say. A party as aggrieved as the students of color didn't want to hear any defense or discussion. If Western Culture classes were causing so much pain and casting such vile abuse at a student group that Stanford had worked tirelessly to satisfy, well, then, the direction forward was clear. Western Culture was out, except insofar as the West could be made to appear as but one lineage among others.

The accusations worked, and Stanford replaced Western Culture with a course called "Cultures, Ideas, and Values." The title had an acronym "CIV" that played off the old General Studies requirement, but the pluralization of "Culture" to "Cultures" was a devastating change. It signaled the demise of any single strand of Great Books, Big Ideas, and masterpieces, the very thing that had made the old General Studies requirement so meaningful. Different sections of each CIV class wouldn't share a common syllabus, and each had to include works by women and minorities, along with some representation of at least one non-European culture. The turn was complete, the triumph of multiculturalism settled.

Except the story doesn't end there. We've seen how youths responded to Frost in the Detroit arena in 1962 and, later, what happened at Stanford in the '70s, after Stanford dropped the General Studies model that had steeped students in the great works of Western Civilization. Now let's look at how youths responded to the further diversification of the curriculum in the '90s.

In September 1994, Stanford issued a fresh review of its curriculum, including the Cultures, Ideas, and Values offerings.[20] The committee appointed to run the review conducted surveys and held focus groups and town halls in the dormitories, in addition to conducting many less formal discussions with professors and students. The nineteen members of this Commission on Undergraduate Education were dutifully honest about the opinions they heard. What the students told them, in fact, follows closely what I've argued about the value of a coherent past imparted to students in a prescriptive, "civilizational" manner.

"Student opinion on CIV was remarkably clear and consistent," the authors say in section 6, "BREADTH REQUIREMENTS: The Cultures Cores." Most of the students with whom they spoke liked the idea of a small course that everyone had to take and for which they would have to read broadly outside their interests and eventual major, but the praise stopped there. In practice, they said, the actual courses annoyed and disappointed them. First of all, students objected to the variety of the offerings, claiming that "the tracks differed too widely in purpose, workload[,] and grading policy." Think hard on that response and set it against faculty assumptions about students' wanting to shape their own undergraduate careers. More choice did not please these students—they wanted more uniformity. Second, it bothered them that the materials on the syllabi didn't jell into a body of works with some common tie. The classes had a desirable diversity, yes, "but the course materials—especially the non-Western materials—were not well integrated." Those nontraditional inclusions impressed them as mere "tokens," they said, levelling a charge that must have appalled faculty progressives, who regarded tokenism as a perpetual stumbling block to authentic diversity. Finally, in trying "to meet so many different needs," the in-class presentations came off as "sketchy and superficial."[21]

Were these opinions representative of the whole student population? In light of a *Stanford Daily* poll cited in the report that recorded 72 percent of students believing "CIV should be changed,"[22] it certainly seemed so. One couldn't dismiss these specific dissatisfactions as the grumbling of kids who disliked their teachers and didn't earn decent grades. They were too numerous to discount.

The committee listened and ended up urging that the entire program "must be transformed." What the students specifically wanted, however, the faculty could not recommend. They immediately ruled out any "return to the single-course 'Western Civilization' structure."

Nor would they establish a new binding list of core readings. CIV did have certain broad requirements: something from the Bible, an ancient epic, some Renaissance drama, an Enlightenment thinker, and some Marx and Freud. But to specify particular works, to add any more set texts and authors, would start looking prescriptive and nondiverse. It would impose on the course "a definition of culture that many faculty members do not accept." Because such a list would give a limited number of works "privileged status," reform would stall, producing "endless debates about relative value and appropriate representation."[23] The commonality that students desired would have to come from something besides a canon of Great Books or a grand design such as Western Civilization.

The committee found that educational adhesive in a move that has become so commonplace that we might easily overlook its sweeping implications. They took a step back, to what we might characterize as a meta-disciplinary approach to tradition. Instead of compiling a body of creations into a memorable storyline that everyone would follow, teachers would focus on the *process* of compilation, the *methods* of tradition-making. The authors of the new curriculum put it like this: "The common intellectual experience of the course, therefore, would be a self-consciousness about the enterprise itself, and awareness of the analytical and ideological issues that the study of culture involves."[24]

In other words, the new curriculum would require critical thinking about culture: not this or that tradition, but "self-consciousness" about the nature and purpose of tradition, reflection upon tradition in the abstract. In this layout we should catch anticipations of the "methods" curriculum of Nicholas Lemann, discussed in chapter three above, and the "material history" assignment given to Ross Douthat, discussed in chapter one above. Pick any tradition, the authors say—"European, Asian, Islamic"—hold up some texts as "fundamental" within that tradition, but remember that the important thing is not to learn the details of the works held up as important, but to analyze how and why that culture has deemed those works important. Be canny; be pensive; don't get too caught up in the materials, in characters and actions and moments of eloquence. Focus on developing your own skills of critical study, not on the contents of the things studied. In sum, "the course should become the proper forum for a critically and historically informed discussion of issues of ethnicity, cultural identity, and political and social values." What Lady Macbeth does at night, the last five minutes of *Tristan*, the proper width of a fluted Greek column...all of these should give way to social generalizations, dogmas about culture and race. Instead of instilling knowledge of what the geniuses and leaders in a coherent tradition have imagined and executed over the ages, a Stanford general education should train students in the proper understanding of the transhistorical workings of identity and politics.

That was the thrust of the recommendations. In a remarkable case of academic obtuseness, the students told the educational authorities what was wrong, and the mentors failed them again. A May 1997 story by reporter Alison Schneider in the *Chronicle of Higher Education* covering discussions subsequent to the release of the report quoted several students and teachers at Stanford, including those on the committee pushing for a revised CIV. None of the people interviewed for the piece seemed content, no matter which side they were on. Some thirty professors teaching in the CIV program, we read, signed a letter objecting to the review process and its criticisms of the course; on the other hand, students who took the course didn't think much of those teachers. Schneider cited another survey of undergraduate opinion, this one from 1996, in which more than 60 percent of respondents judged that the course had only "slight to moderate value," which the reporter called "a grim statistic for the only course that every Stanford undergraduate must take." Things had to change, it was clear, and the article turned to faculty members who served on the review committee for clarification. English professor John Bender reiterated the report's recommendation: an overall revision of CIV into a "critical thinking about tradition" course that would enable Stanford freshman to carry what they learned in CIV into later years. Note the change in learning goals: "We are redefining what the core means, and we're saying that the core of humanistic education is not whether you've read *The Iliad* or Dante. The core is whether you have the skills to read *The Iliad* or Dante. You can learn the skills to read Shakespeare by reading Sophocles." Another English professor on the committee agreed, offering a simple analogy: "What we're trying to do is not to show every variety of fish, but to teach people how to go fishing."[25]

The blindness here is astonishing. The professors acknowledged student dismay, and they agreed with the low appraisals of the CIV curriculum's scattershot approach, but they completely ignored what really made CIV unpopular—and what had made Western Civilization and Western Culture so popular in the bad old days. Students craved a core, but Bender and the committee managed to "redefine" that core as something that isn't really a core.

This was never going to work. Not only was it conceptually incoherent; it also completely misconstrued the minds the professors were supposed to cultivate. Let's say it once more: the skills a sophomore needs in order to read *The Iliad* don't excite him one bit. The promise of analytic prowess doesn't prompt him to turn the page and follow what happens next. No, it is the sight of Hector in the dirt, bleeding to death and pleading to pitiless Achilles:

> ...I beg you, beg you by your life, your parents—
> don't let the dogs devour me by the Argive ships!

Wait, take the princely ransom of bronze and gold,
the gifts my father and noble mother will give you…

To which Achilles growls,

Beg no more, you fawning dog—begging me by my
parents!
Would to god my rage, my fury would drive me now
to hack your flesh away and eat you raw—
such agonies you have caused me![26]

That's what brings freshmen back to the humanities as sophomores. They don't care about *how* to read Dante. They want the image
of three-headed Lucifer deep in the ice of Hell, the heads of Judas
Iscariot, Cassius, and Brutus in each respective mouth, while Dante
and Virgil climb their way to Purgatory. They love the fishing because
of the fish! That was obvious. How did the professors become so
clueless? The evidence of alienation was right in front of them, in
sliding enrollments and students leaving the humanities majors. How
could they ever have come to assume that skills would suffice, that
Shylock's vengeance and "Was this the face that launched a thousand
ships?" could be supplanted by arts of analysis? Had they taught and
written about these works for so long that the power and greatness
of *The Iliad* and the rest had dimmed? Were they too old to imagine
the emotional states of recent high school graduates? Were these
professional analysts of texts so professionalized by the 1990s that
they had forgotten the inspirations that drew them to the fields when
they were nineteen themselves?

What happened to the humanities after the turn away from
canonical works—the sliding enrollments, programs closing, jobs
disappearing—answers these questions in an unhappy way. The

results indicate just how far the thinking of the mentors diverged from the expectations of the mentees. The curricular changes at Stanford and a thousand other schools didn't lift the burden of Eurocentrism from the young people's sagging shoulders—there was no such burden. The gutting of the core didn't respect their desire to experiment with their own learning—no such desire existed. The abandonment of the Western canon didn't elevate other traditions, either. Graduates in 2010 had no more substantive knowledge of African history and art and literature than 1980 graduates—at best, they got a glimpse of a non-Western novel or painting popping up here or there in a token manner.

None of those promises came through. Isaac Barchas, the Stanford student whose article I quoted above, graduated in June 1989. He had served as a young member of the committee created to implement the just-approved Cultures, Ideas, and Values course—the only member who liked the old Western Culture class (which he had taken in 1985). As the committee set about staffing the new courses and constructing the syllabi, he divulges, an unfortunate reality surfaced. When CIV was originally proposed, it was said that assistant professors at Stanford couldn't wait to teach a multicultural course like that. But after the Western Culture requirement was successfully abolished and it was time to get to work on the new curriculum, Barchas reported, "the great pool of innovative young faculty eager to teach a year-long course to freshmen never materialized."[27] Having knocked down the dominant tradition, the faculty apparently considered their work done. Erecting other traditions and teaching them to incoming students didn't motivate them. "Western Culture is history," Barchas wrote in 1989, "and whether CIV ever attains its radical potential is not a common topic of campus conversation."[28] His essay tells not the wondrous accomplishments of diversity, but a different story: the eclipse of the very idea of general education. They took a tradition away and never replaced it with another tradition, not even with a consistent assemblage one could recognize as multicultural. The professors had lost interest, and the youths lost what every youth needs and deserves: a patrimony, any patrimony. Multiculturalism didn't multiply heritages and enhance each one; it left the students with no heritage at all, no relationship to past greatness. And there was an emotional consequence to this presumably progressive reform: students could no longer take any pride in what they were studying. They had to be more critical than that. They couldn't plod their way through *The Aeneid* and boast at the end, "Wow, I have finished one of the monuments of the millennia." Monuments, or rather, "monumentality," had to be analyzed, criticized—debunked. Watching Olivier's *Richard III* was no better than watching episodes of *Lost*. By what standard could you rank the first above the second? Their teachers had flattened and demystified the world.

One wonders what these professors would have said twenty-five years later, when a group of Stanford undergraduates sought to revive Western Civilization in the curriculum and were subjected to a smear campaign that displayed a lot less historical knowledge and political awareness than students possessed in the days of Western Civ but a whole lot more vitriol. The episode is a fair specimen of the wages of utopian disappointment.

It started on March 14, 2015, with an article in the *Stanford Review*, the conservative student paper, under the title "The Death of Stanford's Humanities Core." Its author, Justin Lai, an undergraduate double-majoring in symbolic systems and history, compared the current Thinking Matters curriculum, which we discussed in chapter three, to the old Western Civ and Western Culture curricula and pronounced it not even a humanities requirement. Many of the Thinking Matters alternatives, he wrote, "lack even a single work of substantial literature or reading, and are often focused on non-humanities disciplines." Lai blamed conformist Stanford administrators who had "modified its curriculum to appease critics at the expense of the rigor and quality of its programs." It is up to the students, then, Lai suggested, to pressure the leaders to change it.[29]

One year later, the editors of the *Review* did just that, creating a petition to revive the Western Civ requirement, with 350 signatures needed to bring the proposal to a vote by the student body as a whole. The editors issued a manifesto backing the proposal on February 21, 2016, under the heading "The Case for a Western Civilization Requirement at Stanford." The manifesto included blunt language about the historical ignorance of undergraduates ("uninformed engineers"), the Western origins of technology and science, the pointless jumble of existing Ways courses, and the Western basis of individual freedoms. The editors promised that the two-course requirement would not gloss over the facts of slavery and colonialism.[30] Conservative students proceeded to drift around campus and ask peers in cafeterias and on pathways to sign, and many of them did, enough to get the proposal on the ballot.

In early April the vote results came in: 342 in favor of Western Civ, 1,992 opposed (interestingly, fewer voted in favor than signed the petition). The *Review* kids weren't surprised; they hadn't expected to win. One of them told me in a phone interview that the idea struck them at first as a nifty way to tweak the easily triggered leftists in the activist organizations and at the other paper, the *Stanford Daily*, though a serious and sad subtext to everything the editors said was consistent. Heavily outnumbered, as conservatives always are at the twenty-first-century research university, these young people saw themselves as gadflies and dissenters. They recognized that a proposal to revive Western Civ would hit hard at Millennial grievance and irritation. So they set out to tease their fellow students: *Besides democracy, education, philosophy, logic, mathematics, engineering,*

literature, and theater, what has Western civilization ever done for us?
Let's start a petition!

The 6–1 loss ended the affair, but it evoked a response from the other side that set a pattern that has been repeated on 100+ campuses since then: "When I first read your petition, I thought it was too obviously harmful to garner any support.... Then I went and looked at the number of people who signed it...186 and counting in just a few days. I felt sick. I felt like crying. I felt so hurt and betrayed that so many people, so many of my Stanford peers would support such a disgusting initiative." That was written for the *Stanford Arts Review* in late February of that year by an undergraduate of Native American background. Stanley Kurtz quotes this and similar responses to the proposal at length in *The Lost History*. The petitioners were accused of "elitism," "classism," and "hatred."[31] An op-ed in the *Stanford Daily* stated that the manifesto's claim that it was "Western values" that had undone the intellectual case for colonialism "blatantly insults, among others, the post-colonial, feminist, anti-racist, and Marxist movements that challenge many of the worst elements of Western thought."[32] Another op-ed, from just the day before, "The White Civ's Burden," alleged that the editors' praise of Western freedom ignored the fact that "such noble aspirations are inherently hampered by their position within a racist, sexist, and classist system which sought—and still seeks—to explicitly uphold white supremacy and the subjugation of all others."[33]

Three days later, the editor in chief of the *Stanford Review*, Harry Elliott, told the *College Fix* that "intimidation tactics by students against the effort are already in full swing." Some students who signed the petition asked that their names be removed after getting harassing messages. Social media were particularly nasty: "I've been called racist, I've been called a joke, I've been told to put Western Civilization up my ass, it's quite hilarious," Elliott remarked.[34]

These reactions hadn't come from nowhere, of course. The accusations had too much of a preprogrammed tenor to them; the charges of racism were too shallow and insipid for them to be reasoned judgments made by independent minds. In all the responses I read when I went back to review the affair, not one unexpected observation popped up. The accusations followed a script that claimed a more accurate knowledge of the past but in fact delved no further than a few details and generalizations about white villainy. The student who asked on Facebook whether *Mein Kampf* would be required reading if the proposal passed didn't think it necessary to give any evidence for his surmise.[35] Some angry students seemed to think it was enough to throw obscenities at Elliott and the *Review* editors. Furious young critics of the proposal often maintained that they had already had Western Civ packed into their heads from first through twelfth grade, but their remarks demonstrated very little acquaintance with it. Consider, for instance, the authors of the *Stanford Daily* op-ed quoted above, who seem ignorant of the fact that feminism and Marxism are thoroughly Western inventions. Indeed, the entire historiographical side of the controversy was downright dull. The old justification for dumping Western Civilization—because it narrowed the past and obscured other traditions—gave way to crude and agitated sallies against Western devilry. The critics didn't have the knowledge to make their case interesting, and they didn't need the knowledge, either. They had something better: offense, outrage, disgust.

That's what this latest battle at Stanford revealed most of all: nothing political, just the ascendance of feeling. This was an emotional contest, not an intellectual one, and Western Civ had lost it long before the *Review* petition came along. Back in 1960, the professors spoke boldly of the West. By 1970, not so boldly. By 2010, Western civilization was met with skepticism at best, damnation at worst. The dogma told leftist kids that the actions of conservative students need be addressed only within a climate of shame, which was extra-thick throughout 2015 and 2016 for reasons other than the new fight over general education: the death of Michael Brown in Ferguson, Missouri, the rise of Donald Trump, and more. The controversy over Western Civ took place in this bigger context of preexisting unrest. One important factor in the anti-conservative hostility was a student group that had materialized earlier and aggressively primed undergraduates to react to the Western Civ petitioners in exactly the virulent way that they did. The main target of this group was not the *Stanford Review*, in fact, but the Stanford administration and its putative systemic racism. The nature and purpose of the project came through in a link in the "White Civ's Burden" op-ed that took you to a document entitled "Who's Teaching Us?" The document was a seven-page list of demands issued by a coalition of existing student identity groups that had begun forming two years before in opposition to Stanford's continuing intention, it alleged, "to perpetuate racial injustice." As with many other "demand lists" issued at the time, the items in the document were audacious, the tone of high indignation forbidding, and the demands threatening. Among other things, the coalition called for "a recurring and comprehensive identity and cultural humility training to be instated as a requirement for all faculty" ("humility"?). The next president and provost, they continued, must be lesbians of color (to "break both the legacy of white leadership and cisgender male leadership"). Departments outside the School of Humanities and Sciences were ordered to "double their quantities of faculty of color." The Wells Fargo branch on campus had to be expelled (because Wells Fargo invested in prisons). And so on. The statement demanded that the administration respond by 3:00 p.m. on Friday, April 8.[36]

As with the reactions to the *Review* petition, much of the expression of this statement was irrational. The authors spoke of "dire needs" and "a state of emergency," and they pledged that if the president didn't meet their demands, they would "proceed accordingly." They wanted a system for "reporting and tracking microaggressions from faculty," too, with each professor's record on that score playing a part in faculty evaluations. These were impossible requests, of course. Imagine a Stanford historian who had blasted patriarchy for thirty years forced to undergo "humility training." Imagine a provost sitting down with the authors and trying to tell them that hiring quotas are un-Constitutional. But the impossibility and high-handedness of it all were precisely the point. As we saw earlier with the #Students-AgainstHate letter, they had tactical value. Hot feelings were a source of strength. The *Review* editors had gotten past the point of caring, so they were free to laugh at the melodrama, but school officials couldn't do that. In fact, the *Review* editors answered the "Who's Teaching Us?" list with a demand list of their own, including: "WE DEMAND that Stanford renames White Plaza as Black Plaza," "WE DEMAND that Stanford recognizes that half-lives matter, and establishes a committee to fund the Chemistry and Physics Departments accordingly," and "WE DEMAND that Stanford builds a wall around El Centro Chicano and makes MEChA pay for it," an echo of Trump's campaign promise to build a wall and make Mexico pay for it.[37] As might have been expected, the mockery incensed the activists, who hated the opposition's laughter more than anything. It only amplified their outrage, and the fury they expressed helps explain why administrators at Stanford and every other institution indulged the protesters throughout that season of protest.[38]

When I look back at that final episode at Stanford, and then further back to those occasions when the faculty had voted to drop Big Picture requirements and set diversity above any one tradition and "skills" over the content of Great Books, a question for the mentors comes to mind: *Are you happy with the outcome?* These angry, half-educated seniors who could muster so little knowledge and no wit at all in their confrontations but sputtered their offense with gusto—were they the prophesied result of your curricular reforms? When you insisted that twenty-year-olds be given control over their own formation, is this how you wanted them to exercise their freedom? Did you think that releasing them from the burdens of Western Culture would make them more worldly, more liberal? Did you not anticipate how the denial of a coherent and monumental background would disable them from intelligent controversy? You righteously dismantled one grand narrative in the name of diversity and choice, and diversity and choice wouldn't allow any other overarching scheme or storyline to take its place. The multiculturalism you hailed did what it was supposed to do: multiplied and randomized the books, heroes, artworks, and settings, leaving sophomores to assemble them into a meaningful whole—something they couldn't do. You may not have cared about meaningful wholes, judging them exclusionary, the concoction of narrow interests, not the historical truth, but the nineteen-year-olds just released from the structures of family and home and high school needed those wholes to ease their way into the world. All they ended up with in their heads was Western guilt, a slender and brittle sense of the past that didn't deepen their experience. It attenuated it. These wispy appeals to "systemic racism" and "historic injustice" didn't sweeten their relationships. They poisoned them. The guilt kept them from sharing Juliet's passion and Gatsby's dream. It blunted their experience and their very selves. They can't even admire their own native tongue: it's the "masters'" language.

Let us understand, then, the relationship between the vitriol and nausea launched at conservative students and the very thing the professors demolished. What in the petition affair set the activists off? You're wrong if you think it was Western Civilization, historical injustice, or racial insult. The reaction was more psychologically complex than that. It had to do with a particular relationship to the past, exacerbated by a dose of peer group dynamics. Here's what happened: They saw a group of students doing something they couldn't do—claiming an inheritance, a unified body of great works and events and individuals, and it maddened them down to their toes. Those smug little conservatives had received the past as their bequest; the noble but damaged activists couldn't do any such thing, and it drove them crazy. Western Civilization exalted books they hadn't read and artworks they hadn't appreciated, and their ignorance sparked a panicky insecurity. The "privilege" of the conservative students only punctuated the shortage the other students were suffering, which felt all the worse in such a hypercompetitive domain as the super-selective campus. Their teachers had told them that they had no heritage, no honored past to call their own, only spite and indignity, tales of slaves whipped, women assaulted, and peoples decimated. How could they not envy peers with better luck, with a past that made them proud? The *Stanford Review* gang appeared so secure—no whining or resentment. They could even find humor in the attacks, and a lot of that confidence stemmed from their ownership of Plato and the rest. Their conservative mentors, however few in number, told them so. What had the activists heard? That Plato belongs to *them*, not to you. That *they* can identify with Jane Austen's girls; *you* can't. That when Americans memorialize D-Day, you shouldn't because the couple thousand black troops who hit the beach back then aren't ever acknowledged.

It doesn't take a profound understanding of human nature to realize that the message would only dissatisfy them unless they discovered another usable past. You can't leave nineteen-year-olds with no anchors. They need aged things that stabilize and ennoble them, such as American youth used to find in *The Columbian Orator*, the collection of ancient and modern writings and speeches used in nineteenth-century classrooms and which served teenage slave Frederick Douglass as a treasured (and secret) intellectual roadmap to freedom. This was the experience of countless Americans, not just great writers like Douglass and retired humanists like me. The students of color in 2016 expressed that need themselves, over and over. When they demanded the expansion of "studies" programs, their own dormitories and centers, and more teachers and advisors of color, they were pleading for a community of their own, traditions of their own, not some watery vision of diversity. In the "Who's Teaching Us?" document, the students asserted, "Please do not respond to our demands by highlighting diversity and social-justice related measures the University has in place." They had had enough of that already. They wanted a more distinctive, authentic affirmation of their identity. They craved a more meaningful and epochal framework, one that went well into the past, that had stature and majesty, that underscored greatness, not victimhood. Their problem wasn't white supremacy; it was nothing-supremacy, relativism in matters of culture, history, and art, no legacy inherently better than any other.

The mentors missed the point entirely. They believed that taking down Western Culture would yield a gladsome inclusiveness, not a melting pot, but a salad, in which each ingredient would retain its integrity, the kind of tolerance that welcomes all, but none too deeply, because that might end up favoring some over others. That was and is the liberal way, a managerial approach to group tensions, with inequities remedied by acts of recognition ("We're here to listen") and new allocations of resources (hiring counselors who are experts in disadvantaged populations). The enduring vexation of students of color should have told them long ago that it wasn't working. In truth, the activist groups didn't have a problem unique to their group. This is a universal need. The soul must have more: faith in immortals, a sharing of greatness, contact with sympathetic forebears. When the bureaucrats promised them tolerance and inclusion, they replied, *To hell with inclusion!* What they really wanted is what everybody wants: his own precious inheritance, his own supremacy.

In his famous autobiography, in the midst of describing his underworld life before his January 1946 arrest for larceny and breaking and entering, Malcolm X singles out for a moment a peculiar deficiency in himself. He was obviously intelligent, with sure instincts. Though only twenty years old, he recalls, he coursed through the network of drug dealers, gamblers, thugs, fences, and prostitutes with studious discernment. He followed the rules of criminal conduct like a veteran and scoped the personalities he encountered with the skill of someone with twenty years of experience. When he organized a gang to break into houses in upscale Boston, he says, "I wasn't rushing off half-cocked. I had learned from some of the pros, and from my own experience, how important it was to be careful and plan. Burglary, properly executed, though it had its dangers, offered the maximum chances of success with minimum risk."[39] He adds, "Within the residence burglary category, there are further specialty distinctions," sounding like an expert explaining professional methods to an intern. The operation had to be "perfect," and that required a slow and deliberate weighing of risks and handling of personnel. Except for a few occasions, the many drugs he took didn't shake that mindfulness.

And yet, he admits, "I would bet that my working vocabulary wasn't two hundred words."[40] He had the street lingo down pat, but that was all. "Every word I spoke was hip or profane," he says, and there weren't many of them. The streets and clubs didn't require more. He didn't even realize the problem until he left the scene, entered prison, and met Bimbi, a longtime prisoner, older and steadier, "the first Negro convict I'd known who didn't respond to 'What'cha know, Daddy?'"[41] Bimbi demanded respect, and black and white prisoners both gave it, ready to hear what he had to say about human behavior, the local history of Concord, Thoreau, and religion. Malcolm cursed the guards and savored his nickname among the other prisoners—"Satan"—but all that stopped in the presence of this sober man of knowledge. "What fascinated me most of all," Malcolm says, "was that he was the first man I had ever seen command total respect...with his words."[42] Malcolm stopped cursing.

Bimbi urged him to use his brains a little bit, suggesting an English correspondence course, and Malcolm was so impressed with the man's demeanor that he proceeded to take the course until he could write a grammatical letter (it took him a year to get to that point). Bimbi would often teach prisoners the derivation of words (words, again), something that lead to the next, even more improbable step for Malcolm: a correspondence course in Latin. At the same time, letters and visits from family members commenced, and they informed him of "something called 'the Nation of Islam,'"[43] a curious religion he had never heard about before, but whose first instructions were simple: no more pork or cigarettes. He complied; the other prisoners and the guards noticed and were mystified. Malcolm hungered to learn more as his brother talked about Mr. Elijah Muhammad and delivered in a whisper the first principle that a member of the Nation must understand: "The white man is the devil."[44] That axiom grabbed Malcolm, and his curiosity went back in time, to books about Africa and the slave trade, the British in India and the Opium Wars in China. But once again, the words got in the way. He checked out volumes from the library, but they contained so many terms he didn't know that the books "might as well have been in Chinese." At this point Malcolm thought "some of the first serious thoughts [he] had ever had in [his] life," but he didn't possess the language to pursue them. In prison, trying to communicate with people on the outside, Malcolm lacked the weapons, and he knew it. "In the street," he boasts, "I had been the most articulate hustler out there—I commanded attention when I said something. But now, trying to write simple English, I not only wasn't articulate. I wasn't even functional."[45]

So began the next step in self-training. He secured a dictionary and started to copy out every word in it, every definition from *aardvark* forward. He didn't consult the dictionary each time he hit an unfamiliar word in the books he had. No, he closed all the other books, stuck with the dictionary alone, and kept transcribing. It sounds like drudgery, but for him it wasn't. It opened his eyes to words "that I never knew were in the world," he remembered, and to people and places, too, for "the dictionary is like a miniature encyclopedia." Each morning he would review the definitions that he had copied the day before, then move on to the next page. Months passed, the dictionary task was complete, and now he found he could comprehend the books that had mystified him before.

The family visits taught him something bigger, too: the myths of creation and world development that the Nation of Islam espoused, the narrative of white devils enslaving Africans and obliterating African civilization, "whitening" history and obscuring its revealing contents, the "twenty-four wise scientists," "Mr. Yacob," the secret truth about Moses and what had taken place on the island of Patmos and other tales that Malcolm would later recognize as foreign to authentic Muslim teaching but that at the time provided him with a framework that gave his present condition a reason and a purpose. Seeing the white man as superior not in all things, only at manipulation and abuse, put his criminal past and incarcerated present in a different light. His days had been chaotic, violent, cruel, drug-addled, and sordid—all true, but now they had a rationale. There was a Big

Picture coming into focus. He was no longer just a rootless rogue bouncing from one hustle to another. His new understanding of the world gave his actions an air of design. He had been proud to be "Satan," until he found out that Satan was exactly what the Man wanted him to be, what a thousand years of racial stratagems had determined for him.

Nothing better could have happened to him than prison, he said after it was over. Malcolm stuck to his room most of the day, reading history, philosophy, and religion until lights out at 10:00 p.m., and then he continued by the corridor light deep into the night, logging so many hours that his 20/20 vision deteriorated and he developed an astigmatism. "I knew right there in prison that reading had changed forever the course of my life," he concluded. "As I see it today, the ability to read awoke some long dormant craving to be mentally alive."[46]

That's the sequence recounted in chapters ten and eleven in the *Autobiography*, "SATAN" and "SAVED." We have evil and recovery, a craving and a birth—or rebirth (he had been a top student when he was a boy). Reading changed everything about Malcolm. Reality itself was altered. The cell he occupied was no longer a confinement, but a refuge allowing him to read, read, read: "I had never been so truly free in my life."[47] This is the language of conversion—"It was like a blinding light"[48]—and later, when he was transferred to another prison and he took up the Bible, Malcolm read over and over again the story of the most famous conversion in history, Saul on the road to Damascus. Malcolm didn't become a Christian, but he sympathized with how Paul felt after he heard the voice of God and was struck blind: "I do understand his experience." Like any conversion, Malcolm's divided his life in two: the man before and the man after. "It's as though someone else I knew of had lived by hustling and crime," he marvels. "I would be startled to catch myself thinking in a remote way of my earlier self as another person."[49]

This is just the transformation that Millennials should consider—this is why I bring it up—but they can't. It requires, first, that they come to dislike who they are, and that doesn't go with the self-affirmations on which they've been raised. More basic than that is, of course, the reading problem. I've cited the number of Millennials who, as adolescents, found reading an insignificant activity. Imagine what Malcolm X would say to them—and how disinclined they would be to listen. Millennials didn't read very much on their own in 2006, when they were teens, and now that they're in their late twenties and thirties, they still don't read very much. As we saw above, the 2019 American Time Use Survey clocks them at four hours and seventeen minutes of leisure time per day, and they devote only seven of those minutes to reading. The approach of middle age hasn't aroused any bookish traits, no heightened curiosity. Games and computers for fun garner more than thirty minutes a day, while television collects two hours. That reading could burst into their lives and become a hyper-intense habit like that of Malcolm in his cell is inconceivable to them. It wasn't a leisure option for him. It was the key to enlightenment. When he left prison and hit his thirties, he never stopped: "If I weren't out here every day battling the white man, I could spend the rest my life reading."[50] Wherever he went he carried a book.

Malcolm's father died (he may have been killed) when he was six years old, and his mother was institutionalized seven years later. At age twenty, he admits, he was belligerently atheist, a nihilist about life and about people, too: "I believed that a man should do anything that he was slick enough, or bad and bold enough, to do and that a woman was nothing but another commodity."[51] His sense of the past ran no further back than the guy who lent him money the week before, his sense of the future no further forward than the robbery he would commit the week after. The world was meaningless, his own existence purposeless: "Deep down, I actually believed that after living as humanly as possible, one should then die violently."[52] Faith, sacrifice, humility—that was the way of chumps. Cynicism was wisdom. In fact, the toughest thing for him to do during his conversion in prison was not recording in his own squiggly hand every word in the dictionary. It was kneeling down to pray, "the hardest test I ever faced in my life."[53] His family told him he must turn east and bow to Allah, but that was nearly impossible for a man who was at that time a "personification of evil." It took him a week: "I had to force myself to bend my knees. And waves of shame and embarrassment would force me back up."[54]

When, in late 1965, the world heard the story of Malcolm's youth of crime and his transformation in prison, he was already dead, assassinated February 21 of that year while delivering a speech in Harlem. Sales took off, eighteen printings in the next five years, and ensuing controversies over the Nation of Islam and a surging Black Power movement raised the reputation of the man ever higher. A 2012 biography of him won the Pulitzer Prize. The life of Malcolm X is no less relevant fifty-seven years after his death, in another age striving and failing to achieve racial harmony, but I cite it here for a different reason. It relates directly to the core of this book, the problems that Millennials have suffered and the cloudy and frustrating notions they embraced when the mentors failed to do their job. For if we evaluate the "wisdom" that our twenty-first-century teachers typically offer in their classrooms and through personal counsel in light of Malcolm's experience, we can see immediately just how empty and unsatisfying that wisdom is. Take the words and deeds of the elders that we have recounted in the preceding pages—the encouragement of Millennials fifteen years ago to dive into their screens all they wanted, the failure of the purveyors of culture to uphold the literary world, the withdrawal of "civilization" from the curriculum—and apply them to the twenty-two-year-old prisoner suddenly realizing how ignorant, imperceptive, and incompetent he is, and you can't help but see their utter uselessness. The current wisdom would never give a young man like Malcolm an overarching worldview—the Nation of Islam outlook included. On the contrary, today's mentors have made it their job to demystify such worldviews, to undermine such over-asserted unity. They have no strong gods or deep myths to pass along, and they laugh at talk of the meaning of life. Their pedagogy wouldn't serve him, no matter how much it might cater to his black identity. The mavens of multiculturalism may insert a diversity course into the general education requirements, they may stipulate that humanities syllabi must include some non-Western materials, they may pledge to hire more teachers of color and commence diversity training for all, but none of that would have impressed Malcolm, either before or after his conversion. "Finding a community" on social media would have struck him as nothing more than a diversion (and the profanity and insults of online comments would disgust him; Malcolm was unfailingly polite after he left prison). It certainly wouldn't have made him rethink his position in the world, and it wouldn't have inspired him to read. And the postconversion Malcolm would have scoffed at multiculturalism as nothing more than a sop to Cerberus, a bit of bland recognition for beaten spirits. The preconversion Malcolm wouldn't have bothered with any of it, either. And, crucially, it would have meant nothing to him while he was in the midst of his climb out of the pit. A soul so uprooted and demoralized doesn't need diversity or virtual friends. It needs faith. It doesn't need "critical thinking" or an iPhone. It needs something to believe in. It doesn't need "equity, tolerance, inclusion." It needs a history, literature, philosophy, religion, a tradition complete and concrete, a meaningful framework.

This is what I called "The Betrayal of the Mentors" in the title of the fifth chapter of *The Dumbest Generation*, and nothing I've seen since 2008 has persuaded me to change my mind. I criticized the young back then for their leisure choices, but they appear to me now to be victims of an older generation of mentors who didn't know how to be mentors—and still don't. The authorities who ought to be the guardians of the dead and the stewards of tradition don't define themselves that way, and so they have little to offer the young. They don't fire up their juniors to read and learn, to plunge into books with even one-tenth the ardor of "Satan" in his cell. They can't; it's a matter of principle. The postmodern outlook that holds sway among our academics and Digital Age intellectuals and journalists rests on a cardinal assumption that completely estranges them from the lost and striving adolescent: no grand narratives. What would they say about the mythmaking of Elijah Muhammad? That it's a fantastical invention. They'd be right about that, but that doesn't change the fact that that mythmaking set Malcolm Little on the road to Damascus. The Malcolm X that they generally honor wouldn't have emerged without it. Our enlightened mentor of 2021 doesn't like myths of origin, and he doesn't like teleological ends, but that doesn't make the adolescent hankering for genesis and closure go away. Malcolm didn't want to read different interpretations of the Gospels to unearth their various ideological underpinnings—he wanted the truth. The point of his critical thinking was to reach a belief, solid and fixed, not to keep going and going and going like an ironist who can't stop ironizing. The mentors of the twenty-first century favor "methods" over fate and design and providence, the very things that give existential comfort to the young, whether they be thugs in prison in 1947 or high achievers at Berkeley this coming fall. As the mentors glance at their shrinking class rosters at the beginning of each semester, they should say, "It's not them—it's us."

How pallid and prosaic must the mentors' talk of diversity and "Ways of Thinking" sound in the ears of nineteen-year-olds gripped by awakenings of mortality, love and rejection, and hopes of success. And how predictable is it that, in the absence of a holistic tradition such as Western Civilization, they latch onto anything and everything (various "injustices," climate fears, Antifa, and the like) as a substitute to provide some meaning to their lives. The mentors won't give them meaning, and so they must find it on their own. The world is not coherent, they hear. History is chancy and heterogeneous, religion is stupid and often evil, and your nation is guilty. That's what they've heard, and that's what they subsequently know. They're not happy with this state of affairs, and who can blame them? The mentors won't help us, but we can still make the world a just and happy unity, they think. History can be overcome, a better religion is possible, and the nation can be perfected. We don't need the materials of the (not-so-good) past in order to progress in the present. They got it wrong, and we can make it right. Expel the bad guys, enforce a few woke dogmas, and everything will be fixed.

Elijah Muhammad's vision, it is true, was shot through with the dogma of white wickedness—even more so than the current teaching about "white supremacy" and "white fragility" in the Woke Age, in fact. Compare, however, the effects of the two ideologies on their respective votaries. When Malcolm Little heard the premise, "The white man is the devil," it excited in him a veritable mania to learn more. He sought the details, the facts of past conquest and exploitation, the philosophies that excused it, the religions that moralized it. He put his heart into it; he persisted in his research all day, every day for years, digging through the corpus of Western civilization to understand its devilish course from long ago to the present. The guilt of the West didn't keep him from exploring the West, no sir. He couldn't put it away! And along the way, he couldn't help finding counter-elements of truth and goodness. He read Schopenhauer, Kant, and Nietzsche. He read W. E. B. Du Bois's *Souls of Black Folk* and Carter Woodson's *Negro History*, Will Durant's

Story of Civilization and H. G. Wells's *Outline of History*. Elijah Muham-mad pictured a white devil out to ruin the harmony of black innocents; Malcolm opened *Paradise Lost* and found that "Milton and Elijah Muhammad were actually saying the same thing." He read Homer and Aesop, Shakespeare and the King James Bible, and in one prison debate argued that King James, "the greatest king who ever sat on the British throne," might have been the real author of Shakespeare's plays.[55] He attended Bible class and enjoyed catching the teacher admitting that St. Paul wasn't really white—or Jesus, either (the teacher admitted he was "brown," a compromise Malcolm let stand with a smile). After he left prison, built the membership of the Nation of Islam, and became the most sought-after college speaker in the country save for Senator Barry Goldwater, he didn't ignore or cut off his antagonists. No, he sought them out. He loved the arguments, which he called "exhilarating." "It was like being on the battlefield—with intellectual and philosophical bullets," he wrote. "It was an exciting battling with ideas."[56]

No such pleasures are available to our Millennials. They share the white-guilt narrative, but it doesn't ignite their curiosity: it kills it. They don't savor debate; it hurts them. The kids at Stanford don't want any more Shakespeare or Milton or King James Bible, and they don't even want to discuss why. They're just through with it. Or rather, they haven't read enough to know they're not through with it, that they've barely scratched the surface. But they do know they don't want any more, period. The mentors have divided them from the past, and the young possess neither the disposition nor the tools to heal the divide. Malcolm X's path through the great works of the Western heritage is no model for them; their horizons are limited to their online peer group. The connections they form online, the friends with whom they share a house, and coworkers of their own age group do not and cannot make up for this absence—nor does the woke religion, but where else can they find purpose and reason? If the woke religion did serve, if it did provide the "metaphysical comfort" that Nietzsche saw as the core appeal of faith, they wouldn't react so viscerally against their antagonists. If they could discover another religion, meaning, crusade, or vision out there for them, one that forsook the endless guilt and resentment of wokeness (it's an unforgiving sect), they would chase it with the very fervor with which they hated Donald Trump. But they can't.

That makes for another contrast with Malcolm X. When you watch clips of him on television in the months before his murder, on CBC's *Front Page Challenge* in 1965, for instance,[57] you see a man responding to sharp questions with no apprehension and with patient resolve. He corrects his interlocutors' misconceptions, and he acknowledges their points as correct, too, when he thinks they're speaking the truth. He smiles, and he explains, listens, and measures his own words. In a 1963 interview at Berkeley, a more congenial setting, Malcolm is more animated, but still deliberate.[58] When a black teacher there asks him about the Nation of Islam's reputation for advocating violence, Malcolm's voice doesn't rise, nor does his posture tighten. "The Muslims," he says, "who have accepted the religion of Islam and follow the religious guidance of the Honorable Elijah Muhammad have never bombed any churches, have never murdered any little girls, as was done in Birmingham, have never lynched anybody, have never at any time been guilty of initiating any aggressive acts of violence during the entire 33 years or more that the Honorable Elijah Muhammad has been teaching us." The words are piercing, but the demeanor remains steady and analytical. He proceeds to ascribe the accusation of violence to the "guilt complex" of white people in America, who realize their own brutality and fear that someday blacks will wake up and do unto them as they have done unto others. At moments his tone becomes strident—for instance, when he describes black demonstrators attacked by police dogs—but he soon settles back and quietly awaits the next question. He doesn't interrupt anyone; there's no wild outrage.

His demeanor is a sign of intellectual confidence. Malcolm is clearly a man who has read widely and built his convictions on years of open books and contemplation. The remark about a "guilt complex" couldn't be made by an individual who hadn't studied the psyche of his adversaries and who didn't believe that that psyche is a rightful object of study. In the CBC show, you can tell when Malcolm stares at his interlocutors that he is trying to imagine what goes on in their heads. It's the same inquisitiveness that drew him to *Paradise Lost* and Francis Bacon. The mythical history of Elijah Muhammad, wacky as it is, didn't make the Western tradition any less compelling to his protégé. Malcolm could sit across from eminent white men, whom he believed were the beneficiaries of black exploitation, and proceed to converse with all the composure of a professor. That's because he was deeply interested in their "reasons," as Renoir and Welles put it. At the end of the CBC show, when the host thanks him, Malcolm breaks into a big smile. He enjoyed the dialogue.

This is a pleasure beyond the reach of our heated Millennials. They haven't prepared for it. They haven't engaged intellectually with the editors of the *Stanford Review* or with Milo or Charles Murray or Heather Mac Donald—because they can't. Their mentors didn't train them for it. Today's young people aren't interested in the racist or sexist or otherwise benighted mind; they don't want to know—or rather, they know it all already. Malcolm saw racism as a psychological phenomenon with social, political, and economic extensions. For all his denunciation of white fiendishness, he was drawn to it as a scientific observer. It was kinetic, in his eyes, sinewy and intriguing. It called for observation. He never stopped reading about it. The utopian, on the other hand, doesn't read a word about it; he doesn't need to. Racism is no more intriguing to him than a rubber mallet. It doesn't have "reasons." It just is, and it's evil.

The intellectual fall from the '60s militant to the utopian Millennial is one of the great cultural catastrophes of our time. This decline is clearly the fault of our teachers and professors, the school boards and entertainment industry, our politicians and journalists. Every time they scoffed when a traditional guy warned against screen time, or when they killed a Great Books initiative, or put sneer quotes around the American Dream, they hurt and discouraged the youths nearby. We see the results every day. Compare the disquisitions of Malcolm X on television with those of the leading Millennial political figure of our time, Alexandria Ocasio-Cortez, and the decay is sadly manifest. The congresswoman is, I believe, highly intelligent—lots of brainpower there—but it is clear that she did not receive a strong humanities education. She never studied the best orators, she hasn't read very many novels, and apparently nobody has told her that she needs more such exercise. She should be much more articulate and knowledgeable, and she would have been if she had had better mentors. When conservatives mock her speech and point out errors of fact and gaps in basic knowledge, they can blame the teachers she had who didn't tell her what Marcuse told the young radicals: you have great potential, but you have much more reading to do.

What have we done to this generation? We have handed the young a history that is miserable—so forget about it. Our country has done many wrongs—so drop the patriotism. The literary canon excluded women and minorities—so skip it. The future is uncertain—so look out for yourself and trust that the "-isms" and phobias that demean and deny will soon end, and do your part to make that happen. We have told them that Great American Novels aren't so great, that the Old Masters had some real problems, and that Western Civilization was built on the labor of the oppressed. The mentors seem to believe that the more we denigrate the past, the more we shall escape its errors and make the twenty-first century the so-much-better antidiscrimination community that the world ought to be. But that's not how progress works. Social progress requires not just indictments of injustices, but positive inspirations as well—from the very past that utopians condemn in toto. Without them, young people lose their balance, fall sway to *ressentiment*. This woke gospel won't help them get through life. It's a false promise of goodness and comfort, and one hears little laughter coming from its high priests. The discrepancy between their utopia and current facts is too wide, and it's not closing quickly enough. The evils keep sticking around. At no point in the near future will blacks in America have proportionate representation in the elite professions, for the achievement gap has been large and stable for decades, and it runs from graduate school all the way down to kindergarten. Men and women will never be friends in the way the utopians envision—not when the burdens of childbearing are borne by women's bodies, not men's, and not when the darker aspects of sexual desire are so persistent. The mad competition for college admissions and plum positions continues, too, leaving a whole lot of losers in the game of success—and utopia isn't supposed to have any losers. God is an answer—another lesson of Malcolm—but the numbers of young Americans who claim no religious affiliation keep going up.

What we see before us is exactly what was going to happen once the elders decided not to pass along the world that had been passed along to them. For the Millennials' Boomer parents and mentors, the inherited cultural universe—Western Civilization, the Great American Novel, the Christian churches, and America from Plymouth Rock to the Founding to the Civil Rights Movement—was already deteriorating, but the remnants were still there for transmission. A sweeping self-mistrust set in, however; the mentors refused to be mentors any more, and they justified their irresponsibility as antiauthoritarian liberation. They didn't consider how the kids who thanked them at the time for the freedom not to be tutored would feel ten years later. The fractious, know-nothing thirty-year-old is what we got when we let the twelve-year-old drop his books and take up the screen and didn't even ask the classroom to counteract it. The dangerous utopian arises precisely out of this stew of abdicating elders, multicultural relativism, and superficial diversity. This formation—or malformation, rather—was set, and nothing challenged it, nothing of meaning and coherence and tradition. And there is no answer for it now. The Millennials have exited young adulthood forever; their intellectual habits are formed for life. They're lost, they're gone, it's over for them. They won't regret their youth; they won't look in the mirror. No matter how punishing life feels, they won't change their expectations, their beliefs, or their behavior. They don't believe their habits are the problem. It's the world that must change. They will "keep waiting / Waiting on the world to change," as the song says.[59] It's going to be a long wait.

Works Cited

ACT. *ACT College and Career Readiness Standards: English*. ACT. https://www.act.org/content/dam/act/unsecured/documents/CCRS-EnglishStandards.pdf.

———. *ACT College and Career Readiness Standards: Reading*. ACT. https://www.act.org/content/act/en/college-and-career-readiness/standards/reading-standards.html.

———. *The Condition of College & Career Readiness 2013*. ACT, 2013. https://files.eric.ed.gov/fulltext/ED558039.pdf.

Adkins, Amy. "What Millennials Want from Work and Life." Gallup Workplace, 10 May 2016. https://www.gallup.com/workplace/236477/millennials-work-life.aspx.

Adler, Margot. "Cuts to University's Programs Draw Outcry." NPR, 16 November 2010. https://www.npr.org/2010/11/15/131336270/cuts-to-university-s-humanities-program-draw-outcry.

Aldric, Anna. "SAT Scores over Time: 1972–2020." PrepScholar, 1 October 2020. https://blog.prepscholar.com/average-sat-scores-over-time.

Allen, Jeff, Brad Bolender, Yu Fang, Dongmei Li, and Tony Thompson. *Relating the ACT Indicator Understanding Complex Texts to College Course Grades*. ACT, 2016. https://www.act.org/content/dam/act/unsecured/documents/2016-Relating-the-ACT-Indicator-Understanding-Complex-Texts.pdf.

Anderson, Sherwood. *Winesburg, Ohio*. New York: Viking, 1958.

Arendt, Hannah. "The Crisis in Education." *Partisan Review* 25 (Fall 1958): 493–513.

Arnold, Matthew. "Preface to the First Edition of *Poems* [1853]." In Arnold, Matthew. *Poetry and Criticism of Matthew Arnold*, 203–14. Edited by A. Dwight Culler. Boston: Houghton Mifflin, 1961.

———. "The Function of Criticism at the Present Time." In Arnold, Matthew. *Poetry and Criticism of Matthew Arnold*, 237–58. Edited by A. Dwight Culler. Boston: Houghton Mifflin, 1961.

Arum, Richard, and Josipa Roksa. *Academically Adrift: Limited Learning on College Campuses*. Chicago: University of Chicago Press, 2010.

Associated Press. "Penn Campus Police Call University President's 'Die-In' Display 'Slap in the Face.'" Fox News, 12 December 2014. https://www.foxnews.com/us/penn-campus-police-call-university-presidents-die-in-display-slap-in-the-face.

Astin, Alexander W., Leticia Oseguera, Linda J. Sax, William S. Korn. *The American Freshman: Thirty-Five Year Trends, 1966–2001*. Los Angeles: Higher Education Research Institute, University of California, Los Angeles, 2002.

Badger Pundit. "The 'Shrieking Girl': Yale Student Expresses Her Need to Be 'Safe' from Halloween Costumes." YouTube, 8 November 2015. Video, 7:21. https://www.youtube.com/watch?v=V6ZVEVufWFI.

Barchas, Isaac D. "Stanford after the Fall: An Insider's View." *Academic Questions* 3, no. 1 (Winter 1989–90): 24–34.

Barlow, John Perry. "Leaving the Physical World" (speech delivered in Japan). Electronic Frontier Foundation, 1993. https://www.eff.org/pages/leaving-physical-world.

Bauerlein, Mark. *The Dumbest Generation: How the Digital Age Stupefies Young Americans and Jeopardizes Our Future; Or, Don't Trust Anyone under 30*. New York: Tarcher Penguin, 2008.

———. "Guilty of Cultural Appropriation in an 'Insensitive' Facebook Post." Minding the Campus, 25 November 2019. https://www.mindingthecampus.org/2019/11/25/guilty-of-cultural-appropriation-in-an-insensitive-facebook-post/.

———. "Nations Need a National Literature." The Agonist, 31 December 2019. http://theagonist.org/essays/2019/12/31/essays-bauerlein.html.

———. "Why Do American Students Lose Ground over Time?" *Atlanta Journal-Constution*, 15 December 2013. https://www.ajc.com/news/opin

ion/why-american-students-lose-ground-over-time/NAw9EKV5QxYx
cq7HvxybXL/.

Bauerlein, Mark, and Sandra Stotsky. *How Common Core's ELA Standards Place College Readiness at Risk*. Pioneer Institute, September 2012. https://irving tonparentsforum.files.wordpress.com/2013/04/bauerlein-stotsky -common-core-ela-standards-1.pdf.

Bauerlein, Mark, and Sunil Iyengar, "There's Good Reason to Worry about Declining Rates of Reading." *Guardian*, 19 February 2008. https:// www.theguardian.com/commentisfree/2008/feb/20/digitalmedia.internet.

Bennett, Sara, and Nancy Kalish. *The Case against Homework: How Homework Is Hurting Our Children and What We Can Do about It* (Crown, 2006). http:// www.thecaseagainsthomework.com/.

Beverley, John. *Against Literature*. Minneapolis, Minnesota: University of Minnesota Press, 1993.

Black Students at Emory. "List of Demands." *Emory Wheel*, 2 December 2015. https://emorywheel.com/black-students-at-emory-list-of-demands/.

Bowles, Nellie. "A Dark Consensus about Screens and Kids Begins to Emerge in Silicon Valley." *New York Times*, 26 October 2018. https://www.nyt imes.com/2018/10/26/style/phones-children-silicon-valley.html.

———. "The Digital Gap Between Rich and Poor Kids Is Not What We Expected." *New York Times*, 26 October 2018. https://www.nytimes.com /2018/10/26/style/digital-divide-screens-schools.html.

Boyack, Connor. "Why Socialism Is So Popular among Young People." Fox Business, 15 May 2019. https://www.foxbusiness.com/politics/ socialism-capitalism-youth-ocasio-cortez.

Bradshaw, Tom, and Bonnie Nichols. *Reading at Risk: A Survey of Literary Reading in America*. National Endowment for the Arts (Mark Bauerlein, Director, Office of Research and Analysis), June 2004. https://www.arts .gov/sites/default/files/ReadingAtRisk.pdf.

Cal State LA University Times. "Ben Shapiro Protest at Cal State LA." YouTube, 25 February 2016. Video, 2:43. https://www.youtube.com/wa tch?v=NRVe6UCmq2I.

Carlson, Scott. "The Net Generation Goes to College." *Chronicle of Higher Education*, 7 October 2005. https://www.chronicle.com/article/the-net-generation-goes-to-college/.

Carlson, Tucker, and Neil Patel. "Why Kids Are Socialists and How to Start Fixing It." Daily Caller, 1 November 2019. https://dailycaller.com/2019/10/31/tucker-carlson-and-neil-patel-why-kids-are-socialists-and-how-to-start-fixing-it/.

CBC. "Malcolm X on Front Page Challenge, 1965: CBC Archives | CBC." YouTube, 7 April 2010. Video, 7:48. https://www.youtube.com/watch?v=C7IJ7npTYrU.

Center for Teaching Innovation. "The Millennial Generation: Understanding & Engaging Today's Learners." Cornell University. https://teaching.cornell.edu/resource/millennial-generation-understanding-engaging-todays-learners.

CIRCLE Staff. *The Youth Vote in 2012*. CIRCLE (Center for Information & Research on Civic Learning & Engagement), 10 May 2013. https://circle.tufts.edu/sites/default/files/2019-12/youth_vote_2012.pdf.

CNBC. "Milo Yiannopoulos: What the 'Alt Right' Is Really About (Full Interview) | Power Lunch." YouTube, 8 September 2016. Video, 7:44. https://www.youtube.com/watch?v=Lgl53EXInPc.

The College Fix. "TheCollegeFix.com: Milo Yiannopoulos Enters UCSB." YouTube, 27 May 2016. Video, 0:42. https://www.youtube.com/watch?v=zK6wkAfNwn0.

College Pulse, FIRE, RealClear Education. *2020 College Free Speech Rankings: What's the Climate for Free Speech on College Campuses?* College Pulse, Foundation for Individual Rights in Education (FIRE), and RealClearEducation, 2020. https://marketplace.collegepulse.com/img/2020_college_free_speech_rankings.pdf.

Collins, Allan, and Richard Halverson. *Rethinking Education in the Age of Technology: The Digital Revolution and Schooling in America*. New York and London: Teachers College Press, Columbia University, 2009.

Conrad, Joseph. *The Shadow-Line and Two Other Tales: Typhoon, The Secret Sharer.* Edited by Morton Dauwen Zabel. Garden City, New York: Doubleday Anchor Books, 1959.

Crèvecoeur, J. Hector St. John de. *Letters from an American Farmer.* Philadelphia: Matthew Carey, 1793.

Cultural Research Center. "American Worldview Inventory 2020—At a Glance." Arizona Christian University, 22 September 2020. https://www .arizonachristian.edu/wp-content/uploads/2020/09/CRC_AWVI2020 _Release10_Digital_01_20200922.pdf.

Dare, Michael. "Touch of Evil's Second Tracking Shot, Just As Long and Impressive As the Opening." YouTube, 16 February 2018. Video, 5:23. https:// www.youtube.com/watch?v=tzcNU_1KqG0.

Dean, Katie. "Maine Students Hit the IBooks." *Wired*, 9 January 2002. https:// www.wired.com/2002/01/maine-students-hit-the-ibooks/.

Dillon, Sam. "A Great Year for Ivy League Schools, but Not So Good for Applicants to Them." *New York Times*, 4 April 2007. https://www.nyt imes.com/2007/04/04/education/04colleges.html.

Donnelly, Grace. "Half of Millennials Support Colleges [*sic*] Restricting Free Speech 'In Extreme Cases.'" *Fortune*, 12 September 2017. https://fortune.com /2017/09/12/millennials-hate-speech-freedom-of-speech/.

Douthat, Ross. "The Truth about Harvard," *Atlantic*, March 2005, 95–99. https:// www.theatlantic.com/magazine/archive/2005/03/the-truth -about-harvard/303726/.

Dretzin, Rachel, and John Maggio, prods. *Frontline*. Season 26, episode 6, "Growing Up Online." Aired 22 January 2008 on PBS. https://www.pbs .org/wgbh/pages/frontline/kidsonline/.

Duberman, Martin. "An Experiment in Education." *Daedalus* 97 (Winter 1968): 318–41.

Du Bois, W. E. B. *The Souls of Black Folk*. In Du Bois, W. E. B. *W. E. B. Du Bois, Writings*. Edited by Nathan Irvin Huggins. New York: Viking Press, Library of America, 1986.

Durst, Jacob. "Breitbart Editor Brings Crowd, Protesters to White Hall." *Emory Wheel*, 14 April 2016. https://emorywheel.com/milo-yian nopoulos-speaks/.

Eagan, Kevin, Jennifer B. Lozano, Sylvia Hurtado, and Matthew Case. *The American Freshman: National Norms Fall 2013*. Los Angeles: Higher Education Research Institute, University of California, Los Angeles, 2013. https://www.heri.ucla.edu/monographs/TheAmericanFreshman2013.pdf.

Eakin, Emily. "More Ado (Yawn) about Great Books," *New York Times*, 8 April 2001. https://www.nytimes.com/2001/04/08/education/more-ado -yawn-about-great-books.html.

Eberstadt, Mary. "The New Intolerance." *First Things*, March 2015. https:// www.firstthings.com/article/2015/03/the-new-intolerance.

Ekins, Emily. "What Americans Think about Poverty, Wealth, and Work." Cato Institute, 24 September 2019. https://www.cato.org/publications /survey-reports/what-americans-think-about-poverty-wealth-work.

Ekins, Emily, and Joy Pullman. "Why So Many Millennials Are Socialists." The Federalist, 15 February 2016. https://thefederalist.com/2016/02/15 /why-so-many-millennials-are-socialists/.

Elliott, Harry. "The Western Civilization Witch Hunt," *Stanford Review*, 7 March 2016. https://stanfordreview.org/the-western-civilization-witch-hunt/.

Epstein, Joseph. "The Tyranny of the 'Tolerant.'" *Wall Street Journal*, 9 October 2020. https://www.wsj.com/articles/the-tyranny-of-the -tolerant-11602278220.

Ferguson, Andrew. *Crazy U: One Dad's Crash Course in Getting His Kid into College*. New York: Simon & Schuster, 2011.

FilMagicians. "Orson Welles Talks Touch of Evil, James Cagney & Jean Renoir." YouTube, 1 October 2017. Video, 13:14. https://www.youtube .com/watch?v=niMGXhS28YI.

FIRE. "Religious Liberty in Peril on Campus, National Surveys Reveal." Foundation for Individual Rights in Education (FIRE), 10 November 2003. https://www.thefire.org/religious-liberty-in-peril-on-campus -national-surveys-reveal/.

Fitzgerald, F. Scott. *The Great Gatsby*. New York: Scribner's, 1925.

Flaherty, Colleen. "Major Exodus." Inside Higher Ed, 26 January 2015. https://www.insidehighered.com/news/2015/01/26/where-have-all-english-majors-gone.

———. "Suspended for Using N-Word." Inside Higher Education, 31 August 2018. https://www.insidehighered.com/news/2018/08/31/n-word-simply-be-avoided-or-emory-wrong-suspend-law-professor-who-used-it.

Forster, E. M. *Aspects of the Novel*. New York: Harcourt, 1956.

Galston, William A., and Clara Hendrickson. "How Millennials Voted This Election." Brookings Institution, 21 November 2016. https://www.brookings.edu/blog/fixgov/2016/11/21/how-millennials-voted/.

GenDIY. "Millennials Are Tolerant, Educated, Enterprising, and Hyphenated." HuffPost, 21 February 2015. https://www.huffpost.com/entry/millennials-are-tolerant-_b_6350434.

Gleick, James. *Faster: The Acceleration of Just About Everything*. New York: Pantheon, 1999.

Greenberg, Eric, and Karl Weber. "Why the Youth Vote Is the Big Story—for 2008 and for Decades to Come." HuffPost, 25 May 2011. https://www.huffpost.com/entry/why-the-youth-vote-is-the_b_158273.

Greene, Graham. *A Burnt-Out Case*. New York: Bantam, 1962.

Hagan, Melissa J., Michael R. Sladek, Linda J. Luecken, and Leah D. Doane. "Event-Related Clinical Distress in College Students: Responses to the 2016 U.S. Presidential Election." *Journal of American College Health* 68, no. 1 (2018): 21–25.

Hartman, Andrew. "The Millennial Left's War against Liberalism." *Washington Post*, 20 July 2017. https://www.washingtonpost.com/news/made-by-history/wp/2017/07/20/the-millennial-lefts-war-against-liberalism/.

Hawthorne, Nathaniel. *The Marble Faun: or, The Romance of Monte Beni*. 2 vols. Boston: Ticknor & Fields, 1864.

Hayot, Eric. "The Humanities as We Know Them Are Doomed. Now What?" *Chronicle of Higher Education*, 1 July 2018. https://www.chronicle.com/article/the-humanities-as-we-know-them-are-doomed-now-what/.

Heller, Nathan. "The Big Uneasy: What's Roiling the Liberal-Arts Campus?" *New Yorker*, 30 May 2016, 48–57.

Herold, Benjamin. "1-to-1 Laptop Initiatives Boost Student Scores, Study Finds." *Education Week*, 17 May 2016. https://www.edweek.org/techno logy/1-to-1-laptop-initiatives-boost-student-scores-study-finds/2016/05.

Herbert, Bob. "Here Come the Millennials." *New York Times*, 13 May 2008. https://www.nytimes.com/2008/05/13/opinion/13herbert.html.

Hirsch, E. D., Jr. *Cultural Literacy: What Every American Needs to Know*. New York: Houghton Mifflin, 1987.

———. "Introduction—The Knowledge Requirement: What *Every* American Needs to Know." In *The State of the American Mind: 16 Leading Critics on the New Anti-Intellectualism*, 1–16. Edited by Mark Bauerlein and Adam Bellow. West Conshohocken, PA: Templeton Press, 2015.

Hodge, Dawn. "Camille Paglia—Student Protest (Shouting and Screaming at 48:00)." YouTube, 16 April 2019. Video, 50:34. https://www.youtube .com/watch?v=mLsQHQfPYW4.

Hoffower, Hillary, and Allana Akhtar. "Lonely, Burned Out, and Depressed: The State of Millennials' Mental Health 2020." Business Insider, 10 October 2020. https://www.businessinsider.com/millennials-mental -health-burnout-lonely-depressed-money-stress?op=1.

Homer. *The Iliad*. Translated by Robert Fagles. New York: Viking, 1990.

Horowitz, Michael. "Portrait of the Marxist as an Old Trouper." *Playboy*, March 1970: 23–32, 175–76, 228. https://www.marcuse.org/herbert/new sevents/1970/709PlayboyInt.htm.

Howe, Neil. "Who Is the Real 'Dumbest Generation'?" *Washington Post*, 7 December 2008. https://www.washingtonpost.com/wp-dyn/content/ar ticle/2008/12/05/AR2008120502601.html.

Howe, Neil, and William Strauss. *Millennials Rising: The Next Great Generation*. New York: Vintage: 5 September 2000.

Ireland, Corydon. "Welcoming Gen Ed: Harvard Forum Extols New General Education Requirements." *Harvard Gazette*, 4 September 2009. https:// news.harvard.edu/gazette/story/2009/09/welcoming-gen-ed/.

Ito, Joichi. "In an Open-Source Society, Innovating by the Seat of Our Pants." *New York Times*, 5 December 2011. https://www.nytimes.com/2011/12/06/science/joichi-ito-innovating-by-the-seat-of-our-pants.html.

Ito, Mizuko, Sonja Baumer, Matteo Bittanti, danah boyd, Rachel Cody, Becky Herr-Stephenson, Heather A. Horst et. al. *Hanging Out, Messing Around, and Geeking Out: Kids Living and Learning with New Media*. Boston: MIT Press, 2010.

Iyengar, Sunil, Sarah Sullivan, Bonnie Nichols, Tom Bradshaw, Kelli Rogowski, Mark Bauerlein. *To Read or Not to Read: A Question of National Consequence* (National Endowment for the Arts, November 2007). https://www.arts.gov/sites/default/files/ToRead.pdf.

Jaschik, Scott. "Grade Inflation, Higher and Higher." Inside Higher Ed, 29 March 2016. https://www.insidehighered.com/news/2016/03/29/survey-finds-grade-inflation-continues-rise-four-year-colleges-not-community-college.

Johnson, Steven. "Colleges Lose a 'Stunning' 651 Foreign-Language Programs in 3 Years." *Chronicle of Higher Education* 22 January 2019. https://www.chronicle.com/article/colleges-lose-a-stunning-651-foreign-language-programs-in-3-years/.

Johnson, Steven. "Dawn of the Digital Natives." *Guardian*, 7 February 2008. https://www.theguardian.com/technology/2008/feb/07/internet.literacy.

Kabbany, Jennifer. "Stanford Erupts in Controversy After Student Petition Calls for Mandatory Western Civ Classes." The College Fix, 25 February 2016. https://www.thecollegefix.com/stanford-erupts-controversy-student-petition-calls-mandatory-western-civ-classes/.

———. "Stanford Snowflakes Meltdown over April Fool's Joke Mocking Leftist Campus 'Demands.'" The College Fix, 1 April 2016. https://www.thecollegefix.com/stanford-snowflakes-meltdown-april-fools-joke-mocking-leftist-campus-demands/.

Kaufman, Elliot, and Harry Elliott. "Who's Teaching Stanford?" *National Review*, 7 April 2016. https://www.nationalreview.com/2016/04/whos-teaching-stanford-campus-activists-issue-diversity-demands/.

Keen, Andrew. *The Internet Is Not the Answer*. New York: Atlantic Monthly Press, 2015.

Kemp, Amanda. "Blacks Feel Unwanted." *Stanford Daily*, 28 April 1987.

Kenny, Sarah. "'We Demand More': Student Leaders across the Country Challenge Politicians to Combat Hate." *Washington Post*, 13 November 2017. https://www.washingtonpost.com/news/grade-point/wp/2017/11/13/we-demand-more-student-leaders-across-the-country-challenge-political-leaders-to-do-more-to-combat-hate/.

Kravitz, Kayley. "Ambitious Millennials." HuffPost, 7 March 2013. https://www.huffpost.com/entry/ambitious-millennials_b_2812937.

Kirby, Emily Hoban, and Kei Kawashima-Ginsberg. *The Youth Vote in 2008*. CIRCLE (The Center for Information & Research on Civic Learning & Engagement), 17 August 2009. http://www.whatkidscando.org/youth_on_the_trail_2012/pdf/CIRCLE%20youith%20vote%202008.pdf.

Kreeger, Erika Lynn Abigail Persephone Joanna. "The White Civ's Burden." *Stanford Daily*, 22 February 2016. https://www.stanforddaily.com/2016/02/22/the-white-civs-burden/.

Kurtz, Stanley. *The Lost History of Western Civilization*. New York: National Association of Scholars, 11 January 2020. https://www.nas.org/storage/app/media/Reports/Lost%20History%20of%20Western%20Civ/The%20Lost%20History%20of%20Western%20Civilization.pdf.

Lai, Justin. "The Death of Stanford's Humanities Core." *Stanford Review*, 14 March 2015. https://stanfordreview.org/the-death-of-stanfords-humanities-core/.

Lambert, Craig. "Nonstop: Today's Superhero Undergraduates Do '3,000 Things at 150 Percent.'" *Harvard Magazine*, March–April 2010. https://www.harvardmagazine.com/2010/03/nonstop.

Lanham, Richard A. "The Electronic Word: Literary Study and the Digital Revolution." *New Literary History* 20, no. 2 (Winter 1989): 265–90.

Learning and Academic Resource Center. "Learning and Academic Resource Center." University of California, Irvine. www.larc.uci.edu.

Leavis, F. R. *The Common Pursuit*. New York: NYU Press, 1964.

Lemann, Nicholas. "The Case for a New Kind of Core." *Chronicle of Higher Education*, 27 November 2016. https://www.chronicle.com/article/the-case-for-a-new-kind-of-core/.

Lenhart, Amanda, Rich Ling, Scott Campbell, and Kristen Purcell. *Teens and Mobile Phones*. Pew Research Center, 20 April 2010. https://www.pew research.org/internet/2010/04/20/teens-and-mobile-phones/.

Levitz, Eric. "This One Chart Explains Why the Kids Back Bernie." *New York*, 15 February 2020. https://nymag.com/intelligencer/2020/02/this-one-chart-explains-why-young-voters-back-bernie-sanders.html.

Lewis, Sinclair. *Main Street*. New York: Signet, 1961.

Lindemann, Erika. "Freshman Composition: No Place for Literature." *College English* 55, no. 3 (March 1993): 311–16.

Lock, Samantha. "'To Kill a Mockingbird,' Other Books Banned from California Schools over Racism Concerns." *Newsweek*, 13 November 2020. https://www.newsweek.com/kill-mockingbird-other-books-banned-california-schools-over-racism-concerns-1547241?amp=1&__twitter_impression=true.

Logue, Josh. "Chalk It Up to Trump." Inside Higher Ed, 25 March 2016. https://www.insidehighered.com/news/2016/03/25/debate-grows-over-pro-trump-chalkings-emory.

Lougee, Carolyn C. "Women, History, and the Humanities: An Argument in Favor of the General Studies Curriculum." *Women's Studies Quarterly* 9, no. 1 (Spring 1981): 4–7.

Lowrey, Annie. "Millennials Don't Stand a Chance." *Atlantic*, 13 April 2020. https://www.theatlantic.com/ideas/archive/2020/04/millennials-are-new-lost-generation/609832/.

Ludden, Jennifer. "Why Aren't Teens Reading Like They Used To?" NPR, 12 May 2014. https://www.npr.org/2014/05/12/311111701/why-arent-teens-reading-like-they-used-to.

Lukianoff, Greg, and Jonathan Haidt. *The Coddling of the American Mind: How Good Intentions and Bad Ideas Are Setting Up a Generation for Failure*. New York: Penguin, 2018.

Maguire, Jessica. "MIT's Jenkins, Johnson Talk Community, Creativity." Gamasutra, 17 March 2008. https://www.gamasutra.com/php-bin/news _index.php?story=17829.

Marcinek, Andrew. "Project-Based Learning for Digital Citizens: Collaboration, Networking and Results." Edutopia, 9 December 2011. https://www.edutopia.org/blog/PBL-digital-citizens-andrew-marcinek.

Marcuse, Herbert. *An Essay on Liberation*. Boston: Beacon Press, 1969.

Martin, Steven, Nan Marie Astone, and H. Elizabeth Peters. "Fewer Marriages, More Divergence: Marriage Projections for Millennials to Age 40." Urban Institute, 29 April 2014. https://www.urban.org/research /publication/fewer-marriages-more-divergence-marriage-projections -millennials-age-40.

Mayer, John. "Waiting on the World to Change." Track 1 on *Continuum*. Aware/ Columbia/Sony, 2006, compact disc.

Molyneux, Guy, Ruy Teixeira, and John Whaley. *The Generation Gap on Government*. Center for American Progress, 27 July 2010. https://www .americanprogress.org/wp-content/uploads/issues/2010/07/pdf/dww _millennials_execsumm.pdf.

Moran, Lee. "Bill Maher Blasts Social Media Tycoons for Creating Such Addictive Products." HuffPost, 13 May 2017. https://www.huffingtonpost .ca/entry/bill-maher-social-media-drug-dealers_n_5916a78ce4b0 031e737dd975.

Morning Consult and Politico. *National Tracking Poll #200766*. Morning Consult and Politico, 17–19 July 2020. https://www.politico.com/f/?id= 00000173-7329-d26c-af77-7b7f646a0000.

National Assessment Governing Board. *Reading Framework for the National Assessment of Educational Progress*. U.S. Department of Education, September 2010. https://www.nagb.gov/content/nagb/assets/documents /publications/frameworks/reading/2011-reading-framework.pdf.

National Center for Education Statistics. *NAEP 2012 Trends in Academic Progress: Reading 1971–2012, Mathematics 1973–2012*. U.S. Department of Education, 2013. https://nces.ed.gov/nationsreportcard/subject/pub lications/main2012/pdf/2013456.pdf.

———. *The Nation's Report Card: U.S. History 2010.* U.S. Department of Education, June 2011. https://nces.ed.gov/nationsreportcard/pubs/main 2010/2011468.asp#section2.

———. "The Nation's Report Card: 2018 U.S. History, Geography, and Civics at Grade 8, Highlights Reports." U.S. Department of Education, 23 April 2020. https://nces.ed.gov/pubsearch/pubsinfo.asp?pubid=2020017.

National Commission on Excellence in Education. *A Nation at Risk: The Imperative for Education Reform.* U.S. Department of Education, April 1983. https://edreform.com/wp-content/uploads/2013/02/A_Nation_At _Risk_1983.pdf.

National Survey of Student Engagement. *Fostering Student Engagement Campuswide—Annual Results 2011.* Bloomington, Indiana: Indiana University Center for Postsecondary Research, 2011. https://scholarwo rks.iu.edu/dspace/bitstream/handle/2022/23408/NSSE_2011_Annual _Results.pdf?sequence=1&isAllowed=y.

TheNexusInstitute. "George Steiner on Myths and Music." YouTube, 23 June 2010. Video, 6:37. https://www.youtube.com/watch?v=oKh7edvRvFQ.

Nielsen. "U.S. Teen Mobile Report Calling Yesterday, Texting Today, Using Apps Tomorrow." Nielsen, 14 October 2010. https://www.nielsen.com/us/en/insi ghts/article/2010/u-s-teen-mobile-report-calling-yesterday-texting -today-using-apps-tomorrow/.

Noel-Levitz, Inc.. *2008 National Freshman Attitudes Report.* Noel-Levitz, Inc., 2008. https://accreditation.uni.edu/sites/default/files/documents /national_freshmen_attitudes_report_noel-levitz_208_1.pdf.

Novak, Michael. *Writing from Left to Right: My Journey from Liberal to Conservative.* New York: Image, 2013.

O'Reilly, Tim. "What Is Web 2.0: Design Patterns and Business Models for the Next Generation of Software." O'Reilly, 30 September 2005. https:// www.oreilly.com/pub/a/web2/archive/what-is-web-20.html.

O'Rourke, P. J. "This Is Why Millennials Adore Socialism." *New York Post,* 12 September 2020. https://nypost.com/2020/09/12/pj-orourke-this-is -why-millennials-adore-socialism/.

OU Student Government Association. "In Solidarity, We Are #StudentsAgainstHate." Facebook, 12 November 2017. Video, 7:29. https://www.facebook.com/watch/live/?v=879056162253125&ref=watch_perma link.

Paglia, Camille. *Sexual Personae: Art and Decadence from Nefertiti to Emily Dickinson*. New York: Vintage Books, 1991.

Palfrey, John, and Urs Gasser. *Born Digital: Understanding the First Generation of Digital Natives*. New York: Basic Books, 2008.

Perie, Marianne, Rebecca Moran, Anthony D. Lutkus, and William Tirre. *NAEP 2004 Trends in Academic Progress: Three Decades of Student Performance in Reading and Mathematics*. National Center for Education Statistics, U.S. Department of Education, July 2005. https://nces.ed.gov/nationsreportcard/pdf/main2005/2005464.pdf.

Pew Research Center. *Millennials in Adulthood: Detached from Institutions, Networked with Friends*. Pew Research Center, 7 March 2014. https://www.pewsocialtrends.org/2014/03/07/millennials-in-adulthood/.

Phelps, William Lyon. "As Mrs. Wharton Sees Us." Review of *The Age of Innocence*, by Edith Wharton. *New York Times*, 17 October 1920. https://timesmachine.nytimes.com/timesmachine/1920/10/17/113314519.html?pageNumber=26.

Pogue, David. "Smartphones Mean You Will No Longer Have to Memorize Facts." *Scientific American*, 1 August 2013. https://www.scientificameri can.com/article/smartphones-mean-no-longer-memorize-facts/.

Pound, Ezra. *Hugh Selwyn Mauberley*. London: Ovid Press, 1920.

———. "What I Feel about Walt Whitman." In Pound, Ezra. *Selected Prose, 1909–1965*, 145–46. Edited and with and introduction by William Cookson. New York: New Directions, 1973.

Poushter, Jacob. "40% of Millennials OK with Limiting Speech Offensive to Minorities." Pew Research Center, 20 November 2015. https://www.pew research.org/fact-tank/2015/11/20/40-of-millennials-ok-with-limiting -speech-offensive-to-minorities/.

Prensky, Marc. "Digital Natives, Digital Immigrants." *On the Horizon* 9, no. 5 (October 2001). https://www.marcprensky.com/writing/Prensky%20-%20 Digital%20Natives,%20Digital%20Immigrants%20-%20Part1.pdf.

Price, Leah. "You Are What You Read." *New York Times*, 23 December 2007.

Pryor, John H., Sylvia Hurtado, Victor B. Saenz, Jessica S. Korn, José Luis Santos, and William S. Korn. *The American Freshman: National Norms Fall 2006.* Los Angeles: Higher Education Research Institute, University of California, Los Angeles, 2006. https://www.heri.ucla.edu/PDFs/pubs/TFS/Norms/ Monographs/TheAmericanFreshman2006.pdf.

Rainie, Lee, Scott Keeter, and Andrew Perrin. *Trust and Distrust in America.* Pew Research Center, 22 July 2019. https://www.pewresearch.org/polit ics/2019/07/22/trust-and-distrust-in-america/.

reelblack. "Malcolm X—Interview at Berkeley (1963)." YouTube, 11 June 2018. Video, 40:57. https://www.youtube.com/watch?v=FZMrti8QcPA&t=739s.

Reich, Charles A. "Reflections: The Greening of America." *New Yorker*, 26 September 1970. https://www.newyorker.com/magazine/1970/09/26/ reflections-the-greening-of-america.

Richardson, Will. "World without Walls: Learning Well with Others." Edutopia, 3 December 2008. https://www.edutopia.org/collaboration-age-technology-will-richardson.

Rideout, Victoria J., Ulla G. Foehr, and Donald F. Roberts. *Generation M²: Media in the Lives of 8- to 18-Year-Olds.* Kaiser Family Foundation, 20 January 2010. https://www.kff.org/other/event/generation-m2-media-in-the-lives-of/.

Right News Network. "Evergreen Top 20 Monstrous Moments." YouTube, 2 June 2017. Video, 9:08. https://www.youtube.com/watch?v=8YnSYvhSeyI.

Robbins, Alexandra. *The Overachievers: The Secret Lives of Driven Kids.* New York: Hyperion, 2006.

Rosenthal, Zach, and Debnil Sur. "History Not Only by the Victors." *Stanford Daily*, 23 February 2016. https://www.stanforddaily.com/2016/02/23 /history-not-only-by-the-victors/.

Rougemont, Denis de. *Love in the Western World.* Princeton, New Jersey: Princeton University Press, 1983.

Saad, Lydia. "Socialism as Popular as Capitalism among Young Adults in U.S." Gallup News, 25 November 2019. https://news.gallup.com/poll/268766/socialism-popular-capitalism-among-young-adults.aspx.

Safer, Morley. "Here Come the Millennials." In *60 Minutes*. Season 40, episode 8, "Superbug/Insanity on Death Row/Here Come the Millenials." Aired 11 November 2007 on CBS. https://www.cbsnews.com/news/the-millennials-are-coming/.

Sanburn, Josh. "Millennials: The Next Greatest Generation?" *Time*, 9 May 2013. https://nation.time.com/2013/05/09/millennials-the-next-greatest-generation/.

Sanders, Sam. "Obama Warns Campus Protesters against Urge to 'Shut Up' Opposition." NPR, 21 December 2015. https://www.npr.org/2015/12/21/460282127/obama-warns-campus-protesters-against-urge-to-shut-up-opposition.

Satia, Priya. "The Whitesplaining of History Is Over." *Chronicle of Higher Education*, 28 March 2018. https://www.chronicle.com/article/the-whitesplaining-of-history-is-over/.

Schmidt, Benjamin M. "The History BA since the Great Recession: The 2018 AHA Majors Report." *Perspectives on History*, 26 November 2018. https://www.historians.org/publications-and-directories/perspectives-on-history/december-2018/the-history-ba-since-the-great-recession-the-2018-aha-majors-report.

Schneider, Alison. "Stanford Revisits the Course That Set Off the Culture Wars." *Chronicle of Higher Education*, 9 May 1997. https://www.chronicle.com/article/stanford-revisits-the-course-that-set-off-the-culture-wars/.

Scholastic. *2010 Kids & Family Reading Report: Turning the Page in the Digital Age*. Scholastic, 2010. http://mediaroom.scholastic.com/files/KFRR_2010.pdf.

Smith, Christian, with Monica Lundquist Denton. *Soul Searching: The Religious and Spiritual Lives of American Teenagers*. New York: Oxford University Press, 2005.

Smith, M. Earl. "Millennials Are the 'Most Tolerant Generation,' Hillary Clinton Says at West Phila. Rally." *Daily Pennsylvanian*, 16 August 2016. https://www.thedp.com/article/2016/08/hillary-clinton-west-phila-rally.

Snyder, Thomas D., Cristobal del Brey, and Sally A. Dillow. *Digest of Education Statistics: 2018*. National Center for Education Statistics, December 2019. https://nces.ed.gov/pubs2020/2020009.pdf.

Soeiro, Loren. "Why Are Millennials So Anxious and Unhappy?" *Psychology Today*, 24 July 2019. https://www.psychologytoday.com/us/blog/i-hear-you/201907/why-are-millennials-so-anxious-and-unhappy.

Standage, Tom. "The Culture War: How New Media Keeps [*sic*] Corrupting Our Children." *Wired*, 1 April 2006. https://www.wired.com/2006/04/war/.

Stanford Review editors. "The Case for a Western Civilization Requirement at Stanford." *Stanford Review*, 21 February 2016. https://stanfordreview.org/the-case-for-a-western-civilization-requirement-at-stanford/.

Stanford University. "Degrees Conferred." Institutional Research & Decision Support. https://irds.stanford.edu/data-findings/degrees-conferred.

———. "General Education Requirements for Undergrads." Stanford University. https://undergrad.stanford.edu/academic-planning/degree-requirements/general-education-requirements-undergrads.

———. *Report of the Commission on Undergraduate Education*. Commission on Undergraduate Education, 1994. https://gcasper.stanford.edu/pdf/CUE Report.pdf.

———. *The Study of Education at Stanford, No. 1*. Stanford University, November 1968. https://files.eric.ed.gov/fulltext/ED032844.pdf.

———. *The Study of Education at Stanford, No. 2*. Stanford University, November 1968. https://files.eric.ed.gov/fulltext/ED032845.pdf.

Steinmann, Jeff. "What Old People Can Learn from Millennials." HuffPost, 24 July 2014. https://www.huffpost.com/entry/life-lessons-_b_5588193.

Strauss, Valerie. "As Homework Grows, So Do Arguments against It." *Washington Post*, 12 September 2006. https://www.washingtonpost.com/archive/politics/2006/09/12/as-homework-grows-so-do-arguments-against-it/6e8517d8-e989-4b47-abf6-83ce4654f6a6/.

Student Government Association [JMU]. "Charlottesville Statement from Jewel Hurt, JMU Student Body President." Facebook, 12 November 2017. Video, 3:24. https://www.facebook.com/watch/?v=10154740781306920.

Sunstein, Cass R. "The Law of Group Polarization." John M. Olin Program in Law and Economics Working Paper No. 91, 7 December 1999. https://chicagounbound.uchicago.edu/cgi/viewcontent.cgi?article=1541&context=law_and_economics.

Tapscott, Don. *Grown Up Digital: How the Net Generation Is Changing Your World.* New York: McGraw-Hill, 2009.

Taylor, Paul, and Scott Keeter, eds. *Millennials: A Portrait of Generation Next: Confident. Connected. Open to Change.* Pew Research Center, 24 February 2010. https://www.pewsocialtrends.org/2010/02/24/millennials-confident-connected-open-to-change/.

Thomas, Alex. "Authoritarian Leftist 'Activists' Demand the End of Free Speech, Extensive Re-Education." The Burning Platform, 17 November 2015. https://www.theburningplatform.com/2015/11/17/authoritarian-leftist-activists-demand-the-end-of-free-speech-extensive-re-education/.

Thompson, Charles. "Lawmaker Demands Penn State President Eric Barron Apologize for 'Hands-Up' Gesture at Protest," *Patriot-News*, 9 December 2014. https://www.pennlive.com/midstate/2014/12/state_representative_to_psu_pr.html.

Tocqueville, Alexis de. *Democracy in America.* Translated, edited, and with an introduction by Harvey C. Mansfield and Delba Winthorp. Chicago: University of Chicago Press, 2000.

Tolstoy, Leo. *War and Peace.* Translated by Richard Pevear and Larissa Volokhonsky. New York: Vintage, 2008.

Turchin, Peter. "Blame Rich, Overeducated Elites as Our Society Frays." Bloomberg Opinion, 20 November 2013. https://www.bloomberg.com/opinion/articles/2013-11-20/blame-rich-overeducated-elites-as-our-society-frays.

Twenge, Jean. *iGen: Why Today's Super-Connected Kids Are Growing Up Less Rebellious, More Tolerant, Less Happy—and Completely Unprepared for Adulthood (and What This Means for the Rest of Us).* New York: Atria, 2017.

Twenge, Jean, Nathan T. Carter, and W. Keith Campbell. "Time Period, Generational, and Age Differences in Tolerance for Controversial Beliefs and Lifestyles in the United States, 1972–2012." *Social Forces* 94, no. 1 (September 2015): 379–99.

UC Berkeley Graduate Assembly. "Statement of Solidarity with Student Body Presidents across the Country, Remembering Charlottesville." Facebook, 12 November 2017. https://www.facebook.com/watch/live/?v=1015476 8704036213&ref=watch_permalink.

UCSB Associated Students. "UCSB #StudentsAgainstHate." KZClip, 16 November 2017. https://kzclip.com/video/hPC3EO4wEWg /ucsb-studentsagainsthate.html.

University of Texas at Austin. "Academic Policies and Procedures." School of Undergraduate Studies. . https://catalog.utexas.edu/undergraduate/ undergraduate-studies/academic-policies-and-procedures.

U.S. Bureau of Labor Statistics. *American Time Use Survey—2010 Results*. U.S. Department of Labor, 22 June 2011. https://www.bls.gov/news.rele ase/archives/atus_06222011.pdf.

———. *American Time Use Survey—2019 Results*. U.S. Department of Labor, 25 June 2020. https://www.bls.gov/news.release/pdf/atus.pdf.

UVA Student Council. "#StudentsAgainstHate." Facebook, 12 November 2017. Letter of protest. https://www.facebook.com/uvastudco/photos/pcb.101558 49298669715/10155849294604715.

———. "Signatures of Solidarity." Facebook, 12 November 2017. Letter of protest. https://www.facebook.com/uvastudco/photos/pcb.1015584929 8669715/10155849294729715.

Van Dam, Andrew. "The Unluckiest Generation in U.S. History." *Washington Post*, 5 June 2020. https://www.washingtonpost.com/business/2020/05/27/ millennial-recession-covid/.

Vice Staff. "53 Reasons Life Sucks for Millennials." Vice, 30 March 2018. https://www.vice.com/en/article/8xkx43/53-reasons-life-sucks -for-millennials.

Victims of Communism Memorial Foundation and YouGov. *U.S. Attitudes toward Socialism, Communism, and Collectivism*. Victims of Communism

Memorial Foundation and YouGov, 20 October 2020. https://victimsofco
mmunism.org/wp-content/uploads/2020/10/10.19.20-VOC
-YouGov-Survey-on-U.S.-Attitudes-Toward-Socialism-Communism
-and-Collectivism.pdf.

Villasenor, John. "Views among College Students Regarding the First
Amendment: Results from a New Survey." Brookings Institution, 18
September 2017. https://www.brookings.edu/blog/fixgov/2017/09/18
/views-among-college-students-regarding-the-first-amendment-
results-from-a-new-survey/.

Virgil. *The Aeneid*. Translated by Robert Fitzgerald. New York: Random House,
1983.

Wang, Victor. "Student Petition Urges English Department to Diversify
Curriculum." *Yale Daily News*, 26 May 2016. https://yaledailynews.com
/blog/2016/05/26/student-petition-urges-english-department-to
-diversify-curriculum/.

Welles, Orson. "Jean Renoir: 'The Greatest of All Film Directors.'" *Los Angeles
Times*, 18 February 1979. https://www.wellesnet.com/thanksgiving-treat
-orson-welles-on-jean-renoir/.

Whitman, Walt. *Leaves of Grass*. Brooklyn, New York: Walt Whitman, 1855.

Who's Teaching Us Coalition. "Who's Teaching Us?" Google Docs. https://
docs.google.com/document/d/1LdN8g3dnB6kIo8saGyJpmYjFd8bjvuU
QTZE2V6NU45U/edit.

Wilde, Oscar. *De Profundis*. New York: Vintage, 1964.

Wolf, Maryanne. *Reader, Come Home: The Reading Brain in a Digital World*. New
York: HarperCollins, 2018.

Wong, Matteo. "Protesting, at Home and on the Streets." *Harvard Magazine*, 3
June 2020. https://www.harvardmagazine.com/2020/06/protesting-at
-home-and-on-the-streets.

Wulfsohn, Joseph A. "Target Reverses Decision to Pull Book Called
'Transphobic' by Twitter User after Facing Censorship Backlash." Fox
News, 16 November 2020. https://www.foxnews.com/media
/tartet-reverses-decision-pull-book-transphobic-censorship-backlash.

X, Malcolm. *The Autobiography of Malcolm X: As Told to Alex Haley*. New York: Ballantine Books, 2015.

Yale University. *We Out Here Film Screening March*. Photograph. Yale University. https://artgallery.yale.edu/sites/default/files/event-images/we_out_here_fi lm_screening_march_10_0_0.jpg.

Yandoli, Krystie. "I'm a Millennial, and I'm Disappointed in Obama." Bustle, 6 December 2013. https://www.bustle.com/articles/10255-obamas -losing-it-im-a-millennial-and-im-disappointed-in-obama.

Yazzie-Mintz, Ethan. *Voices of Students on Engagement: A Report on the 2006 High School Survey of Student Engagement*. Center for Evaluation and Education Policy, Indiana University, 2007. https://files.eric.ed.gov/fullt ext/ED495758.pdf.

Zheng, Binbin, Mark Warschauer, Chin-Hsi Lin, and Chi Chang. "Learning in One-to-One Laptop Environments: A Meta-Analysis and Research Synthesis." *Review of Educational Research* 86, no. 4 (1 December 2016): 1052–1084.

Zuckerman, Phil. "Religion, Secularism, and Homophobia." *Psychology Today*, 21 July 2017. https://www.psychologytoday.com/us/blog/the -secular-life/201707/religion-secularism-and-homophobia.

Notes

Chapter One: Making Unhappy—and Dangerous—Adults

1. Paul Taylor and Scott Keeter, eds., *Millennials: Confident. Connected. Open to Change*, Pew Research Center, 24 February 2010, https://www.pewsocialtrends.org/2010/02/24/millennials-confident-connected-open-to-change/.

2. Vice Staff, "53 Reasons Life Sucks for Millennials," Vice, 30 March 2018, https://www.vice.com/en/article/8xkx43/53-reasons-life-sucks-for-millennials.

3. Neil Howe and William Strauss, *Millennials Rising: The Next Great Generation* (New York: Vintage, 2000); see also Josh Sanburn, "Millennials: The Next Greatest Generation?" *Time*, 9 May 2013, https://nation.time.com/2013/05/09/millennials-the-next-greatest-generation/.

4. Bob Herbert, "Here Come the Millennials," *New York Times*, 13 May 2008, https://www.nytimes.com/2008/05/13/opinion/13herbert.html.

5. Marc Prensky, "Digital Natives, Digital Immigrants," *On the Horizon* 9, no. 5 (October 2001), https://www.marcprensky.com/writing/Prensky%20-%20Digital%20Natives,%20Digital%20Immigrants%20-%20Part1.pdf.

6. Will Richardson, "World without Walls: Learning Well with Others," Edutopia, 3 December 2008, https://www.edutopia.org/collaboration-age-technology-will-richardson.

7. *Frontline*, season 26, episode 6, "Growing Up Online," directed by Rachel Dretzin and John Maggio, written by Rachel Dretzin, aired 22 January 2008 on PBS, https://www.pbs.org/wgbh/pages/frontline/kidsonline/etc/script.html.

8. Jessica Maguire, "MIT's Jenkins, Johnson Talk Community, Creativity," Gamasutra, 17 March 2008, https://www.gamasutra.com/php-bin/news_index.php?story=17829.

9. Jeff Steinmann, "What Old People Can Learn from Millennials," HuffPost, 24 July 2014, https://www.huffpost.com/entry/life-lessons-_b_5588193.

10. TheNexusInstitute, "George Steiner on Myths and Music," YouTube, 23 June 2010, https://www.youtube.com/watch?v=oKh7edvRvFQ.

11. National Center for Education Statistics, "The Nation's Report Card: 2018 U.S. History, Geography, and Civics at Grade 8, Highlights Reports," U.S. Department of Education, 23 April 2020, https://nces.ed.gov/pubsearch/pubsinfo.asp?pubid=2020017.

12. David Pogue, "Smartphones Mean You Will No Longer Have to Memorize Facts," *Scientific American*, 1 August 2013, https://www.scientificamerican.com/article/smartphones-mean-no-longer-memorize-facts/.

13. Tom Standage, "The Culture War: How New Media Keeps [*sic*] Corrupting Our Children," *Wired*, 1 April 2006, https://www.wired.com/2006/04/war/.

14. Joichi Ito, "In an Open-Source Society, Innovating by the Seat of Our Pants," *New York Times*, 5 December 2011, https://www.nytimes.com/2011/12/06/science/joichi-ito-innovating-by-the-seat-of-our-pants.html.

15. Andrew Keen, *The Internet Is Not the Answer* (New York: Atlantic Monthly Press, 2015).

16. John Perry Barlow, "Leaving the Physical World" (speech delivered in Japan), Electronic Frontier Foundation, 1993, https://www.eff.org/pages/leaving-physical-world.

17. Tom Bradshaw and Bonnie Nichols, *Reading at Risk: A Survey of Literary Reading in America* (National Endowment for the Arts; Mark Bauerlein, Director, Office of Research and Analysis), June 2004, https://www.arts.gov/sites/default/files/ReadingAtRisk.pdf.

18. John Palfrey and Urs Gasser, *Born Digital: Understanding the First Generation of Digital Natives* (New York: Basic Books, 2008), 257.

19. Emily Eakin, "More Ado (Yawn) about Great Books," *New York Times*, 8 April 2001, https://www.nytimes.com/2001/04/08/education/more-ado-yawn-about-great-books.html.

20. Mizuko Ito et al., *Hanging Out, Messing Around, and Geeking Out: Kids Living and Learning with New Media* (Boston: MIT Press, 2010).

21. Ibid., 4.

22. Ibid., 69.

23. Ibid.

24. Nellie Bowles, "The Digital Gap between Rich and Poor Kids Is Not What We Expected," *New York Times*, 26 October 2018, https://www.nytimes.com/2018/10/26/style/digital-divide-screens-schools.html.

25. Nellie Bowles, "A Dark Consensus about Screens and Kids Begins to Emerge in Silicon Valley," *New York Times*, 26 October 2018, https://www.nytimes.com/2018/10/26/style/phones-children-silicon-valley.html.

26. Lee Moran, "Bill Maher Blasts Social Media Tycoons for Creating Such Addictive Products," HuffPost, 13 May 2017, https://www.huffingtonpost.ca/entry/bill-maher-social-media-drug-dealers_n_5916a78ce4b0031e737dd975.

27. Bowles, "The Digital Gap"; Bowles, "A Dark Consensus."

28. Promotional copy for Allan Collins and Richard Halverson, *Rethinking Education in the Age of Technology: The Digital Revolution and Schooling in America* (New York and London: Teachers College Press, Columbia University, 2009).

29. Richard Lanham, "The Electronic Word: Literary Study and the Digital Revolution," *New Literary History* 20, no. 2 (Winter 1989): 265–90, at 265.

30. Nielsen, "U.S. Teen Mobile Report Calling Yesterday, Texting Today, Using Apps Tomorrow," Nielsen, 14 October 2010, https://www.nielsen.com/us/en/insights/article/2010/u-s-teen-mobile-report-calling-yesterday-texting-today-using-apps-tomorrow/.

31. Victoria J. Rideout, Ulla G. Foehr, and Donald F. Roberts, *Generation M²: Media in the Lives of 8- to 18-Year-Olds*, Kaiser Family Foundation, 20 January 2010, https://www.kff.org/other/event/generation-m2-media-in-the-lives-of/.

32. Bradshaw and Nichols, *Reading at Risk*.

33. Mark Bauerlein, *The Dumbest Generation: How the Digital Age Stupefies Young Americans and Jeopardizes Our Future; or, Don't Trust Anyone under 30* (New York: Tarcher Penguin, 2008).

34. Don Tapscott, *Grown Up Digital: How the Net Generation Is Changing Your World* (New York: McGraw-Hill, 2009).

35. Maryanne Wolf, *Reader, Come Home: The Reading Brain in a Digital World* (New York: HarperCollins, 2018), 2.

36. Center for Teaching Innovation, "The Millennial Generation: Understanding & Engaging Today's Learners," Cornell University, https://teaching.cornell.edu/resource/millennial-generation-understanding-engaging-todays-learners.

37. National Survey of Student Engagement, *Fostering Student Engagement Campuswide: Annual Results 2011* (Bloomington, Indiana: Indiana University Center for Postsecondary Research, 2011), https://scholarworks.iu.edu/dspace/bitstream/handle/2022/23408/NSSE_2011_Annual_Results.pdf?sequence=1&isAllowed=y.

38. Richard Arum and Josipa Roksa, *Academically Adrift: Limited Learning on College Campuses* (Chicago: University of Chicago Press, 2010), 68.

39. Learning and Academic Resource Center, "Learning and Academic Resource Center," University of California, Irvine, www.larc.uci.edu.

40. Michael Novak, *Writing from Left to Right: My Journey from Liberal to Conservative* (New York: Image, 2013), 91.

41. Ibid., 92.

42. Ibid., 93.

43. Ibid.

44. Michael Horowitz, "Portrait of the Marxist as an Old Trouper," *Playboy*, March 1970, 23–32, 175–76, 228, https://www.marcuse.org/herbert/newsevents/1970/709PlayboyInt.htm.

45. Ibid.

46. Herbert Marcuse, *An Essay on Liberation* (Boston: Beacon Press, 1969), 6.

47. Horowitz, "Portrait of the Marxist."

48. Novak, *Writing*, 107.

49. Charles Reich, "Reflections: The Greening of America," *New Yorker*, 26 September 1970, https://www.newyorker.com/magazine/1970/09/26/ref lections-the-greening-of-america.

50. Andrew Marcinek, "Project-Based Learning for Digital Citizens: Collaboration, Networking and Results," Edutopia, 9 December 2011, https://www.edutopia.org/blog/PBL-digital-citizens-andrew-marcinek.

51. Amanda Lenhart et al., *Teens and Mobile Phones*, Pew Research Center, 20 April 2010, https://www.pewresearch.org/internet/2010/04/20/teens -and-mobile-phones/.

52. Hannah Arendt, "The Crisis in Education," *Partisan Review* 25 (Fall 1958): 500.

53. Bauerlein, *Dumbest Generation*, 236.

54. Neil Howe, "Who Is the Real 'Dumbest Generation'?" *Washington Post*, 7 December 2008, https://www.washingtonpost.com/wp-dyn/content/ar ticle/2008/12/05/AR2008120502601.html.

55. Loren Soeiro, "Why Are Millennials So Anxious and Unhappy?" *Psychology Today*, 24 July 2019, https://www.psychologytoday.com/us/bl og/i-hear-you/201907/why-are-millennials-so-anxious-and-unhappy.

56. Hillary Hoffower and Allana Akhtar, "Lonely, Burned Out, and Depressed: The State of Millennials' Mental Health 2020," *Business Insider*, 10 October 2020, https://www.businessinsider.com/millennials-mental -health-burnout-lonely-depressed-money-stress?op=1.

57. Annie Lowrey, "Millennials Don't Stand a Chance," *Atlantic*, 13 April 2020, https://www.theatlantic.com/ideas/archive/2020/04/millennials-are-new -lost-generation/609832/.

58. Lee Rainie, Scott Keeter, and Andrew Perrin, *Trust and Distrust in America*, Pew Research Center, 22 July 2019, https://www.pewresearch.org/politics/2019/07/22/trust-and-distrust-in-america/.

59. Jean Twenge, *iGen: Why Today's Super-Connected Kids Are Growing Up Less Rebellious, More Tolerant, Less Happy—and Completely Unprepared for Adulthood (and What This Means for the Rest of Us)* (New York: Atria, 2017).

60. Amy Adkins, "What Millennials Want from Work and Life," Gallup Workplace, 10 May 2016, https://www.gallup.com/workplace/236477/millennials-work-life.aspx.

61. Peter Turchin, "Blame Rich, Overeducated Elites as Our Society Frays," Bloomberg Opinion, 20 November 2013, https://www.bloomberg.com/opinion/articles/2013-11-20/blame-rich-overeducated-elites-as-our-society-frays.

62. Steven Martin, Nan Marie Astone, and H. Elizabeth Peters, *Fewer Marriages, More Divergence: Marriage Projections for Millennials to Age 40* (Urban Institute, 29 April 2014), https://www.urban.org/research/publication/fewer-marriages-more-divergence-marriage-projections-millennials-age-40.

63. Andrew Van Dam, "The Unluckiest Generation in U.S. History," *Washington Post*, 5 June 2020, https://www.washingtonpost.com/business/2020/05/27/millennial-recession-covid/.

64. Badger Pundit, "The 'Shrieking Girl': Yale Student Expresses Her Need to Be 'Safe' from Halloween Costumes,," YouTube, 8 November 2015, https://www.youtube.com/watch?v=V6ZVEVufWFI.

65. Melissa J. Hagan et al. "Event-Related Clinical Distress in College Students: Responses to the 2016 U.S. Presidential Election," *Journal of American College Health* 68, no. 1 (2018): 21–25.

66. Matthew Arnold, "Preface to *Poems* [1853]," in Matthew Arnold, *Poetry and Criticism of Matthew Arnold*, ed. A. Dwight Culler (Boston: Houghton Mifflin, 1961) 37–58, 203–14, at 212.

67. James Gleick, *Faster: The Acceleration of Just About Everything* (New York: Pantheon, 1999).

68. Matthew Arnold, "The Function of Criticism at the Present Time," in Matthew Arnold, *Poetry and Criticism of Matthew Arnold*, ed. A. Dwight Culler (Boston: Houghton Mifflin, 1961), 237–58, at 256.

69. W. E. B. Du Bois, *The Souls of Black Folk*, in W. E. B. Du Bois, *W. E. B. Du Bois, Writings*, ed. Nathan Irvin Huggins (New York: Viking Press, Library of America, 1986), 438.

70. Ross Douthat, "The Truth about Harvard," *Atlantic* (March 2005): 95–99.

71. Ibid., 97.

72. Alexis de Tocqueville, *Democracy in America*, trans. and ed. Harvey C. Mansfield and Delba Winthorp (Chicago: University of Chicago Press, 2000), 510.

73. Ibid.

74. Nathaniel Hawthorne, *The Marble Faun: or, The Romance of Monte Beni*, 2 vols. (Boston: Ticknor & Fields, 1864), vii.

75. F. Scott Fitzgerald, *The Great Gatsby* (New York: Scribner's, 1925), 112.

76. Pew Research Center, *Millennials in Adulthood: Detached from Institutions, Networked with Friends* (Pew Research Center, 7 March 2014), https://www.pewsocialtrends.org/2014/03/07/millennials-in-adulthood/.

77. Rainie, Keeter, and Perrie, *Trust and Distrust*.

Chapter Two: They Have a Dream

1. William A. Galston and Clara Hendrickson, "How Millennials Voted This Election," Brookings Institution, 21 November 2016, https://www.brookings.edu/blog/fixgov/2016/11/21/how-millennials-voted/.

2. Josh Logue, "Chalk It Up to Trump," Inside Higher Ed, 25 March 2016, https://www.insidehighered.com/news/2016/03/25/debate-grows-over-pro-trump-chalkings-emory.

3. The College Fix, "TheCollegeFix.com: Milo Yiannopoulos Enters UCSB," YouTube, 27 May 2016, https://www.youtube.com/watch?v=zK6wkAf Nwno.

4. CNBC, "Milo Yiannopoulos: What the 'Alt Right' Is Really About (Full Interview) | Power Lunch," YouTube, 8 September 2016, https://www.yo utube.com/watch?v=Lgl53EXInPc.

5. Jacob Durst, "Breitbart Editor Brings Crowd, Protesters to White Hall," *Emory Wheel*, 14 April 2016, https://emorywheel.com/milo-yiannopou los-speaks/.

6. Nathan Heller, "The Big Uneasy: What's Roiling the Liberal-Arts Campus?" *New Yorker*, 30 May 2016, 52.

7. Ibid., 57.

8. Ibid.

9. Walt Whitman, *Leaves of Grass* (Brooklyn, New York: self-pub., 1855).

10. Cal State LA University Times, "Ben Shapiro Protest at Cal State LA," YouTube, 25 February 2016, https://www.youtube.com/watch?v=NRVe6 UCmq2I.

11. The original post appears to have disappeared, but much of its message is reproduced at Alex Thomas, "Authoritarian Leftist 'Activists' Demand the End of Free Speech, Extensive Re-Education," The Burning Platform, 17 November 2015, https://www.theburningplatform.com/2015/11/17/aut horitarian-leftist-activists-demand-the-end-of-free-speech-extensive-re -education/#more-109447).

12. Associated Press, "Penn Campus Police Call University President's 'Die-In' Display 'Slap in the Face,'" Fox News, 12 December 2014, https:// www.foxnews.com/us/penn-campus-police-call-university-presidents -die-in-display-slap-in-the-face; Charles Thompson, "Lawmaker Demands Penn State President Eric Barron Apologize for 'Hands-Up' Gesture at Protest," *Patriot-News*, 9 December 2014, https://www.pennl ive.com/midstate/2014/12/state_representative_to_psu_pr.html.

13. Oscar Wilde, *De Profundis* (New York: Vintage, 1964), 8–9.

14. Virgil, *The Aeneid*, trans. Robert Fitzgerald (New York: Random House, 1983), (IV 1–3).

15. Denis de Rougemont, *Love in the Western World* (Princeton, New Jersey: Princeton University Press, 1983), 15.

16. Sarah Kenny, "'We Demand More': Student Leaders across the Country Challenge Politicians to Combat Hate," *Washington Post*, 13 November 2017, https://www.washingtonpost.com/news/grade-point/wp/2017/11/13/we -demand-more-student-leaders-across-the-country-challenge-political-le aders-to-do-more-to-combat-hate/; UVA Student Council, "Signatures of Solidarity," Facebook, 12 November 2017, https://www.facebook.com/uvas tudco/photos/pcb.10155849298669715/10155849294729715; UC Berkeley Graduate Assembly, "Statement of Solidarity with Student Body Presidents across the Country, Remembering Charlottesville," Facebook, 12 November 2017, https://www.facebook.com/watch/live/?v=10154768704036213&ref= watch_permalink; UCSB Associated Students, "UCSB #StudentsAgainstHate," KZClip, 16 November 2017, https://kzclip.com/video/hPC3EO4wEWg/ucsb-studentsagainsthate.html; Student Government Association [JMU], "Charlottesville Statement from Jewel Hurt, JMU Student Body President," Facebook, 12 November 2017, https://www.facebook.com /watch/?v=10154740781306920; OU Student Government Association, "In Solidarity, We Are #StudentsAgainstHate," Facebook, 12 November 2017, https://www.facebook.com/watch/live/?v=879056162253125&ref=watch_per malink.

17. UVA Student Council, "#StudentsAgainstHate," Facebook, 12 November 2017, https://www.facebook.com/uvastudco/photos/pcb.1015584929866 9715/10155849294604715.

18. Ezra Pound, *Hugh Selwyn Mauberley* (London: Ovid Press, 1920).

19. Victor Wang, "Student Petition Urges English Department to Diversify Curriculum," *Yale Daily News*, 26 May 2016, https://yaledailynews.com /blog/2016/05/26/student-petition-urges-english-department-to-diversi fy-curriculum/.

20. Eric Levitz, "This One Chart Explains Why the Kids Back Bernie," *New York*, 15 February 2020, https://nymag.com/intelligencer/2020/02/this -one-chart-explains-why-young-voters-back-bernie-sanders.html.

21. Guy Molyneux, Ruy Tuxeira, and John Whaley, *The Generation Gap on Government* (Center for American Progress, 27 July 2010), https://www .americanprogress.org/wp-content/uploads/issues/2010/07/pdf/dww _millennials_execsumm.pdf.

22. Emily Hoban Kirby and Kei Kawashima-Ginsberg, *The Youth Vote in 2008* (The Center for Information & Research on Civic Learning & Engagement, 17 August 2009), http://www.whatkidscando.org/youth_on _the_trail_2012/pdf/CIRCLE%20youith%20vote%202008.pdf.

23. Eric Greenberg and Karl Weber. "Why the Youth Vote Is the Big Story— for 2008 and for Decades to Come," HuffPost, 25 May 2011, https://www .huffpost.com/entry/why-the-youth-vote-is-the_b_158273.

24. Kirby and Kawashima-Ginsberg, *The Youth Vote*.

25. Krystie Yandoli, "I'm a Millennial, and I'm Disappointed in Obama," Bustle, 6 December 2013, https://www.bustle.com/articles/10255-obamas -losing-it-im-a-millennial-and-im-disappointed-in-obama.

26. Emily Ekins, "What Americans Think about Poverty, Wealth, and Work," Cato Institute, 24 September 2019, https://www.cato.org/publications/sur vey-reports/what-americans-think-about-poverty-wealth-work.

27. Lydia Saad, "Socialism as Popular as Capitalism among Young Adults in U.S.," Gallup News, 25 November 2019, https://news.gallup.com/poll/26 8766/socialism-popular-capitalism-among-young-adults.aspx.

28. Victims of Communism Memorial Foundation and YouGov, *U.S. Attitudes toward Socialism, Communism, and Collectivism* (Victims of Communism Memorial Foundation and YouGov: 20 October 2020), https://victimsofcommunism.org/wp-content/uploads/2020/10/10.19.20 -VOC-YouGov-Survey-on-U.S.-Attitudes-Toward-Socialism-Communi sm-and-Collectivism.pdf.

29. P. J. O'Rourke, "This Is Why Millennials Adore Socialism," *New York Post*, 12 September 2020, https://nypost.com/2020/09/12/pj-orourke-this-is -why-millennials-adore-socialism/.

30. Connor Boyack, "Why Socialism Is So Popular among Young People," Fox Business, 15 May 2019, https://www.foxbusiness.com/politics/sociali sm-capitalism-youth-ocasio-cortez.

31. Tucker Carlson and Neil Patel, "Why Kids Are Socialists and How to Start Fixing It," Daily Caller, 1 November 2019, https://dailycaller.com/2019/10 /31/tucker-carlson-and-neil-patel-why-kids-are-socialists-and-how-to-st art-fixing-it/.

32. Emily Ekins and Joy Pullman, "Why So Many Millennials Are Socialists," The Federalist, 15 February 2016, https://thefederalist.com/2016/02/15/ why-so-many-millennials-are-socialists/.

33. M. Earl Smith, "Millennials Are the 'Most Tolerant Generation,' Hillary Clinton Says at West Phila. Rally," *Daily Pennsylvanian*, 16 August 2016, https://www.thedp.com/article/2016/08/ hillary-clinton-west-phila-rally.

34. Jean Twenge, Nathan T. Carter, and W. Keith Campbell, "Time Period, Generational, and Age Differences in Tolerance for Controversial Beliefs and Lifestyles in the United States, 1972–2012," *Social Forces* 94, no. 1 (September 2015): 379–99.

35. GenDIY, "Millennials Are Tolerant, Educated, Enterprising, and Hyphenated," HuffPost, 21 February 2015, https://www.huffpost.com/en try/millennials-are-tolerant-_b_6350434.

36. Andrew Hartman, "The Millennial Left's War against Liberalism," *Washington Post*, 20 July 2017, https://www.washingtonpost.com/news /made-by-history/wp/2017/07/20/the-millennial-lefts-war-against-liber alism/.

37. John Villasenor, "Views among College Students Regarding the First Amendment: Results from a New Survey," Brookings Institution, 18 September 2017, https://www.brookings.edu/blog/fixgov/2017/09/18/vie

ws-among-college-students-regarding-the-first-amendment-results-fr
om-a-new-survey/.

38. Sam Sanders, "Obama Warns Campus Protesters against Urge to 'Shut Up' Opposition," NPR, 21 December 2015, https://www.npr.org/2015/12 /21/460282127/obama-warns-campus-protesters-against-urge-to-shut-up -opposition.

39. College Pulse, Foundation for Individual Rights in Education (FIRE), RealClear Education, *2020 College Free Speech Rankings: What's the Climate for Free Speech on College Campuses?* (College Pulse, FIRE, and RealClear Education, 2020), https://marketplace.collegepulse.com/img /2020_college_free_speech_rankings.pdf.

40. Samantha Lock, "'To Kill a Mockingbird,' Other Books Banned from California Schools over Racism Concerns," *Newsweek*, 13 November 2020, https://www.newsweek.com/kill-mockingbird-other-books-banned-ca lifornia-schools-over-racism-concerns-1547241?amp=1&__twitter_im pression=true.

41. Colleen Flaherty, "Suspended for Using N-Word," Inside Higher Ed, 31 August 2018, https://www.insidehighered.com/news/2018/08/31/n-word -simply-be-avoided-or-emory-wrong-suspend-law-professor-who-used -it.

42. Phil Zuckerman, "Religion, Secularism, and Homophobia," *Psychology Today*, 21 July 2017, https://www.psychologytooday.com/us/blog/the-se cular-life/201707/religion-secularism-and-homophobia.

43. Joseph A. Wulfsohn, "Target Reverses Decision to Pull Book Called 'Transphobic' by Twitter User after Facing Censorship Backlash," Fox News, 16 November 2020, https://www.foxnews.com/media/target-rever ses-decision-pull-book-transphobic-censorship-backlash.

44. Black Students at Emory, "List of Demands," *Emory Wheel*, 2 December 2015, https://emorywheel.com/black-students-at-emory-list-of-dema nds/.

45. Yale University, *We Out Here Film Screening March* (photograph), Yale University, https://artgallery.yale.edu/sites/default/files/event-images/we _out_here_film_screening_march_10_0_0.jpg.

46. Joseph Epstein, "The Tyranny of the 'Tolerant,'" *Wall Street Journal*, 9 October 2020, https://www.wsj.com/articles/the-tyranny-of-the-tolerant -11602278220.

47. Mary Eberstadt, "The New Intolerance," *First Things*, March 2015, https:// www.firstthings.com/article/2015/03/the-new-intolerance.

48. Morning Consult and Politico, *National Tracking Poll #200766* (Morning Consult and Politico, 17–19 July 2020), https://www.politico.com/f/?id= 00000173-7329-d26c-af77-7b7f646a0000.

49. Cass R. Sunstein, "The Law of Group Polarization," John M. Olin Program in Law and Economics Working Paper No. 91, 7 December 1999, https:// chicagounbound.uchicago.edu/cgi/viewcontent.cgi?article=1541&conte xt=law_and_economics.

50. Cultural Research Center, "American Worldview Inventory 2020—At a Glance," Arizona Christian University, 22 September 2020, https://www .arizonachristian.edu/wp-content/uploads/2020/09/CRC_AWVI2020 _Release10_Digital_01_20200922.pdf.

51. J. Hector St. John de Crèvecoeur, *Letters from an American Farmer* (Philadelphia: Matthew Carey, 1793), 13.

52. Ibid., 25.

53. Ibid., 49.

54. Ibid., 52–53.

55. Pew Research Center, *Millennials in Adulthood: Detached from Institutions, Networked with Friends* (Pew Research Center, 7 March 2014), https:// www.pewsocialtrends.org/2014/03/07/millennials-in-adulthood/.

56. Cultural Research Center, "American Worldview Inventory."

Chapter Three: An Anti-Formation

1. U.S. Bureau of Labor Statistics, *American Time Use Survey—2010 Results* (U.S. Department of Labor, 22 June 2011), https://www.bls.gov/news.rele ase/archives/atus_06222011.pdf.

2. Victoria J. Rideout, Ulla G. Foehr, and Donald F. Roberts, *Generation M²: Media in the Lives of 8- to 18-Year-Olds* (Kaiser Family Foundation, 20 January 2010), https://www.kff.org/other/event/generation-m2-media-in -the-lives-of/.

3. The ATUS included "telephone calls, mail, and email" among the group of non-leisure activities, implying that those communications bore upon work- and household-related duties such as paying bills, rather than social contact. Strangely, fifteen-to-nineteen-year-olds turned out to be the age group logging the most time on them, about seventeen minutes per day. This raises the screen portion of a youth's waking moments in the ATUS calculations even higher.

4. Amanda Lenhart et al., *Teens and Mobile Phones* (Pew Research Center, 20 April 2010), https://www.pewresearch.org/internet/2010/04/20/teens -and-mobile-phones/.

5. Rideout, Foehr, and Roberts, *Generation M²*.

6. Lenhart et al., *Teens and Mobile Phones*.

7. Nielsen, "U.S. Teen Mobile Report Calling Yesterday, Texting Today, Using Apps Tomorrow," Nielsen, 14 October 2010, https://www.nielsen .com/us/en/insights/article/2010/u-s-teen-mobile-report-calling-yester day-texting-today-using-apps-tomorrow/.

8. U.S. Bureau of Labor Statistics, *American Time Use Survey—2010 Results*.

9. Rideout, Foehr, and Roberts, *Generation M²*.

10. Scott Carlson, "The Net Generation Goes to College," *Chronicle of Higher Education*, 7 October 2005, https://www.chronicle.com/article/the-net -generation-goes-to-college/.

11. Sara Bennett and Nancy Kalish, *The Case against Homework: How Homework Is Hurting Our Children and What We Can Do about It* (New York: Crown, 2006), http://www.thecaseagainsthomework.com/.

12. Valerie Strauss, "As Homework Grows, So Do Arguments against It," *Washington Post*, 12 September 2006, https://www.washingtonpost.com /archive/politics/2006/09/12/as-homework-grows-so-do-arguments-aga inst-it/6e8517d8-e989-4b47-abf6-83ce4654f6a6/.

13. Sam Dillon, "A Great Year for Ivy League Schools, but Not So Good for Applicants to Them," *New York Times*, 4 April 2007, https://www.nytimes .com/2007/04/04/education/04colleges.html.

14. Andrew Ferguson, *Crazy U: One Dad's Crash Course in Getting His Kid into College* (New York: Simon & Schuster, 2011).

15. Alexandra Robbins, *The Overachievers: The Secret Lives of Driven Kids* (New York: Hyperion, 2006).

16. Josh Sanburn, "Millennials: The Next Greatest Generation?" *Time*, 9 May 2013, https://nation.time.com/2013/05/09/millennials-the-next-greatest -generation/.

17. Craig Lambert, "Nonstop: Today's Superhero Undergraduates Do '3,000 Things at 150 Percent,'" *Harvard Magazine*, March–April 2010, https:// www.harvardmagazine.com/2010/03/nonstop.

18. Kayley Kravitz, "Ambitious Millennials," HuffPost, 7 March 2013, https:// www.huffpost.com/entry/ambitious-millennials_b_2812937.

19. Ethan Yazzie-Mintz, *Voices of Students on Engagement: A Report on the 2006 High School Survey of Student Engagement* (Center for Evaluation & Education Policy, Indiana University, 2007), https://files.eric.ed.gov /fulltext/ED495758.pdf.

20. John Pryor et al., *The American Freshman: National Norms for 2006* (Higher Education Research Institute, University of California–Los Angeles, 2006), https://www.heri.ucla.edu/PDFs/pubs/TFS/Norms/Mo nographs/TheAmericanFreshman2006.pdf.

21. Richard Arum and Josipa Roksa, *Academically Adrift: Limited Learning on College Campuses* (Chicago: University of Chicago Press, 2010), 69.

22. Rideout, Foehr, and Roberts, *Generation M²*.

23. Yazzie-Mintz, *Voices of Students on Engagement*.

24. Ibid.

25. Ibid.

26. Scholastic, *2010 Kids & Family Reading Report: Turning the Page in the Digital Age* (Scholastic, 2010), http://mediaroom.scholastic.com/files/KFRR_2010.pdf.

27. Jeff Allen et al., *Relating the ACT Indicator Understanding Complex Texts to College Course Grades* (ACT, 2016), https://www.act.org/content/dam/act/unsecured/documents/2016-Relating-the-ACT-Indicator-Understanding-Complex-Texts.pdf.

28. Yazzie-Mintz, *Voices of Students on Engagement*.

29. Scholastic, *2010 Kids & Family Reading Report*.

30. Yazzie-Mintz, *Voices of Students on Engagement*.

31. National Center for Education Statistics, *NAEP 2012 Trends in Academic Progress: Reading 1971–2012, Mathematics 1973–2012* (U.S. Department of Education, 2013), https://nces.ed.gov/nationsreportcard/subject/publications/main2012/pdf/2013456.pdf.

32. Marianne Perie et al., *NAEP 2004 Trends in Academic Progress: Three Decades of Student Performance in Reading and Mathematics* (National Center for Education Statistics, U.S. Department of Education, July 2005), https://nces.ed.gov/nationsreportcard/pdf/main2005/2005464.pdf.

33. Jennifer Ludden, "Why Aren't Teens Reading Like They Used To?" NPR, 12 May 2014, https://www.npr.org/2014/05/12/311111701/why-arent-teens-reading-like-they-used-to.

34. National Commission on Excellence in Education, *A Nation at Risk: The Imperative for Education Reform* (U.S. Department of Education, April 1983), https://edreform.com/wp-content/uploads/2013/02/A_Nation_At_Risk_1983.pdf.

35. Ibid.

36. Katie Dean, "Maine Students Hit the IBooks," *Wired*, 9 Jan 2002, https://www.wired.com/2002/01/maine-students-hit-the-ibooks/.

37. Benjamin Herold, "1-to-1 Laptop Initiatives Boost Student Scores, Study Finds," *Education Week*, 17 May 2016, https://www.edweek.org/technology/1-to-1-laptop-initiatives-boost-student-scores-study-finds/2016/05.

38. Binbin Zheng et al., "Learning in One-to-One Laptop Environments: A Meta-Analysis and Research Synthesis," *Review of Educational Research* 86, no. 4 (December 2016): 1052–1084.

39. Mark Bauerlein and Sandra Stotsky, *How Common Core's ELA Standards Place College Readiness at Risk* (Pioneer Institute, September 2012), https://irvingtonparentsforum.files.wordpress.com/2013/04/bauerlein-stotsky-common-core-ela-standards-1.pdf.

40. Steven Johnson, "Dawn of the Digital Natives," *Guardian*, 7 February 2008, https://www.theguardian.com/technology/2008/feb/07/internet.literacy.

41. Mark Bauerlein, "Why Do American Students Lose Ground over Time?" *Atlanta Journal-Constitution*, 15 December 2013, https://www.ajc.com/news/opinion/why-american-students-lose-ground-over-time/NAw9EKV5QxYxcq7HvxybXL/.

42. Mark Bauerlein and Sunil Iyengar, "There Is Good Reason to Worry about Declining Rates of Reading," *Guardian*, 19 February 2008, https://www.theguardian.com/commentisfree/2008/feb/20/digitalmedia.internet.

43. Johnson, "Dawn of the Digital Natives."

44. Tim O'Reilly, "What Is Web 2.0?: Design Patterns and Business Models for the Next Generation of Software," 30 September 2005, https://www.oreilly.com/pub/a/web2/archive/what-is-web-20.html.

45. Anna Aldric, "SAT Scores over Time: 1972–2020," PrepScholar, 1 October, 2020, https://blog.prepscholar.com/average-sat-scores-over-time.

46. ACT, *ACT College & Career Readiness Standards: English* (ACT), https://www.act.org/content/dam/act/unsecured/documents/CCRS-EnglishStandards.pdf.

47. Scott Jaschik, "Grade Inflation, Higher and Higher," Inside Higher Ed, 29 March 2016, https://www.insidehighered.com/news/2016/03/29/survey-finds-grade-inflation-continues-rise-four-year-colleges-not-community-college.

48. ACT, *ACT College & Career Readiness Standards: English*.

49. Aldric, "SAT Scores over Time."

50. ACT, *ACT College & Career Readiness Standards: Reading* (ACT), https://www.act.org/content/act/en/college-and-career-readiness/standards/reading-standards.html.

51. ACT, *The Condition of College & Career Readiness 2013* (ACT, 2013), https://files.eric.ed.gov/fulltext/ED558039.pdf.

52. National Assessment Governing Board, *Reading Framework for the National Assessment of Education Progress* (U.S. Department of Education, September 2010), https://www.nagb.gov/content/nagb/assets/documents/publications/frameworks/reading/2011-reading-framework.pdf.

53. Nellie Bowles, "A Dark Consensus about Screens and Kids Begins to Emerge in Silicon Valley," *New York Times*, 26 October 2018, https://www.nytimes.com/2018/10/26/style/phones-children-silicon-valley.html.

54. U.S. Bureau of Labor Statistics, "Table 11A. Time Spent in Leisure and Sports Activities for the Civilian Population by Selected Characteristics, Averages per Day, 2019 Annual Averages," U.S. Department of Labor, 25 June 2020, https://www.bls.gov/news.release/atus.t11A.htm, a news release excerpted from U.S. Bureau of Labor Statistics, *American Time Use Survey—2019 Results* (U.S. Department of Labor, 25 June 2020), https://www.bls.gov/news.release/pdf/atus.pdf.

55. Benjamin M. Schmidt, "The History BA since the Great Recession: The 2018 AHA Majors Report," *Perspectives on History*, 26 November 2018, https://www.historians.org/publications-and-directories/perspectives-on

-history/december-2018/the-history-ba-since-the-great-recession-the-20 18-aha-majors-report.

56. Margot Adler, "Cuts to University's Programs Draw Outcry," NPR, 16 November 2010, https://www.npr.org/2010/11/15/131336270/cuts-to-univer sity-s-humanities-program-draw-outcry.

57. Colleen Flaherty, "Major Exodus," Inside Higher Ed, 26 January 2015, https://www.insidehighered.com/news/2015/01/26/where-have-all-engl ish-majors-gone.

58. Steven Johnson, "Colleges Lose a 'Stunning' 651 Foreign-Language Programs in 3 Years," *Chronicle of Higher Education*, 22 January 2019, https://www.chronicle.com/article/colleges-lose-a-stunning-651-foreign -language-programs-in-3-years/.

59. Priya Satia, "The Whitesplaining of History Is Over," *Chronicle of Higher Education*, 28 March 2018, https://www.chronicle.com/article/the-whites plaining-of-history-is-over/.

60. Schmidt, "The History BA."

61. Kevin Eagan et al., *The American Freshman: National Norms Fall 2013* (Los Angeles: Higher Education Research Institute, University of California, Los Angeles, 2013).

62. National Center for Education Statistics, "Digest of Education Statistics," https://nces.ed.gov/programs/digest/. This page links to reports from 1990 to 2019.

63. Eric Hayot, "The Humanities as We Know Them Are Doomed. Now What?" *Chronicle of Higher Education*, 1 July 2018, https://www.chronic le.com/article/the-humanities-as-we-know-them-are-doomed-now -what/.

64. Alexander W. Astin et al., *The American Freshman: Thirty-Five Year Trends, 1966–2001* (Los Angeles: Higher Education Research Institute, University of California, Los Angeles, 2002).

65. National Center for Education Statistics, "Digest."

66. Astin et al., *American Freshman*. Earlier in this chapter I cited results on this particular measure for 2006.

67. Ibid.; Eagan et al., *American Freshman*.

68. Stanford University, "General Education Requirements for Undergrads," Stanford University, https://undergrad.stanford.edu/academic-planning /degree-requirements/general-education-requirements-undergrads.

69. E. D. Hirsch Jr., "Introduction—The Knowledge Requirement: What *Every* American Needs to Know," 3, in Mark Bauerlein and Adam Bellow, eds., *The State of the American Mind: 16 Leading Critics on the New Anti-Intellectualism* (West Conshohocken, Pennsylvania: Templeton Press, 2015), 1–16.

70. Ibid., 4.

71. Ibid., 5.

72. Corydon Ireland, "Welcoming Gen Ed: Harvard Forum Extols New General Education Requirements," *Harvard Gazette*, 4 September 2009, https://news.harvard.edu/gazette/story/2009/09/welcoming-gen-ed/.

73. University of Texas at Austin, "Academic Policies and Procedures," School of Undergraduate Studies, https://catalog.utexas.edu/undergraduate/un dergraduate-studies/academic-policies-and-procedures.

74. Hannah Arendt, "The Crisis in Education," *Partisan Review* 25 (Fall 1958): 508.

75. Ibid., 509.

76. Martin Duberman, "An Experiment in Education," *Daedalus* 97 (Winter 1968): 318–41, at 320.

77. Ibid.

78. Ibid., 323.

79. Ibid., 324.

80. Ibid., 321.

81. Ibid., 330.

82. Ibid., 333.

83. Ibid., 338–39.

84. Ibid., 340.

85. Richard Arum and Josipa Roksa, *Academically Adrift: Limited Learning on College Campuses* (Chicago: University of Chicago Press, 2010), 35.

86. Stanford University, "Degrees Conferred," Institutional Research & Decision Support, https://irds.stanford.edu/data-findings/degrees-con ferred.

Chapter Four: The Psychological Novel

1. Greg Lukianoff and Jonathan Haidt, *The Coddling of the American Mind: How Good Intentions and Bad Ideas Are Setting Up a Generation for Failure* (New York: Penguin, 2018), 10.

2. Dawn Hodge, "Camille Paglia—Student Protest (Shouting and Screaming at 48:00)," YouTube, 16 April 2019, https://www.youtube.com/watch?v=mLsQHQfPYW4.

3. Grace Donnelly, "Half of Millennials Support Colleges [*sic*] Restricting Free Speech 'In Extreme Cases,'" *Fortune*, 12 September 2017, https://for tune.com/2017/09/12/millennials-hate-speech-freedom-of-speech/.

4. Right News Network, "Evergreen Top 20 Monstrous Moments," YouTube, 2 June 2017, https://www.youtube.com/watch?v=8YnSYvhSeyI.

5. Leo Tolstoy, *War and Peace*, trans. Richard Pevear and Larissa Volokhonsky (New York: Vintage, 2008), 292–93.

6. Leah Price, "You Are What You Read," *New York Times*, 23 December 2007.

7. Erika Lindemann, "Freshman Composition: No Place for Literature," *College English* 55, no. 3 (March 1993): 311–16, at 311.

8. John Beverley, *Against Literature* (Minneapolis, Minnesota: University of Minnesota Press, 1993).

9. Maryanne Wolf, *Reader, Come Home: The Reading Brain in a Digital World* (New York: HarperCollins, 2018), 51–52.

10. Ibid., 52.

11. Ibid., 51.

12. National Assessment Governing Board, *Reading Framework for the National Assessment of Education Progress* (U.S. Department of Education, September 2010), https://www.nagb.gov/content/nagb/assets/documents/publications/frameworks/reading/2011-reading-framework.pdf.

13. Orson Welles, "Jean Renoir: 'The Greatest of All Film Directors,'" *Los Angeles Times*, 18 February 1979, https://www.wellesnet.com/thanksgiving-treat-orson-welles-on-jean-renoir/.

14. FilMagicians, "Orson Welles Talks Touch of Evil, James Cagney & Jean Renoir," YouTube, 1 October 2017, https://www.youtube.com/watch?v=niMGXhS28YI.

15. Michael Dare, "Touch of Evil's Second Tracking Shot, Just as Long and Impressive as the Opening," YouTube, 16 February 2018, https://www.youtube.com/watch?v=tzcNU_1KqG0&t=210s.

16. Graham Greene, *A Burnt-Out Case* (New York: Bantam, 1962), 182.

17. Ibid., 181.

18. Mark Bauerlein, "Guilty of Cultural Appropriation in an 'Insensitive' Facebook Post," Minding the Campus, 25 November 2019, https://www.mindingthecampus.org/2019/11/25/guilty-of-cultural-appropriation-in-an-insensitive-facebook-post/.

19. E. M. Forster, *Aspects of the Novel* (New York: Harcourt, 1956), 67.

20. Ibid., 68.

21. Ibid., 69.

22. Ibid., 78.

23. Matteo Wong, "Protesting, at Home and on the Streets," *Harvard Magazine*, 3 June 2020, https://www.harvardmagazine.com/2020/06/protesting-at-home-and-on-the-streets.

24. Camille Paglia, *Sexual Personae: Art and Decadence from Nefertiti to Emily Dickinson* (New York: Vintage Books, 1991), 7.

25. Sherwood Anderson, *Winesburg, Ohio* (New York: Viking, 1958), 117.

26. Ibid., 115.

27. Ibid., 119.

28. Ibid., 120.

29. Joseph Conrad, *The Shadow-Line and Two Other Tales: Typhoon, The Secret Sharer*, ed. Morton Dauwen Zabel (Garden City, New York: Doubleday Anchor Books, 1959), 121.

Chapter Five: Multiculturalism or Malcolm X?

1. Mark Bauerlein, "Nations Need a National Literature," The Agonist, 31 December 2019, http://theagonist.org/essays/2019/12/31/essays-bauerlein .html.

2. Ibid.; William Lyon Phelps, "As Mrs. Wharton Sees Us," review of *The Age of Innocence*, by Edith Wharton, *New York Times*, 17 October 1920, https://www.nytimes.com/1920/10/17/archives/as-mrs-wharton-sees-us -as-mrs-wharton-sees-us.html.

3. Ezra Pound, "What I Feel about Walt Whitman," in Ezra Pound, *Selected Prose, 1909–1965*, ed. William Cookson (New York: New Directions, 1973), 145–46.

4. F. R. Leavis, *The Common Pursuit* (New York: NYU Press, 1964), 193.

5. National Center for Education Statistics, *The Nation's Report Card: U.S. History 2010* (U.S. Department of Education, June 2011), https://nces.ed .gov/nationsreportcard/pubs/main2010/2011468.asp#section2.

6. Stanford University, *The Study of Education at Stanford, No. 1* (Stanford University, November 1968), https://files.eric.ed.gov/fulltext/ED032844 .pdf, 14.

7. Ibid., 13.

8. Ibid.

9. Ibid.

10. Stanford University, *The Study of Education at Stanford, No. 2* (Stanford University, November 1968), https://files.eric.ed.gov/fulltext/ED032845 .pdf, 3.

11. Ibid., 9.

12. Ibid., 11.

13. Carolyn C. Lougee, "Women, History, and the Humanities: An Argument in Favor of the General Studies Curriculum," *Women's Studies Quarterly* 9, no. 1 (Spring 1981): 4–7.

14. Ibid., 4–5.

15. Isaac D. Barchas, "Stanford after the Fall: An Insider's View," *Academic Questions* 3, no. 1 (Winter 1989–90): 24–34.

16. Stanley Kurtz, *The Lost History of Western Civilization* (New York: National Association of Scholars, 11 January 2020), https://www.nas.org /storage/app/media/Reports/Lost%20History%20of%20Western%20Civ /The%20Lost%20History%20of%20Western%20Civilization.pdf.

17. Ibid.

18. Ibid., 100.

19. Amanda Kemp, "Blacks Feel Unwanted," *Stanford Daily*, 28 April 1987.

20. Commission on Undergraduate Education, Stanford University, *Report of the Commission on Undergraduate Education* (Stanford University, 1994), https://gcasper.stanford.edu/pdf/CUE_Report.pdf.

21. Ibid.

22. Ibid.

23. Ibid.

24. Ibid.

25. Alison Schneider, "Stanford Revisits the Course That Set Off the Culture Wars," *Chronicle of Higher Education*, 9 May 1997, A10–A12. Available at https://www.chronicle.com/article/stanford-revisits-the-course-that-set -off-the-culture-wars/.

26. Homer, *The Iliad*, trans. Robert Fagles (New York: Viking, 1990), XXII, lines 399–410.

27. Barchas, "Stanford after the Fall," 30.

28. Ibid., 32.

29. Justin Lai, "The Death of Stanford's Humanities Core," *Stanford Review*, 14 March 2015, https://stanfordreview.org/the-death-of-stanfords-huma nities-core/.

30. *Stanford Review* editors, "The Case for a Western Civilization Requirement at Stanford," *Stanford Review*, 21 February 2016, https:// stanfordreview.org/
the-case-for-a-western-civilization-requirement-at-stanford/.

31. Kurtz, *The Lost History*, 107–08.

32. Zack Rosenthal and Debnil Sur, "History Not Only by the Victors," *Stanford Daily*, 23 February 2016, https://www.stanforddaily.com/2016 /02/23/history-not-only-by-the-victors/.

33. Kreeger, Erika Lynn Abigail Persephone Joanna, "The White Civ's Burden," *Stanford Daily*, 22 February 2016, https://www.stanforddaily .com/2016/02/22/the-white-civs-burden/.

34. Jennifer Kabbany, "Stanford Erupts in Controversy After Student Petition Calls for Mandatory Western Civ Classes," The College Fix, 25 February 2016, https://www.thecollegefix.com/stanford-erupts-controversy-stu dent-petition-calls-mandatory-western-civ-classes/.

35. Harry Elliott, "The Western Civilization Witch Hunt," *Stanford Review*, 7 March 2016, https://stanfordreview.org/the-western-civilization-witch -hunt/.

36. Who's Teaching Us Coalition, "Who's Teaching Us?" Google Docs, https://docs.google.com/document/d/1LdN8g3dnB6kI08saGyJpmYjFd 8bjvuUQTZE2V6NU45U/edit.

37. Jennifer Kabbany, "Stanford Snowflakes Meltdown over April Fool's Joke Mocking Leftist Campus 'Demands,'" The College Fix, 1 April 2016, https://www.thecollegefix.com/
stanford-snowflakes-meltdown-april-fools-joke-mocking-leftist-campus-demands/.

38. Elliot Kaufman and Harry Elliott, "Who's Teaching Stanford?" *National Review*, 7 April 2016, https://www.nationalreview.com/2016/04/ whos-teaching-stanford-campus-activists-issue-diversity-demands/.

39. Malcolm X, *The Autobiography of Malcolm X: As Told to Alex Haley* (New York: Ballantine Books, 2015), 144.

40. Ibid., 137.

41. Ibid., 156.

42. Ibid., 157. Ellipsis in original.

43. Ibid., 158.

44. Ibid., 162.

45. Ibid., 174

46. Ibid., 182.

47. Ibid., 176.

48. Ibid., 167.

49. Ibid., 173.

50. Ibid., 183.

51. Ibid., 137.

52. Ibid., 141.

53. Ibid., 172.

54. Ibid., 173.

55. Ibid., 189.

56. Ibid., 288.

57. CBC, "Malcolm X on Front Page Challenge, 1965: CBC Archives | CBC," YouTube, 7 April 2010, https://www.youtube.com/watch?v=C7IJ7npTYrU.

58. reelback, "Malcolm X—Interview at Berkeley (1963)," YouTube, 11 June 2018, https://www.youtube.com/watch?v=FZMrti8QcPA&t=739s.

59. John Mayer, "Waiting on the World to Change," track 1 on *Continuum*, Aware/Columbia/Sony 2006, compact disc.

Index